Adobe® Photoshop®
Lightroom® 4

CLASSROOM IN A BOOK®

The official training workbook from Adobe Systems

Adobe

Adobe Photoshop Lightroom 4 Classroom in a Book

Adobe Systems Incorporated, 345 Park Avenue, San Jose, California 95110-2704, USA

Adobe Press books are published by Peachpit, a division of Pearson Education located in Berkeley, California. For the latest on Adobe Press books, go to www.adobepress.com. To report errors, please send a note to errata@peachpit.com. For information on getting permission for reprints and excerpts, contact permissions@peachpit.com.

Printed and bound in the United States of America

ISBN-13: 978-0-321-81957-4

ISBN-10:   0 321 81957 8

9 8 7 6 5 4 3 2

WHAT'S ON THE DISC

Here is an overview of the contents of the Classroom in a Book disc

The *Adobe Photoshop Lightroom 4 Classroom in a Book* disc includes the lesson files that you'll need to complete the exercises in this book, as well as other content to help you learn more about Adobe Photoshop Lightroom 4 and use it with greater efficiency and ease. The diagram below represents the contents of the disc, which should help you locate the files you need.

These same disc files are available to eBook users via electronic download. Please click here to go to the last page in your eBook for instructions.

Lesson files

Each lesson has its own folder inside the Lessons folder. You will need to copy these lesson folders to your hard drive before you can begin each lesson.

Online resources

Links to Adobe Community Help, product Help and Support pages, Adobe certification programs, Adobe TV, and other useful online resources can be found inside a handy HTML file. Just open it in your Web browser and click on the links, including a special link to this book's product page where you can access updates and bonus material.

Adobe Press

Find information about other Adobe Press titles, covering the full spectrum of Adobe products, in the Online Resources file.

CONTENTS

4   REVIEWING   114

5 ORGANIZING AND SELECTING   138

7 CREATING A PHOTO BOOK   **220**

9 PRINTING IMAGES   **264**

GETTING STARTED

Adobe® Photoshop® Lightroom® delivers a complete workflow solution for the digital photographer—from importing, reviewing, organizing, and enhancing digital images to publishing photos, producing client presentations, creating photo books and web galleries, and outputting high-quality prints. The user interface is highly intuitive and easy to learn, yet Lightroom has all the power and versatility you'd expect from an Adobe application, using state-of-the-art technologies to manage large volumes of digital photographs and to perform sophisticated image processing tasks. Whether you're a home user, a professional photographer, a hobbyist, or a business user, Lightroom enables you to stay in control of your growing digital photo library and to easily produce good-looking pictures and polished presentations for both web and print.

If you've used an earlier version of Lightroom, you'll find that this Classroom in a Book® will teach you advanced skills and covers the many new innovative features that Adobe Systems has introduced in this version. If you're new to Lightroom, you'll learn the fundamental concepts and techniques that will help you master the application.

About Classroom in a Book

Adobe Photoshop Lightroom 4 Classroom in a Book is part of the official training series for Adobe graphics and publishing software developed with the support of Adobe product experts. Each lesson in this book is made up of a series of self-paced projects that give you hands-on experience using Adobe Photoshop Lightroom 4.

Adobe Photoshop Lightroom 4 Classroom in a Book includes a CD attached to the inside back cover. On the CD you'll find all the image files used for the lessons in this book, along with additional learning resources.

Prerequisites

Before starting on the lessons in this book, make sure that you and your computer are ready by following the tips and instructions on the next few pages.

Requirements on your computer

You'll need about 500 MB of free space on your hard disk for the lesson files and the work files that you'll create as you work through the exercises.

Required skills

The lessons in this book assume that you have a working knowledge of your computer and its operating system. Make sure that you know how to use the mouse and the standard menus and commands, and also how to open, save, and close files. Can you scroll (vertically and horizontally) within a window to see content that may not be visible in the displayed area? Do you know how to use context menus, which open when you right-click (Windows) / Control-click (Mac OS) items?

If you need to review these basic and generic computer skills, see the documentation included with your Microsoft® Windows® or Apple® Mac® OS X software.

Installing Adobe Photoshop Lightroom

Before you begin using *Adobe Photoshop Lightroom 4 Classroom in a Book*, make sure that your system is set up correctly and that you've installed the required software and hardware.

You must purchase the Adobe Photoshop Lightroom 4 software separately. For system requirements and complete instructions on installing the software, see the Adobe Photoshop Lightroom 4 Read Me file on the application CD or the Adobe Photoshop Lightroom Support Center on the web at www.adobe.com/support/photoshoplightroom.

Copying the Classroom in a Book files

The CD attached to the inside back cover of this book includes a Lessons folder containing all the image files you'll need for the lessons. You'll import these images into your Lightroom library and learn to organize them using the catalog that is central to many of the projects in this book. Keep the lesson files on your computer until you have completed all the exercises.

Copying the Lesson files from the CD

1 Create a new folder named **LR4CIB** inside the *username*/My Documents (Windows) or *username*/Documents (Mac OS) folder on your computer.

2 Insert the *Adobe Photoshop Lightroom 4 Classroom in a Book* CD into your CD-ROM drive.

3 Locate the Lessons folder on the CD and copy it into the LR4CIB folder you created in step 1.

4 When your computer finishes copying the Lessons folder, remove the CD from your CD-ROM drive and put it away.

Creating a catalog file for working with this book

The catalog file stores information about all the photos in your library. It includes the location of the master files, any metadata you've added in the process of organizing your images, and a record of every adjustment or edit you've made. Most users will keep all their photos in a single catalog, which can easily manage thousands of files. Some might want to create separate catalogs for different purposes, such as home photos and business photos. Although you can create multiple catalogs, you can only have one catalog open in Lightroom at a time.

For the purposes of working with this book, you'll create a new catalog to manage the image files that you'll use in the lessons. This will allow you to leave the default catalog untouched while working through the lessons, and to keep your lesson files together in one easy-to-remember location.

Creating a library folder

First you'll create a folder to contain your new catalog as well as the files that you'll create as you complete the lessons in this book.

1 Locate the LR4CIB folder you've created on your computer.

2 Within that folder, create a new folder called **LR4CIB Library**. This new folder should be located right next to the Lessons folder that you've just copied from the CD.

Creating a new catalog file

When you first launch Lightroom, a catalog file named Lightroom 4 Catalog.lrcat is automatically created on your hard disk. This default Lightroom catalog file is created in the *username*/My Documents/My Pictures/Lightroom (Windows) or *username*/Pictures/Lightroom (Mac OS) folder.

You'll create your new catalog file inside your LR4CIB Library folder.

1 Start Adobe Photoshop Lightroom 4.

2 From the Lightroom menu bar, choose File > New Catalog.

3 In the Create Folder With New Catalog dialog box, navigate to the LR4CIB Library folder inside the LR4CIB folder you created on your hard disk.

Note: In this book, the forward arrow character (>) is used to denote submenus and commands found in the menu bar at the top of the workspace or in context menus; for example, Menu > Submenu > Command.

4 Create a new catalog by doing one of the following:

- On Windows, type **LR4CIB Library Catalog** in the File Name text box, and then click Save.

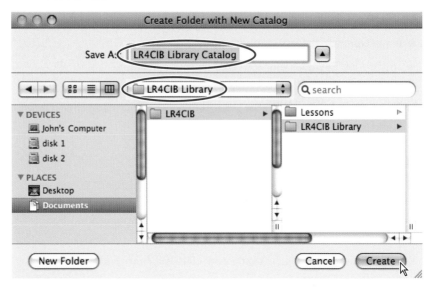

- On Mac OS, type **LR4CIB Library Catalog** in the Save As text box, and then click Create.

Lightroom opens your new library catalog, which is empty as you have not yet imported any photos.

In order to be sure that you're always working with the right catalog as you progress through the lessons in this book, you will now set the preferences so that you will be prompted to specify the LR4CIB catalog each time you launch Lightroom. It is recommended that you keep this preference set as long as you're working through the lessons in this book.

5 Choose Edit > Preferences (Windows) / Lightroom > Preferences (Mac OS).

6 In the Preferences dialog box, click the General tab. From the Default Catalog menu, choose Prompt Me When Starting Lightroom.

● **Note:** In the remainder of this book, instructions that differ for Macintosh users and those working on Windows systems are given in a compact format as follows; the forward slash character (/) is used to separate equivalent terms and commands for Windows / Mac OS, in the order shown here.

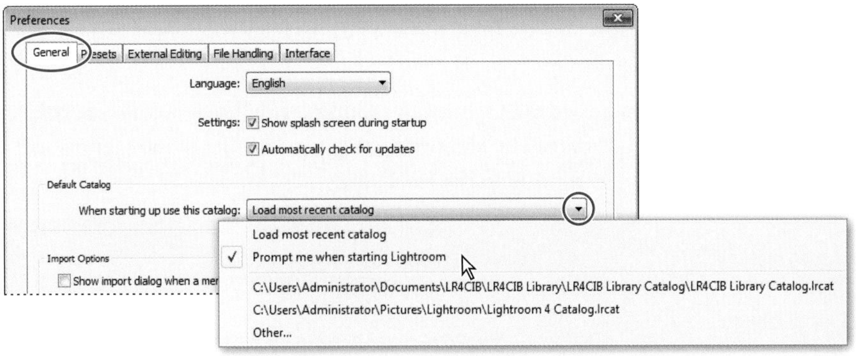

7 Click OK (Windows) / the Close button (⬤) (Mac OS) to close the Preferences dialog box.

Next time you start Lightroom the Select Catalog dialog box will appear, giving you the opportunity to make sure that your LR4CIB Library Catalog is selected before Lightroom launches.

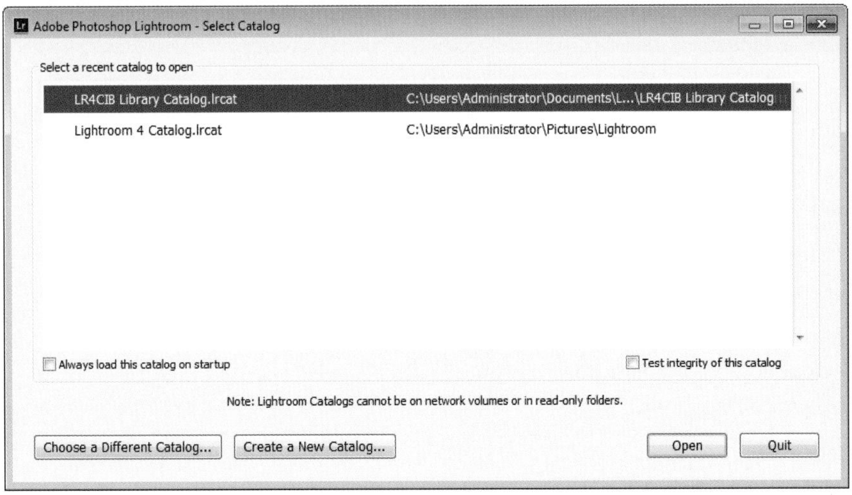

▶ **Tip:** You can hold down the Clrl+Alt / Control+Option keys immediately after you launch Lightroom to open the Select Catalog dialog box regardless of your Default Catalog preference settings.

Getting Help

Help is available from several sources, each one useful to you in different circumstances:

Note: You don't need to be connected to the Internet to view Help in Lightroom. However, with an active Internet connection, you can access the most up-to-date information.

Help in the application: The complete user documentation for Adobe Photoshop Lightroom is available from the Help menu, in the form of HTML content that displays in the Adobe Community Help application. Even without the Community Help application, this content will display in your default browser. This documentation provides quick access to summarized information on common tasks and concepts, and can be especially useful if you are new to Lightroom or if you are not connected to the Internet.

The first time you enter any of the Lightroom modules, you'll see module-specific tips that will help you get started by identifying the components of the Lightroom workspace and stepping you through the workflow.

You can dismiss the tips if you wish, by clicking the Close button (x) in the upper right corner of the floating tips window. Click the Turn Off Tips checkbox at the lower left to disable the tips for all of the Lightroom modules. You can call up the module tips at any time by choosing Help > [*Module name*] Tips.

In the Help menu you can also access a list of keyboard shortcuts applicable to the current module.

Help on the Web: You can also access the most comprehensive and up-to-date documentation on Lightroom via your default browser, whether Lightroom is currently running or not.

Help PDF: Help is also available as a PDF document, optimized for printing; you can download the document at: www.adobe.com/go/learn_lightroom_helppdf_en.

Additional resources

Adobe Photoshop Lightroom 4 Classroom in a Book is not meant to replace documentation that comes with the program or to be a comprehensive reference for every feature. Only the commands and options used in the lessons are explained in this book. For comprehensive information about program features and tutorials, please refer to these resources:

Adobe Community Help Community Help brings together active Adobe product users, Adobe product team members, authors, and experts to give you the most useful, relevant, and up-to-date information about Adobe products.

To access Community Help To invoke Help in the application, press F1 or choose Help > Lightroom help.

Adobe Community Help content is updated based on community feedback and contributions. You can add your own comments to content or forums—including links to web content. You can also publish your own content using Community Publishing, or contribute Cookbook Recipes. Find out how you can contribute at www.adobe.com/community/publishing/download.html

See http://community.adobe.com/help/profile/faq.html for answers to frequently asked questions about Community Help.

Adobe Photoshop Lightroom 4 Help and Support www.adobe.com/support/ photoshoplightroom where you can find and browse Help and Support content on adobe.com.

Adobe Forums http://forums.adobe.com lets you tap into peer-to-peer discussions, questions and answers on Adobe products.

Adobe TV http://tv.adobe.com is an online video resource for expert instruction and inspiration about Adobe products, including a How To channel to get you started with your product.

Resources for educators www.adobe.com/education includes three free curriculums that use an integrated approach to teaching Adobe software and can be used to prepare for the Adobe Certified Associate exams.

Also check out these useful links:

Adobe Photoshop Lightroom 4 product home page
http://www.adobe.com/products/photoshoplightroom.

Adobe Labs http://labs.adobe.com gives you access to early builds of cutting-edge technology, as well as forums where you can interact with both the Adobe development teams building that technology and other like-minded members of the community.

Adobe certification

The Adobe training and certification programs are designed to help Adobe customers improve and promote their product-proficiency skills. There are four levels of certification:

- Adobe Certified Associate (ACA)

- Adobe Certified Expert (ACE)

- Adobe Certified Instructor (ACI)

- Adobe Authorized Training Center (AATC)

The Adobe Certified Associate (ACA) credential certifies that individuals have the entry-level skills to plan, design, build, and maintain effective communications using different forms of digital media.

The Adobe Certified Expert program is a way for expert users to upgrade their credentials. You can use Adobe certification as a catalyst for getting a raise, finding a job, or promoting your expertise.

If you are an ACE-level instructor, the Adobe Certified Instructor program takes your skills to the next level and gives you access to a wide range of Adobe resources.

Adobe Authorized Training Centers offer instructor-led courses and training on Adobe products, employing only Adobe Certified Instructors. A directory of AATCs is available at http://partners.adobe.com.

For information on the Adobe Certified programs, visit www.adobe.com/support/certification/main.html.

1 A QUICK TOUR OF PHOTOSHOP LIGHTROOM

Lesson overview

The first part of this lesson will help you understand how Lightroom works and familiarize you with the workspace, providing an introduction to the seven Lightroom workspace modules:

- The Library Module, where you'll import, review, and organize your images so that you can access them quickly and easily

- The Map Module, where you can make use of GPS information recorded by your camera to help manage your photos

- The Develop Module, a digital darkroom where you can correct, adjust, retouch, and enhance your photos

- The Book Module, where it's easy to produce stylish photo books

- The Slideshow Module, where you can quickly create dynamic, expressive presentations to showcase your work

- The Print Module, where you can quickly set up professional-looking print layouts and manage output settings with ease

- The Web Module, where you'll find everything you need to share your photos in your own interactive web gallery

The exercises in the second part of the lesson will guide you through a typical workflow: you'll import, review, organize, and edit images, and then share them as e-mail attachments.

 You'll probably need between one and two hours to complete this lesson.

In this lesson, you'll get an overview of how Lightroom works. You'll familiarize yourself with the workspace, panels, tools, and controls, as you explore the Library, Develop, Map, Book, Slideshow, Print and Web Modules.

Understanding how Lightroom works

Working with Lightroom will be easier and more productive if you have an overview of how Lightroom works—and how it differs from other image processing applications in the way it handles digital images.

About catalog files

Note: A single catalog can easily manage thousands of files but you can create as many catalogs as you wish, depending on the way you prefer to work. For example, you may wish to use different catalogs to separate your personal library from your professional work.

Lightroom stores information about your images in a catalog file. The catalog file is central to the way Lightroom works: when you bring a photo into your library, Lightroom does not actually import the image file itself but merely creates a new entry in the library catalog to record the file's location. Once an image has been registered in this way as part of your Lightroom library, any operation you perform on the photo in Lightroom will be recorded in its catalog entry. Whenever you assign a rating, tag, or flag to the image, group it in a collection with other photos, or publish it online, your actions are recorded in the catalog file.

The images in your Lightroom library can be located anywhere on your computer hard disk, or even on external storage media; the catalog file stores references to their locations. If you wish to rename or move an image file that you've already imported into your library, you should only do so from within Lightroom so that the changes can be tracked by the catalog file; otherwise, Lightroom will report the renamed or moved file as missing and you'll be asked to reestablish the link so that the information in the catalog file can be updated.

Managing photos in a library

To work with a photo in Lightroom you must first add it to your library catalog by importing it from your computer hard disk or from external storage media, or by downloading it directly from a digital camera or card reader.

Even during the import process, Lightroom offers you a range of options to help you manage your photos. The intuitive import interface (see the illustration below) makes it quick and easy to set up your own import presets that will save you time and effort by batch-processing your image files as they are imported.

You can choose to leave your image files at their current locations, copy them to a new location leaving the originals intact (the option illustrated below), or move them and delete the originals to avoid duplicating files. If you choose to copy or move your files during the import process, you can either have Lightroom replicate the original folder structure in which they are stored, reorganize them into subfolders based on capture date, or consolidate them into a single folder.

You can also have Lightroom rename your image files during import, create duplicates for backup purposes, attach keyword tags and other metadata, and even apply a wide range of developing presets—all before you've opened a single image! You'll learn more about the import options in Lesson 3, "Importing."

Non-destructive editing

The catalog file also records each step you take when you modify or edit a photo. When you crop the image, correct the color, adjust exposure, or apply effects, Lightroom writes the changes to the photo's library catalog entry—effectively saving a set of instructions for the edits you make—rather than applying the changes directly to the original image file. This is called non-destructive editing.

As you work on your photo, Lightroom will show you a preview of the effects of your work, but the original image actually remains unaltered. The modifications you make are applied only when you export or output the image. In this respect, Lightroom works very differently from image processing applications such as Photoshop or Photoshop Elements, which save changes directly to the source file.

There are many advantages in storing modifications separately from the image data. Non-destructive editing frees you to experiment with your images. Crop an image and later change your mind—no problem! You can undo, redo, or tweak any modification that you've made without ever losing any information from the original file.

The changes you make to an image will be applied only during output—while it is being exported as a preview to be displayed on-screen in Lightroom, as part of a print or book layout, or as a low-resolution JPEG image to be used in a web page. The original image data remains intact; the editing instructions captured in the catalog file are applied only to copies of the image created in the rendering process.

Should you wish to edit an image using an external image processing application, you should always launch the process from within Lightroom. In this way, you can be sure that Lightroom will keep track of changes made to the file, and the edited copy will automatically be added to your Lightroom library. For a JPEG, TIFF, or PSD image, Lightroom gives you the option to edit the original file, or a copy—either with or without the adjustments that you've already applied in Lightroom. For files in any other file format, you can edit a copy to which your Lightroom adjustments have already been applied.

► **Tip:** You can specify your favorite external editor in the External Editing preferences. Photoshop or Photoshop Elements will be preselected by default, if either application is installed on your computer.

The Lightroom workspace

The Lightroom workspace is divided into six main panels. At the center of the workspace is the work area, flanked by the left and right panel groups. Above the work area and the left and right panel groups is the top panel, with an identity plate at the left and the Module Picker to the right. Immediately below the work area is the Toolbar, and below that, across the bottom of the workspace, the Filmstrip.

● **Note:** The illustration at the right shows the Windows version of Lightroom. On Mac OS, the arrangement of the workspace is the same except for minor differences in style between the two operating systems. On Windows, for example, the menu bar is located under the title bar of the application window, whereas on Mac OS the menu bar is anchored at the top of the screen, above the title bar of the application window.

The basic arrangement of the panels is identical in all of the seven Lightroom workspace *modules*. Only the contents of the panels vary from module to module, to address the specific requirements of each working mode.

The top panel

The top panel displays an identity plate on the left and the Module Picker on the right. The identity plate can be customized to feature your own company name or logo and will be temporarily replaced by a progress bar whenever Lightroom is performing a background process. You'll use the Module Picker to move between the different workspace modules by clicking their names. The name of the currently active module is always highlighted in the Module Picker.

The work area

At center-stage is the main preview and working area. This is where you select, review, sort, compare, and apply adjustments to your images, and where you preview the work in progress. From module to module, the work area offers different viewing options, allowing you to see either one photo or multiple images at a range of magnification levels, and to preview your book designs, slideshows, web galleries, and print layouts.

You can increase the size of the work area by hiding any or all of the surrounding panels. The work area is the only element of the Lightroom workspace that can't be hidden from view.

The left and right panel groups

The content of the side panel groups changes as you switch between the workspace modules. As a general rule, you'll use panels in the left group to find and select items, and panels in the right group to edit or customize settings for your selection.

In the Library Module for example, you'll use the panels below the Navigator panel in the left group (Catalog, Folders, Collections, and Publish Services) to locate, select, and group the images you want to work with, and the panels below the Histogram panel in the right panel group (Quick Develop, Keywording, Keyword List, Metadata, and Comments) to apply changes to them. In the Develop Module, you can choose from develop presets on the left, and fine-tune their settings on the right. In the Slideshow, Print and Web Modules, you can select templates on the left, and customize their appearance on the right.

The Toolbar

The tools available in the Toolbar also vary as you move from module to module. You can customize the Toolbar for each module independently to suit your working habits, choosing from a variety of tools and controls for switching viewing modes, setting ratings, flags, or labels, adding text, and navigating through preview pages. You can show or hide individual controls, or hide the Toolbar altogether until you need it. Most of the options presented in the Toolbar are also available as menu commands or keyboard shortcuts.

▶ **Tip:** The first time you enter any of the Lightroom modules, you'll see module tips that will help you get started by identifying the components of the Lightroom workspace and stepping you through the workflow. Dismiss the tips by clicking the Close button. To reactivate the tips for any module, choose [*Module name*] Tips from the Help menu.

The Filmstrip

The Filmstrip always displays the same set of images as the Grid view in the Library module; it can show every image in the library, the contents of a selected folder or collection, or a selection filtered by subject, date, keyword, or a range of other criteria. You can work directly with the thumbnails in the Filmstrip—or the Grid view in the Library module—to assign ratings, flags and color labels, apply metadata and developing presets, and rotate, move, or delete photos.

The Filmstrip keeps the images you're working with accessible when you're using a view other than the Grid view in the Library Module, and while you're working in one of the other modules. Whichever module you're working in, you can use the Filmstrip to quickly navigate through a selection of images, or to move between different sets of images.

Customizing the workspace

All of the workspace panels are highly customizable. You can expand, collapse, resize, hide, and show panels and groups of panels, either manually or automatically. You can add or remove control elements, change the font size, background color, and more. All of these options will be covered in more detail in Lesson 2, "Introducing the Workspace."

The Lightroom modules

Lightroom has seven workspace modules: Library, Develop, Map, Book, Slideshow, Print, and Web. Each module offers a specialized set of tools and features tailored to the different phases of your workflow: importing, organizing and publishing, adjusting and enhancing, and generating output for screen, print, or web.

You can move effortlessly between modules to suit the task at hand. Some operations, such as creating backup copies or exporting images in various file formats, are not tied to any specific module and are always accessible via menu commands.

The Library module

In the Library module you can review and organize the images in your photo library. The work area offers several different viewing modes so you can browse, inspect, compare, or select images with ease.

You can move between the different viewing modes either using menu commands or the View Mode buttons at the left of the Toolbar.

From left to right, the buttons invoke the Grid, Loupe, Compare, and Survey views.

You can customize the Toolbar for each of the viewing modes independently, choosing features, tools, and controls from the menu at the far right of the Toolbar.

Tools and controls that are currently visible in the Toolbar have a check mark beside their names in the menu. The order of the tools and controls from left to right in the Toolbar corresponds to their order from top to bottom in the menu.

In the Library module, the left panel group consists of the Navigator panel and any combination of the Catalog, Folders, Collections, and Publish Services panels, which help you to find, organize, and share the images in your library. At the top of the group, the Navigator panel is always available but you can show or hide any of the other four panels as you create additional folders and collections and move your photos between them.

The right panel group contains the Histogram panel, which can be collapsed but not hidden, and any combination of the Quick Develop, Keywording, Keyword List, Metadata, and Comments panels. Use these five panels to quickly apply developing presets, to make color corrections and tonal adjustments, and to review or edit any keyword tags, metadata, or published comments that are attached to an image.

▶ **Tip:** To specify which panels are expanded, collapsed, displayed, or hidden in a panel group, right-click (Windows) or Control-click (Mac OS) any panel header in the group, and choose from the context menu.
To choose from options that affect the behaviour of the panel group as a whole, Right-click / Control-click the outer edge of the panel group (beyond the scrollbar).

The buttons below the panel groups give quick access to the Import, Export, Synchronize Metadata, and Synchronize Settings dialog boxes.

The Develop module

Although the Quick Develop panel in the Library module offers some basic image editing options, you'll work in the Develop module when you wish to make more detailed adjustments and modifications to your photos. You can correct the color balance or tonal range, crop or straighten an image, remove red eye, and apply a range of selective local adjustments—all non-destructively.

In the Develop module, the work area offers two viewing modes: the Loupe view, which enables you to view a single image at different levels of magnification, and the Before/After view (with a variety of layout options), which makes it easy to compare the original and edited versions of a photo. You can move between these viewing modes using the controls at the left of the Toolbar.

The Toolbar can be customized for each viewing mode independently by choosing from an array of controls—Flagging, Rating, Color Label, Navigate, Slideshow, and Zoom—available in the menu at the right of the Toolbar. Some tools are available only in one module, such as the Painter tool, which can be used to apply attributes and settings directly to your images in the Library module. Others appear only in a particular viewing mode, such as the Before & After controls, which let you swap or copy develop settings between the original and edited versions of a photo in the Before/After view of the Develop module.

Tip: You can make more space available for your working view by hiding any panels that you're not currently using, as has been done with the Filmstrip in the illustration below.

The left panel group contains the Navigator panel, which can be collapsed but not hidden, and any combination of the Presets, Snapshots, History, and Collections panels, which can be shown or hidden to suit the way you prefer to work.

Develop presets are used to apply a series of develop settings with a single click. Lightroom ships with a set of default presets, and also allows you to add your own. Snapshots are development stages that you have chosen to save during the editing process. The History panel enables you to selectively undo or redo changes.

The right panel group always contains the Histogram panel and an array of editing tools—the Crop Overlay, Remove Spots, Remove Red Eye, Graduated Filter, and Adjustment Brush tools—but you can select any combination of the Basic, Tone Curve, Adjustments (HSL / Color / B&W), Split Toning, Detail, Lens Corrections, Effects, and Camera Calibration panels. You can use these panels to fine-tune many aspects of your photos: adjust the tonal balance, create special dual tone effects, correct lens vignetting, or add film grain. The buttons below the panel groups simplify the process of copying and pasting settings between photos, applying previously used settings to an image, and resetting an edited photo to its original state.

The Map module

Lightroom 4 introduces geotagging in the new Map module, where you can see or mark where your photos were taken. Photos already tagged with GPS coordinates will automatically appear on the map. You can drag images captured without GPS information directly onto the map from the Filmstrip, and edit location details and other metadata in the panel at the right. The Filter bar above the map view lets you highlight just those photos at locations currently visible on the map or filter for tagged or untagged shots. In the Saved Locations panel at the left, you can save a list of your favorite places for easy access.

Tip: You can also load a GPS tracklog from a mobile device and have Lightroom tag your photos automatically by matching their capture times to the locations recorded in the tracklog.

The Book module

The Book module, also new in Lightroom 4, delivers a suite of layout and type tools to help you create sophisticated photo book designs that can either be uploaded directly from Lightroom for printing through the online book vendor Blurb, or saved to PDF and printed on your own printer.

You can work with a multi-page preview of your book layout, focus on your design spread-by-spread, or view single pages in the Book module's central work area, switching between these viewing modes and moving through the pages of your book using the controls in the Toolbar.

In the left panel group, the Preview panel displays a thumbnail preview of the page or spread you're editing and helps you to navigate the layout when you're working at high magnification. The Collections panel provides easy access to your photo collections and saved book designs. The right panel group presents the tools and controls you'll use to customize your photo book. Once you've chosen from size, cover style, and paper type options, you can either have Lightroom generate a layout and place your photos automatically or choose from a wide range of preset page templates, and then tweak your design with the controls in the Page, Guides, Cell, and Background panels. The Caption and Type panels let you customize page and photo captions and edit type characteristics for titles and body text. The Book module Filmstrip has markers to show which images are included in your layout.

The Slideshow module

In the Slideshow module you can easily create stylish presentations from any image collection in your library. The images in your collection are displayed in the Filmstrip, where you can choose which photos you wish to include in your slideshow, and drag their thumbnails to change the order in which they will appear. The work area shows one image at a time in the Slide Editor view, where you can work on the slides individually, or preview your slideshow as a whole.

The left panel group contains the Preview, Template Browser, and Collections panels. The Template Browser offers a list of customizable slide layouts and the Collections panel allows you to navigate between your collections or create new ones. The right panel group can contain any combination of the Options, Layout, Overlays, Backdrop, Titles, and Playback panels. Use the Options, Layout, Overlays, and Backdrop controls to customize your slides. You can specify the way text or ratings appear, choose a background, or change the layout, and then save your customized settings as a new template. The Titles panel lets you add intro and ending screens, and the Playback panel offers options for adding a soundtrack, and controls for fades and timing. In the Toolbar below the Slide Editor view you'll find playback controls for the slideshow preview and tools for rotating images and adding text to your slides. Buttons below the left panel group make it simple to export a single slide or the whole presentation in either PDF or video formats.

The Print module

The Print module offers a range of preset templates and all the layout tools you'll need to quickly prepare any selection of images from your library for printing.

The photos in your collection are displayed in the Filmstrip, where you can select the images you want to print. You can drag the thumbnails in the Filmstrip to change the placement of your photos in the layout. The work area—the Print Editor view—shows your print layout, which may include only one image, a single image repeated at a variety of sizes, or multiple images.

The left panel group contains the Preview panel, the Template Browser, and the Collections panel. You can use the Collections panel to navigate between your collections or to create new ones, and the Template Browser to choose from a list of customizable print layout templates. The right panel group contains the Layout Style panel and a suite of other panels that varies slightly with your choice of layout style. Use the Image Settings, Layout, Rulers, Grid & Guides, Cells, and Page panels to customize your print layout. If you wish, you can save your settings as a custom template. The Print Job panel has settings for print resolution, color management and other output options.

The Toolbar below the Print Editor view contains controls for navigating through multiple-page print previews and buttons below the panel groups provide easy access to page setup and print settings.

The Web module

In the Web module you can build, preview, and then export or upload your own website to showcase your photos interactively.

As in the Slideshow and Print modules, the Template Browser in the left panel group offers a wide range of preset gallery templates which can be previewed in the Preview panel at the top of the group. The Collections panel provides easy access to your images and saved gallery designs. The panels in the right panel group contain settings and controls that enable you to choose between HTML and Flash gallery styles, customize the appearance and functionality of the preset templates, add titles, captions, information, links, and graphics, and manage output.

The main work area—the Gallery Editor view—displays a working interactive preview of your web gallery that is updated as you work. The style and placement of the image thumbnails and playback controls for your gallery depends on your choice of layout style and gallery template. Buttons below the panel groups make it easy to test your gallery on the fly in your choice of web browser, before you export or upload your finished presentation.

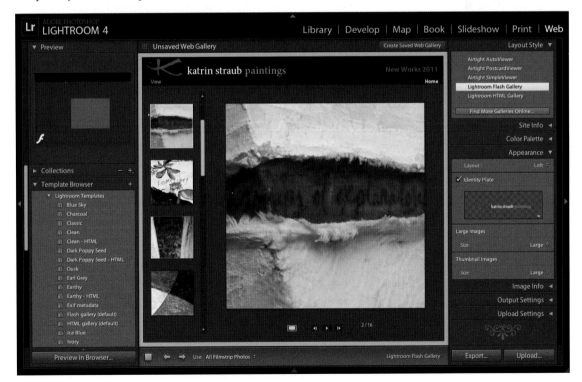

The Toolbar below the Gallery Editor view presents controls for navigating the photos in a collection and a menu offering the option to include all of the images in the Filmstrip, a selected subset, or just those photos you have flagged. You can use the Filmstrip to change the order in which your photos will appear.

The Lightroom workflow

The modular Lightroom interface makes it easy to manage every stage of your workflow, from image acquisition to finished output:

- **Import** The Lightroom workflow begins in the Library module, where you can choose to acquire images from your hard disk or external storage media, or from your camera. You can import photos from another application, grab still frames from video—even bypass your camera's memory card and capture photos directly into Lightroom.

- **Organize** You can set the options in the Import dialog box to apply a basic level of organization to your catalog by adding keyword tags and other meta-data to your photos in batches. Once the photos have been imported, you'll use the Library and Map modules to manage them—to tag, sort, and search your image library by location, keywords, flags, and ratings, and to create collections to group your photos by any association you wish.

- **Process** You'll crop, adjust, correct, retouch, and apply effects to your images in the Develop module. Optionally, you can launch an external image editor from within Lightroom for additional pixel-based editing.

- **Create** In the Book, Slideshow, Print and Web modules, you can put together polished presentations and layouts to showcase your photos.

- **Output** Some output operations—such as exporting your edited images in a variety of digital file formats or sharing them as e-mail attachments—are not tied to any specific module and are always accessible via menu commands. The Book, Slideshow, Print and Web modules each have their own output options and export controls. The Library module hosts the Publish Services panel for sharing your images online.

In the exercises to follow, you'll step through a typical workflow as you familiarize yourself with the Lightroom workspace.

Importing photos

You can import photos into your Lightroom library from your hard disk, your camera, a memory card reader, or from external storage media. During the import process you can choose from many options to help you manage and organize your files. For the purposes of this Quick Tour we will ignore most of these advanced options; Lesson 3, "Importing," will go into more detail.

Before you start on the exercises in this section, make sure that you have correctly copied the Lessons folder from the CD in the back of this book onto your computer's hard disk as detailed in "Copying the Classroom in a Book files" on page 2, and created the LR4CIB Library Catalog file to manage the lesson files as described in "Creating a catalog file for working with this book" on page 3.

1   Start Lightroom. In the Adobe Photoshop Lightroom - Select Catalog dialog box, make sure that the file LR4CIB Library Catalog.lrcat is selected in the Select A Recent Catalog To Open list, and then click Open.

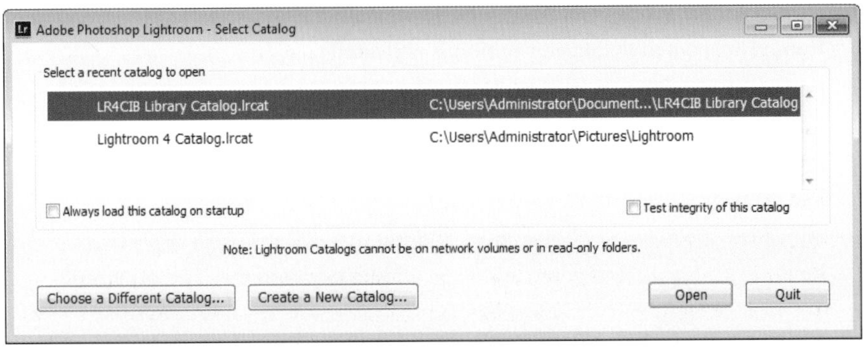

2   Lightroom will open in the screen mode and workspace module that were active when you last quit. If necessary, switch to the Library module by clicking Library in the Module Picker at the top of the workspace.

3   Choose File > Import Photos And Video. If the Import dialog box appears in compact mode, as shown in the illustration below, click the Show More Options button at the lower left of the dialog box to access all of the options available in the expanded Import dialog box.

▶ **Tip:** If you can't see the Module Picker, choose Window > Panels > Show Module Picker, or press the F5 key. Note that on Mac OS the function keys are assigned to specific operating system functions by default and may not work as expected in Lightroom. If you find this to be the case, either press the fn key (not available on all keyboard layouts) together with the F5 key, or change the keyboard behavior in the system preferences.

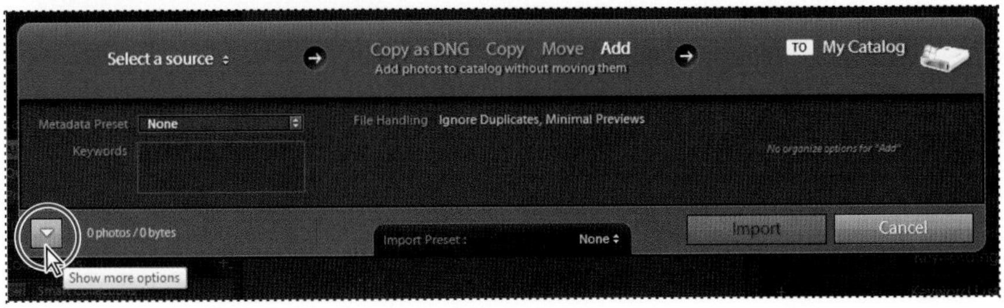

The layout of the header bar of the Import screen reflects the steps in the import process: first specify the source location of the files you wish to import, select the appropriate type of import, and then choose from destination (for Copy and Move imports) and batch processing options.

4   In the Source panel at the left of the expanded Import dialog box, navigate to the Lessons folder that you copied into the LR4CIB folder on your hard disk.

5   Select the Lesson 1 folder. Ensure that all of the images in the Lesson 1 folder are checked for import.

6 In the import options just above the thumbnail previews, select Add so that the imported photos will be added to your catalog without being moved or copied.

7 In the File Handling panel at the right of the expanded Import dialog box, choose Minimal from the Render Previews menu and ensure that the Don't Import Suspected Duplicates option is activated.

8 In the Apply During Import panel, choose None from both the Develop Settings menu and the Metadata menu, and then type **Lesson 1** in the Keywords text box. Make sure that your import is set up as shown in the illustration below, and then click Import.

Thumbnails of the Lesson 1 images appear in the Grid view of the Library module and also in the Filmstrip at the bottom of the Lightroom workspace. If you don't see the Filmstrip, press the F6 key or choose Window > Panels > Show Filmstrip.

Reviewing and organizing

When you're working with a library that contains many images, you need to be able to find exactly what you're looking for quickly. Lightroom delivers numerous tools that will make organizing and finding your files easy and enjoyable.

You should make it a working habit to go through a few cycles of reviewing and organizing your files each time you import a new batch. Investing a little time in this way can save you a lot of effort later, making it much quicker and easier to retrieve the photos you want when you need to work with them.

You've already taken the first step towards structuring your catalog by applying the keyword tag "Lesson 1" to the lesson images as they were imported.

Tagging photos with keywords is perhaps the most intuitive and versatile way to organize your catalog, because it lets you sort and search your library based on whatever words you choose to associate with your images, making it easy to find the files you need, regardless of how they are named or where they are located.

About keyword tags

Keyword tags are labels (such as "Sculpture" or "New York") that you attach to your images to make them easy to find and organize. Shared keywords create virtual groupings within your library, linking related photos although the image files may actually be stored in many separate locations.

There's no need to painstakingly sort your photos into subject-specific folders or rename files according to their content; simply assign one or more keyword tags to each image and you can easily retrieve it by searching your library using the Metadata and Text filters located in the Filter bar across the top of the work area.

You can create keyword tags to sort your photos into photographic categories, organize them according to content by tagging them with the names of people, places, activities or events, or associate them by season, color, or even mood; your imagination is the only limit.

Attach multiple keyword tags to your images to make retrieving the pictures you want even easier; you could quickly find all the photos that you've tagged with the keyword Sculpture, and then narrow the search to return only those that are also tagged New York. The more tags you attach to your photos, the more chances you have of finding exactly the right image when you need it.

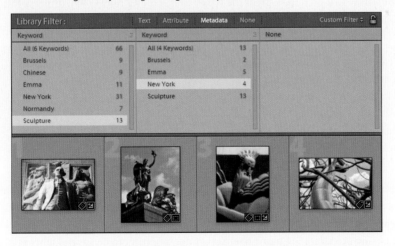

For more detail on using keyword tags, see Lesson 5, "Organizing and Selecting."

Working in slideshow mode

As a convenient way to review the images you've just imported, you can now sit back and enjoy an impromptu slideshow:

1 Check the Catalog panel (below the Navigator preview in the left panel group) to make sure that the Grid view is displaying the images from the previous import. Choose Window > Impromptu Slideshow or press Ctrl+Enter / Command+Return to launch a full-screen slideshow. Press the spacebar to pause and resume playback. Press the left arrow key to return to the previous image or the right arrow key to advance to the next.

Even while the slideshow is playing, you can start organizing your catalog by using keyboard shortcuts to rank your photos with star ratings, flag images as picks or rejects, or attach color labels. This makes the impromptu slideshow a great first-pass review: you can quickly mark your images, and then use a search filter to isolate the shots you want to work with once you return to the Library.

Note: The slideshow plays according to the settings current in the Slideshow module and will repeat until you press the Esc key to return to the Library.

Tip: Whenever you use your keyboard to mark a photo in the impromptu slideshow, the rating, flag, or label you assign appears briefly in the lower left corner of the screen.

2 To quickly assign a rating to the image currently displayed in your slideshow, press a number between 1 (for 1 star) and 5 (for 5 stars) on your keyboard. To remove the rating, press 0. You can attach only one rating to each photo; assigning a new rating will replace the old one. For the purposes of this exercise, mark three or four images with 3, 4, and 5 stars.

Rating stars are displayed under the thumbnail images in all of the Library module views and in the Filmstrip, as shown in the illustration at the left.

3 Press the P key on your keyboard to flag the image currently displayed in your slideshow as a pick (⚑), press the X key to flag it as a reject (⊠), or press the U key to remove any flags. Flag several of the Lesson 1 images as picks, and mark at least one as a reject.

You can choose to display flags, along with other information, in the image cells in the Library views and in the Filmstrip. Images flagged as rejects appear grayed out, while those marked as picks are indicated by a white border.

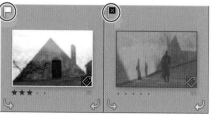

Use color labels to mark photos for specific purposes or projects. You might use a red label for images you intend to crop, green for those that need correction, or blue to identify photos you wish to use in a particular presentation. To help you remember the meaning of your labels, you can assign your own names to the colors by choosing Metadata > Color Label Set > Edit. You can create several label sets, and switch between them as needed. You could customize one set for working in the Library module and another to suit your workflow in the Develop module.

4 To assign a color label to the image currently displayed in your slideshow, use the number keys. Press 6 on your keyboard to assign a red color label, press 7 for yellow, 8 for green, or 9 for blue. There's no keyboard shortcut to assign a purple color label. To remove a color label simply press the same number again. Assign different colored labels to several of the images, and then remove one.

In the Library module's Grid View, and in the Filmstrip, a photo with a color label will be framed in that color when it's selected, and surrounded by a tinted image cell background when it's not, as shown in the illustration at the right.

If you prefer, you can change the view options so that color labels will appear only under the thumbnail images in the Grid view. You'll learn about customizing view options and more about assigning ratings, flags, and color labels, using both menu commands and the controls in the Toolbar, in Lesson 5, "Organizing and Selecting."

5 Press the Esc key to stop the slideshow and return to the Library module.

In the Library, you can user the Filter bar above the thumbnail grid to search your images by text or metadata content, and then refine your search by filtering for one or more of the searchable attributes—rating, flag status, label color, or file type—so that only those photos you want are displayed in the Grid view and the Filmstrip.

6 If the Filter bar is not already visible above the work area, open it by choosing View > Show Filter Bar. Click the Attribute filter. Click the fourth star, and choose Rating Is Greater Than Or Equal To from the Rating menu. Lightroom will now display only those photos with at least a 4 star rating.

7 Experiment a little with the attribute filters. Try searching different star ratings; then varied combinations of ratings, flags, and labels.

When you're working with only a few images, as you are in this lesson, rating, flagging, and filtering seems unnecessary, but as your photo library grows to contain hundreds or even thousands of photos you'll find these tools invaluable. The objective of this step in your workflow is to organize your images so that you can retrieve them easily for processing in the Develop, Slideshow, Print, and Web modules.

Creating a collection

Once you've reviewed and sorted your library, searched your photos by keywords or text, and filtered out unwanted images using the attributes filters, you can group the remaining photos as a *collection*, so that you can easily retrieve the same selection at any time without repeating your search. To group your photos in a collection you can choose between several options:

- The Quick Collection: a temporary holding collection in the Catalog panel, where you can assemble a selection of images.

- A "standard" Collection: a permanent grouping of photos that will be listed in the Collections panel.

- A Smart Collection: a selection of images automatically filtered from your library according to whatever criteria you specify.

- A Publish Collection: a selection of images intended for publishing that will be listed in the Publish Services panel. A Publish Collection will keep track of images you've published, enabling you to check at a glance whether the versions you're sharing are up-to-date.

1 If the star rating filter is still active in the Grid view, clear this setting by choosing Library > Filter by Rating > Reset This Filter, or simply click None in the Filter bar above the Grid view to disable all active filters.

2 Ensure that Previous Import is selected in the Catalog panel; the Grid view and the Filmstrip should display all nine images.

Note: A selected image is highlighted in the Grid view and the Filmstrip by a narrow white border (or a colored border if the image has a color label) and a lighter cell background color. If more than one photo is selected, the active photo is shown with an even lighter background. Some commands will affect only the active photo while others affect all selected photos.

When you next import images, the Previous Import folder will be updated and you'll no longer be able to isolate this particular group of images by choosing from the entries in the Catalog panel.

In this case, you could still retrieve your selection by working with the Folders panel or searching the Lesson 1 tag, but it would not be so easy to retrieve a group of photos (such as the results of a complex search) that didn't share a keyword or were spread across separate folders.

The solution is to create a collection, a virtual grouping that will be permanently listed in the Collections panel, so you'll be able to call up the same set of images at any time with a single click.

3   Choose Edit > Select All; then choose Library > New Collection. In the Create Collection dialog box, type **My First Collection** as the collection name. Under Placement, select Top Level. Under Collection Options, activate Include Selected Photos, disable Make New Virtual Copies, and then click Create.

Your new collection is now listed in the Collections panel. The listing includes an image count showing that the collection My First Collection contains nine photos.

Tip: Folders in the Collections panel can be nested. For example, you could create a Portfolio folder, and then create subfolders named Portraits, Landscape, Product shots, Black & White, etc. Each time you import an outstanding image, add it to one of these collections to slowly build up your portfolio.

Rearranging and deleting images in a collection

While you're working with the images in the Previous Import folder or the All Photographs folder, source locations listed in the Catalog panel, the order of the photos in the Grid view and in the Filmstrip is fixed; the thumbnails are either ordered by capture time (the default) or by your choice of various other criteria from the sort menu in the Toolbar, such as file name, rating, or the order in which the photos were imported into your catalog.

If the image source is a single folder without subfolders, or a collection, however, you're free to rearrange their order in the Grid view and the Filmstrip, and even remove them from the working view without deleting them from the catalog.

1   If your new collection is not already selected in the Collections panel, click to select it now. Choose Edit > Select None.

2   In the Filmstrip, Ctrl-click / Command-click to select the fifth and sixth images, featuring a spiral staircase, and drag them to the left. Drag the selected photos over the space between the first and second thumbnails in the Filmstrip and release the mouse button when the black insertion line appears.

Tip: You need to drag the thumbnail of one of your selected images, rather than the image cell frame.

The selected photos snap to their new positions in the Grid view and the Filmstrip.

3 To deselect the two photos you just moved, click an empty area in the main work area, or choose Edit > Select None. Click to select the first thumbnail in the Grid view and drag it to the right of the last image in the collection. Release the mouse button when the vertical black insertion line appears. In the Toolbar, the Sort criteria has now changed to User Order.

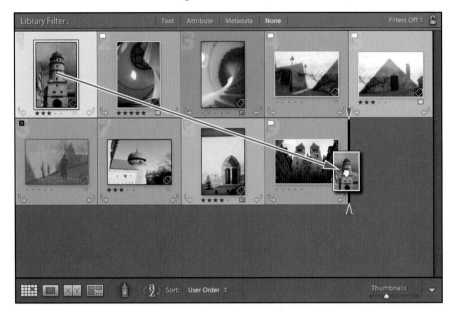

4 Choose Edit > Select None. Right-click / Control-click the seventh image in the Grid view and choose Remove From Collection from the context menu.

In the Collections panel (and in the header bar of the Filmstrip) the image count shows that My First Collection now contains only 8 images.

Although you've removed a photo from the collection, it hasn't been deleted from your catalog. The Previous Import folder and the All Photographs folder in the Catalog panel still contain all nine images. A collection contains only references to the files in your catalog; deleting the reference does not affect the file in the catalog.

▶ **Tip:** Should you wish to edit the same image differently in two collections, you'll first need to make a virtual copy—an additional catalog entry for the image—for inclusion in the second collection. You'll learn about this in Lesson 6, "Developing and Editing."

You can include a single image in any number of collections—each collection will then contain its own reference to the same file. If you apply a modification to a photo in a collection, the modification will be visible in each folder and collection that references the same photo. This is because Lightroom stores only one entry for each image file in its library catalog, and a record of all modifications is associated with that entry; any collection including that image links to the same catalog entry, and therefore displays the modified photo. Although the original image file itself remains untouched, its catalog entry has changed to include your modifications. For more information on collections, please refer to "Using collections to organize images" in Lesson 5.

Comparing photos side by side

Often you'll have two or more similar photos that you'd like to compare side by side. The Library module features a Compare view for exactly this purpose.

1 If you have any images selected in the Grid view, choose Edit > Select None. Click the Compare View button (⊠Y) in the Toolbar to switch to the Compare view. Alternately, choose View > Compare, or press C on your keyboard. By default, Lightroom selects the first two images in the collection for comparison.

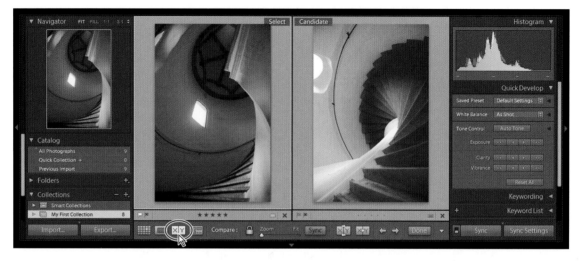

2 The Select pane is active by default. In the Filmstrip, click on the third thumbnail, DSC_3637.jpg, to replace the current Select image. Press the right arrow key on your keyboard to view the next photo to the right in the Candidate pane.

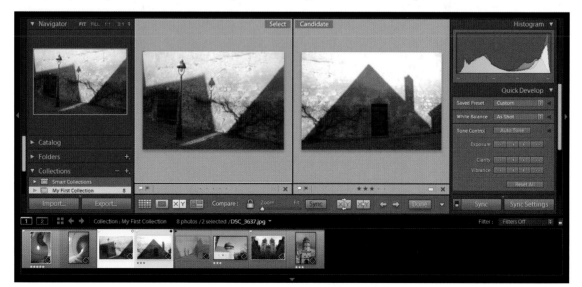

3   Press the Tab key on your keyboard to quickly hide the side panel groups so that your photos can be displayed at a larger size in the Compare view.

4   Click the Swap button () in the Toolbar below the Candidate image to swap the Candidate and Select images; then, use the right arrow key to compare the new Select photo with next candidate from the collection.

5   When you've made your choice, click the Done button at the right end of the Toolbar. The Select image will appear in the single-image Loupe view.

Comparing several photos

The Survey view lets you compare and select from several photos at the same time; you can narrow your selection one by one, until only the best photo remains. Even while you're working in the Compare and Survey views, you can continue to organize your photos by using menu commands and the controls in the Toolbar to assign star ratings, flags, and color labels. If necessary, use the Content menu at the right of the Toolbar to show the controls you need.

1   Choose Edit > Select None. In the Filmstrip, Ctrl-click / Command-click the three photos of the shadowed wall, and then click Survey view (▦) in the Toolbar. Alternatively, choose View > Survey, or press N on your keyboard.

The Survey view will display all the selected images; the more images you select the smaller the individual preview images in the Survey view. You can make more room for the images you're reviewing by hiding the Filmstrip and side panel groups as necessary, though the right panel group can be useful for viewing additional information about the active photo—from a histogram graphing tonal distribution to metadata about the camera, lens, and settings that were used. The active image is indicated by a thin white border; to activate a different photo, you can either click its thumbnail in the Filmstrip or click the image directly in the work area.

2 Drag any of the images to reposition it in the Survey view. The other images will be shuffled automatically to accommodate your action.

3 As you move the pointer over each of the images, a Deselect Photo icon () appears in the lower right corner. Click this icon to remove a photo from the selection in the Survey view.

4 Continue to eliminate photos from the Survey view until you've narrowed your selection to a single image, and then press E on your keyboard to switch to the single-image Loupe view.

> ▶ **Tip:** If you eliminate a photo accidentally, choose Edit > Undo to return it to the survey selection, or Ctrl-click / Command-click the image in the Filmstrip. You can easily add a photo to the selection in the same way.

As you eliminate candidates the remaining photos are progressively resized and shuffled to fill the space available in the work area. Eliminating a photo from the Survey view does not remove it from the collection.

5 Press Shift+Tab (twice if necessary) to show all the workspace panels. Double-click the enlarged image to return to the Grid view. Choose Edit > Select None.

Developing and editing

Without even leaving the Library module, you can use the Quick Develop panel in the right panel group to make some quick, but effective, adjustments. For more advanced image processing, the Develop module offers additional adjustment tools, as well as a more comprehensive and convenient editing environment.

Using Quick Develop in the Library module

The Quick Develop panel offers simple controls for making basic adjustments to color and tone, and a choice of develop settings presets. In the following example you'll quickly improve the tonal balance of an image using the Auto Tone button.

▶ **Tip:** If the Filmstrip is not visible, choose Window > Panels > Show Filmstrip or press F6 on your keyboard.

1   In the Filmstrip, select the file DSC_3637.jpg. You can see the name of the file in the tooltip that appears when you hold the pointer over its thumbnail, and also in the status bar above the Filmstrip when the image is selected.

2   Double-click the selected image in the Filmstrip to open it in the Loupe view. To make more space available for a larger preview, hide the Filmstrip by pressing the F6 key or disable the menu option Window > Panels > Show Filmstrip. Hide the left panel group by pressing the F7 key or disable the menu option Window > Panels > Show Left Module Panels.

As you can see from both the image preview and the distribution curve in the Histogram panel, this photo has a tonal imbalance: the lit area of the wall is overexposed, the shadowed areas are somewhat flat, and there is a lack of mid-tone detail.

3 In the Quick Develop panel, watch the tone distribution curve shift in the Histogram panel as you click the Auto Tone button.

You'll notice an immediate and substantial improvement, especially in the brighter areas of the image; the adjustment has recovered a lot of detail from the overexposed wall. The shadowed areas show some improvement, but are still too dark. The peaks at either end of the histogram curve have shifted, but there is still a very apparent trough in the midtone range.

4 Click the triangle to the right of the Auto Tone button. Click twice each on the left-most button for the Highlights control and the right-most button for Shadows. Click the left-most Whites button once, the second button from the left for Blacks twice, and the right-most Clarity button three times.

The histogram shows a greatly improved tonal distribution; there is more information in the midtone range and no obvious imbalance at either end of the curve. The adjusted image has much more detail in both the lit and shadowed areas.

Working in the Develop module

The controls in the Quick Develop panel let you change settings but don't indicate absolute values for the adjustments you make to your images.

In our example there is no way to tell which parameters were modified by the Auto Tone adjustment, or by how much they were shifted. For finer control, and a more comprehensive editing environment, you need to move to the Develop module.

1 Keeping the image from the previous exercise selected, switch to the Develop module now by doing one of the following:

- Click Develop in the Module Picker.

- Choose Window > Develop.

- Press Ctrl+Alt+2 / Command+Option+2.

2 If necessary, expand the History panel in left panel group and the Basic panel in the right panel group by clicking the white triangle beside each panel's name. Collapse any other panels that are currently open, except the Navigator on the left and the Histogram at the right. Press F6 to hide the Filmstrip.

The History panel not only lists every modification you've made to a photo—even Quick Develop adjustments made in the Library module—but also enables you to return the image to any of its previous states. The most recent entry—the last Clarity adjustment you applied—is at the top of the History list. The earliest entry, at the bottom of the list, records the date and time that the image was imported. Clicking this entry will revert the photo to its original state. As you move the pointer over each entry in the list, the Navigator displays a preview of the image at that stage of development.

The Basic panel displays information about the adjustment settings that was unavailable in the Quick Edit panel. For our image in its most recent state, the Exposure is set to -0.20, Contrast is set to -6, Highlights, Shadows, Whites, Blacks, and Clarity are set to -90, +90, +9, -9, and +60, respectively.

3 In the History panel, click the entry for the first modification you made to this photo: the Auto Tone adjustment: Inspect the settings in the Basic panel.

For this image, clicking Auto Tone modified the Exposure setting only, but applying Auto Tone to another photo will produce different adjustment values.

4 Return the photo to its most recent state by clicking the top entry in the History panel list.

5 In the Toolbar (View > Show Toolbar), click the small triangle to the right of the Before/After button and choose Before/After Top/Bottom from the menu.

▶ **Tip:** If you don't see the Before/After button in the Toolbar, click the triangle at the right of the Toolbar and activate Before And After in the Toolbar content menu.

By comparing the Before and After images, you can see how much you've improved the photo with just a few clicks.

Now let's look at how much difference your manual Quick Develop adjustments made after applying Auto Tone.

6 Leaving the most recent Clarity adjustment activated in the History panel, right-click / Control-click the entry for the Auto Tone adjustment and choose Copy History Step Settings To Before from the context menu.

There's much more to learn about the tools and features in the Develop module, but we'll leave that for later. For now you'll straighten this slightly tilted photo, and then crop it.

Straightening and cropping an image

1 Press D on your keyboard to activate the Loupe view in the Develop module.

2 Click the Crop Overlay Tool (▦), located just below the Histogram in the right panel group. The Crop Overlay Tool enables you to both crop and straighten your image.

3 When the Crop Overlay Tool is active, additional controls become available in a panel below the tool buttons. Click to select the Straighten tool (⬤). The pointer changes to a crosshairs cursor, and the spirit level icon of the Straighten tool follows your movement across the preview.

4 Look for a line in the image that should be either true horizontal or vertical. For this image, the only reliable reference is the post of the street-lamp. Drag a plumb line down through the center of the post with the Straighten tool. Release the mouse button; the image is rotated so that your plumb line becomes vertical and the Straighten tool returns to the Crop Overlay Tool controls.

▶ **Tip:** To maintain the original aspect ratio of an image when you crop it manually, make sure that Original is selected from the cropping Aspect menu and that the aspect ratio is locked.

Lightroom has overlaid a cropping rectangle on the straightened photo, automatically positioned to achieve as large a cropped area as possible while trimming away the angled edges. If you wished to adjust the crop, you could drag any of the six handles on the cropping rectangle. To assist with manual cropping, you can choose from a variety of grid overlays in the Tools > Crop Guide Overlay menu, or hide the grid by choosing Tools > Tool Overlay > Never Show.

5 When you're done, apply the crop by clicking the Crop Overlay tool, the Close button at the lower right of the tool controls, or the Done button in the Toolbar.

You can reactivate and adjust the crop at any time by simply clicking the crop tool.

Adjusting lighting and tonal balance

In a previous exercise you adjusted the Recovery control to darken highlights. For this exercise you will use the Fill Light feature to lighten areas that are too dark without affecting the rest of the tonal range.

1 Press the F6 key to show the Filmstrip, and the F7 key to hide the left panels. In the Filmstrip, click to select the photo DSC_7556.jpg.

Like the image that you adjusted using the controls in the Quick Develop panel, this photo is another difficult case; captured in shadow on an gloomy day, and effectively back-lit by the glare of the overcast sky, the image is too dark and appears flat and dull.

2 Inspect the histogram at the top of the right panel group. It's easy to see that the tonal distribution is uneven: data is clumped at both ends of the curve with a heavy bias towards the shadows and an obvious deficiency of information through most of the midtone range.

3 In the Basic panel below the histogram, click the Auto adjustment button at the top of the Tone controls, noting the effect on the histogram curve as well as the image in the work area.

Although the photo has brightened a little, it still appears flat and lifeless. The darker tones have shifted slightly to the right and the peak in the shadows range is not as sharp. The peak in the highlights is reduced, but the trough in the mid-tones is still a dominant feature.

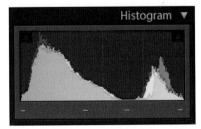

4 Inspect the settings in the Basic panel. The Auto Tone adjustment has affected most of the Tone settings. Press Ctrl+Z / Command+Z to undo the adjustment, or show the left panels and click the Import entry in the History panel.

This image requires an approach that addresses different tonal ranges separately. The Histogram panel can help you to identify the settings that need to be adjusted.

5 In the Histogram panel, move the pointer slowly from left to right from one end of the graphed curve to the other. Each tonal range is highlighted as the pointer passes over it. In the Basic panel, the corresponding control is also highlighted.

You'll start by adjusting the Exposure—the setting indicated for the midtone range, and then work down through the other controls in the Basic panel.

6   In the Basic panel's Tone pane, drag the Exposure slider to the right, or type in the text box, to set a value of **+0.2**, noting the change in the histogram as well as the photo. Set the Contrast value to **+20** and set the Highlights, Shadows, and Blacks to values of **-60**, **+60**, and **+50** respectively.

The Clarity and Vibrance settings in the Basic panel's Presence pane affect the image as a whole, rather than a specific tonal range. Increasing the Clarity adds depth and definition to an image by heightening the local contrast between adjacent areas of the image. The Vibrance slider alters the saturation of color in a non-linear manner, boosting less saturated colors more than bolder areas.

7   Set both the Clarity and Vibrance values to **+50**.

Your adjustments have brightened and intensified our underexposed lesson image. Unfortunately they have also intensified a digital artefact known as *chromatic aberration*, which results in colored fringes around pictured objects, usually most noticeable near the edges of a photo where the lens has been unable to accurately focus the different wavelengths of incoming light on the sensor.

8   Scroll down in the right panel group and expand the Lens Corrections panel; then, select the Profile mode in the picker at the top of the panel and click the check-box to activate the Remove Chromatic Aberration option.

9 Activate any of the before and after views by clicking the triangle to the right of the Before/After button in the Toolbar and choosing from the menu. In the History panel, click between the Import entry and the most recent state, noting the improvement in the tonal distribution in the Histogram panel.

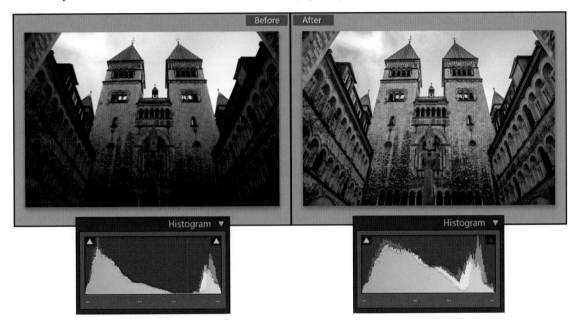

Correcting lens distortion

The combination of perspective and the characteristics of the lens you use to capture a photograph may result in any of several types of distortion in an image.

Our lesson image shows pronounced *keystone distortion*, which occurs when an object is photographed from an angle rather than from a straight-on view. Keystone distortion is common in photos of tall buildings taken from ground level; the edges of the building appear closer to each other at the top than they do at the bottom.

Another common form of distortion is *barrel distortion*: a lens effect that is most noticeable in shots taken with a wide-angle lens, causing straight lines to bow out toward the edges of the image. The opposite of this effect is known as *pincushion distortion*, where straight lines in the image appear to bend inward.

1 In the Lens Corrections panel, select the Manual mode at the top of the panel.

2   Observe the effect on the image as you drag the Distortion slider through its range; then, set a value of **+90**. Set the Vertical Transform value to **-80**. Set a value of **-3** for Horizontal Transform and reduce the scale to **75**(%).

3   Activate the Crop Overlay Tool (▦), below the Histogram panel. In the tool options pane below the tool buttons, click to unlock the padlock icon, if necessary, so that the crop is not constrained to the original aspect ratio.

4   Drag the handles at the corners and sides of the crop overlay rectangle to surround as much of the photo as possible without including any of the gray image canvas; then, bring the left edge inwards a little, referring to the overlay grid to help you center the image in the cropping rectangle.

5 Click the Crop Overlay Tool again to disable it and return to the Loupe view. Choose the Before/After Left/Right view from the menu in the Toolbar. When you're done, click the Loupe view button (▣) at the left of the Toolbar.

This combination of settings is too extreme to really be called a correction, but serves to demonstrate how the Transform controls work. You can see that the change has given the image a very different feel; the Lens Corrections panel's Transform controls can be employed singly, or in any combination, not only to "correct" an image, but also to achieve effects.

Editing in another application

In the process of reducing the keystone distortion in our lesson photo without pushing the top of our towers out of the frame, the image has been compressed horizontally, giving it an uncomfortable, pinched look.

In this exercise, you'll learn how to open a photo from your Lightroom catalog in an external image editing application to find a solution to a problem like this.

Photoshop or Photoshop Elements will be preselected as the default external editor, if either of those applications is installed on your computer, but you can also specify another application in the External Editing preferences.

1 If you wish to specify an application other than Photoshop or Photoshop Elements, choose Preferences from the Edit (Windows) / Lightroom (Mac OS) menu. Under Additional External Editor on the External Editing pane of the Preferences dialog box, click the Choose button beside Application, select your favorite image editor, and then click Open / Choose. Click OK on Windows, or the red Close button on Mac OS, to close the Preferences dialog box.

2 With the image DSC_7556.jpg still selected in the Filmstrip, choose the desired application from the Photo > Edit In menu.

3 In the Edit Photo With... dialog box, activate the option Edit A Copy With Lightroom Adjustments under What To Edit. Under Copy File Options, choose your preferred file format, color space, and bit depth from the options available in the pop-up menus. You can either type a new value for Resolution, or accept the default; then, click Edit.

The image opens in your external editor. For the purposes of this exercise, we'll assume you're working with Photoshop.

4 In Photoshop, choose Image > Image Size. In the Image Size dialog box, disable the Constrain Proportions option. Under Pixel Dimensions, double-click to select the Width value and type a new value of **1100** (pixels). Leave the option Resample Image active and choose Bicubic Smoother (Best For Enlargement) from the resampling menu; then, click OK. Choose File > Close; then, click Save.

The edited copy of the photo opens in Lightroom. In the Filmstrip (and also in the Library module Grid view) the thumbnail for the externally edited copy is stacked with the original image.

5 In the Filmstrip, select the original photo, DSC_7556.jpg. Press the F7 key to show the left panels. In the History panel, click to select the Import entry.

6 Switch to the Library module by clicking Library in the Module Picker across the top of the workspace.

7 Click the Compare View button (⊠Ⓨ) in the Library module Toolbar to compare the original photo with the externally edited copy.

Sharing your work by e-mail

Now that you've edited and enhanced your photos, the final step in your workflow is to present them to your client, share them with your friends and family, or to display them for the world to see on a photo-sharing website or in your own interactive web gallery. In Lightroom, it takes only seconds to create a sophisticated photo book or slideshow, customize a print layout, publish your photos online, or generate a stylish interactive gallery ready to be uploaded directly to your web server from within Lightroom.

Lesson 7, "Creating a Photo Book," Lesson 8, "Creating a Slideshow," Lesson 9, "Printing Images," and Lesson 10, "Publishing your Photos," will provide much more detail on the many Lightroom tools and features that make it simple to create professional-looking presentations, layouts, and galleries to showcase your photos. In this exercise, you'll learn how you can attach your finished images to an e-mail without leaving Lightroom.

1 Press Ctrl+D / Command+D or choose Edit > Select None. In the Filmstrip, select the image DSC_3637.jpg, which you adjusted earlier in this lesson; then, Ctrl-click / Command-click to add the externally edited image DSC_7556-Edit to the selection.

2 Choose File > Email Photos.

Lightroom detects the default e-mail application on your computer and opens a dialog box where you can set up the address, subject, and e-mail account for your message, and specify the size and quality for the attached images.

3 Click Address to open your Lightroom address book; then, enter a contact name and e-mail address and click OK.

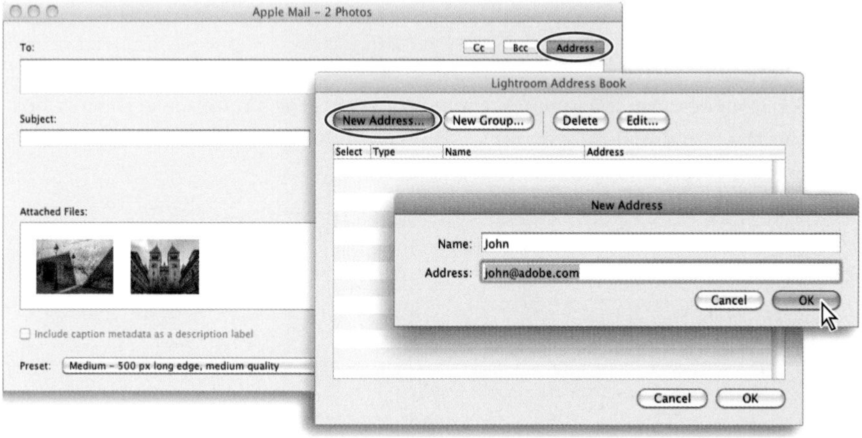

Note: For Windows users: if you have not specified a default e-mail application in Windows, the sequence of dialog boxes you see may differ slightly from that described and illustrated here (from Mac OS). The process is basically the same, but you may need to refer to steps 8, 9, and 10 to set up an e-mail account before returning to this step.

4 In the Lightroom Address Book dialog box, you can specify as many recipients for your message as you wish. For now, select the entry for your new contact by clicking the check box, and then click OK.

5 Now type a subject line for your e-mail.

6 Choose from the image size and quality options in the Preset menu.

7 If you intend to use your default e-mail application, you're ready to click Send and add a text message in a standard e-mail window.

8 If you'd prefer to connect directly to a web-based mail service, you need to set up an account. In the From menu, choose Go To Email Account Manager.

9 In the Lightroom Email Account Manager dialog box, click the Add button at the lower left. In the New Account dialog box, enter your e-mail account name and choose your service provider; then, click OK.

10 Enter your e-mail address and password under Credential Settings in the Lightroom Email Account Manager dialog box, and then click Validate.

Lightroom uses your credential settings to verify your account online. In the Lightroom Email Account Manager dialog box, a green light indicates that your web-based e-mail account is now accessible by Lightroom.

11 Click Done to close the Email Account Manager. Type a message in the text box above the thumbnails of your attached images, change the font, text size, and text color if you wish, and then click Send.

Getting help

Help is available from several sources, each one useful to you in different circumstances:

Help in the application: The complete user documentation for Adobe Photoshop Lightroom is available from the Help menu, in the form of HTML content that displays in the Adobe Community Help application. Even without the Community Help application, this content will display in your default browser. This documentation provides quick access to summarized information on common tasks and concepts, and can be especially useful if you are new to Lightroom or if you are not connected to the Internet.

In the Help menu you can also access a list of keyboard shortcuts for the current module, and module-specific tips that will help you get started by introducing you to the Lightroom workspace and stepping you through the workflow.

Help on the Web: You can also access the most comprehensive and up-to-date documentation on Lightroom via your default browser, whether Lightroom is currently running or not.

Help PDF: Help is also available as a PDF document, optimized for printing; you can download the document at: www.adobe.com/go/learn_lightroom_helppdf_en.

> **Note:** You don't need to be connected to the Internet to view Help in Lightroom. However, with an active Internet connection, you can access the most up-to-date information.

Navigating Help in the application

1   Choose Help > Lightroom Help, or press the F1 key on your keyboard. Even if you are not currently connected to the Internet, the Adobe Community Help application (or, if the Community Help application is not installed, your default web browser) will open to the front page of the Adobe Photoshop Lightroom Help documentation that was installed on your computer together with the Lightroom application.

2   For quick access to Help documentation specific to the module in which you are working, press Ctrl+Alt+/ on Windows, or Command+Option+/ on Mac OS.

3   Press Ctrl+/ on Windows, or Command+/ on Mac OS to see a list of keyboard shortcuts for the current module.

4   Choose a topic from the table of contents. Click the plus sign (+) to the left of any topic heading to see a list of sub-topics. Click a sub-topic to see its content displayed on the right.

If you do have an active Internet connection, the Community Help application gives you access to the most up-to-date information about Lightroom and other Adobe products. You can search and browse Adobe and community content, and comment on or rate any article just as you would in your default browser. Search results will show not only content from Adobe, but also from the community.

You can also download reference content for use offline, and subscribe to new content updates (which can be downloaded automatically) so that you'll always have the most up-to-date information. Adobe content is updated based on community feedback and contributions. You can contribute in several ways: add comments to content or forums—including links to web content, publish your own content using Community Publishing, or contribute Cookbook Recipes. Find out how to contribute at www.adobe.com/community/publishing/download.html.

See http://community.adobe.com/help/profile/faq.html for answers to frequently asked questions about Community Help.

Accessing Help and Support on the Web

You can access Lightroom Help, Support and other useful resources on the Web, even if Lightroom is not currently running.

1 Do one of the following::

- If Lightroom is currently running, choose Help > Lightroom Online.

- If Lightroom is not currently running, point your default web browser to www.adobe.com/support/photoshoplightroom where you can find and browse Lightroom Help and Support content on adobe.com.

2 To search for a particular topic in the Help documentation, enter a search term in the Search text box at the top of the page, and then click Search.

3 Choose from the options just below the search field on the results page to show All Community Content or narrow the search to return Only Adobe Content.

You can find a list of additional resources that will help you to get the most out of Lightroom on page 7.

Congratulations—you've completed the first lesson. You have been introduced to the seven Lightroom workspace modules and learned how they fit into your workflow. You've imported photos, taken the first steps towards organizing your catalog in the Library module, explored some of the powerful editing tools in the Develop module, and seen just how easy it can be to share your images.

Before you move on to the next lesson, take minute or two to refresh your new skills by reading through the lesson review on the facing page.

Review questions

1 What is non-destructive editing?

2 What are the seven Lightroom workspace modules and how do they relate to your workflow?

3 How can you increase the viewing area without resizing the application window?

4 What advantage is there to grouping images in a collection, rather than by keyword?

5 Why is it recommended to create a special collection for each book, slideshow, print, or web project?

Review answers

1 Whatever modifications you make to an image in your library—cropping, rotation, corrections, retouching, or effects—Lightroom records the editing information only in the catalog file. The original image data remains unchanged.

2 The Lightroom workflow begins in the Library module: a hub where you'll import, organize, sort, and search your photos, manage your growing catalog, and keep track of the images you publish. You can leverage GPS metadata to organize your photos by location in the Map module. Move to the Develop module for a comprehensive editing environment with all the tools you need to correct, retouch, and enhance digital images and ready them for output. The Book, Slideshow, Print and Web modules each provide a range of stylish preset templates together with a suite of powerful, intuitive controls to help you customize them so that you can quickly create sophisticated layouts and presentations to share and showcase your work in its best light.

3 You can hide any of the panels and panel groups surrounding the work area. The working view automatically expands into the space available. The work area is the only part of the Lightroom workspace that you cannot hide from view.

4 The difference between grouping images in a collection and applying keyword tags is that, in a collection, you can change the order of the photos displayed in the Grid view and the Filmstrip, and you can remove an image from the group.

5 In a collection, you can change the order in which your images are displayed, which affects their placement in your project or layout. Images that are not included in a collection are displayed in a fixed order reflecting your choice of sorting criteria, such as capture date, file name, or star rating.

2 INTRODUCING THE WORKSPACE

Lesson overview

Whether you prefer to use menu commands, keyboard shortcuts, or buttons and sliders—whether you use a small screen or a large one, one monitor or two—you can customize the flexible Lightroom workspace to suit the way *you* work. Customize each of the modules individually so that you always have your favorite tools and controls at hand, arranged just the way you like them.

To help familiarize you with the Lightroom workspace, this lesson will focus on the interface elements and skills that are common to all the workspace modules:

- Toggling between screen modes

- Adjusting the workspace layout

- Showing and hiding panels and panel groups

- Collapsing or expanding panels

- Changing and customizing view modes

- Working with a second display

- Personalizing the workspace

- Choosing interface options

- Using keyboard shortcuts

 You'll probably need between one and two hours to complete this lesson.

Make working with Lightroom even more pleasurable, and ultimately more productive, by personalizing the workspace so that you always have your favorite tools at hand. Lightroom streamlines your workflow, allowing you to move effortlessly between the different modules and viewing modes and freeing you up to spend less time in front of the computer and more time behind the lens!

Getting started

▶ **Tip:** The first time you enter any of the Lightroom modules, you'll see module tips that will help you get started by identifying the components of the Lightroom workspace and stepping you through the workflow. Dismiss the tips by clicking the Close button. To reactivate the tips for any module, choose [*Module name*] Tips from the Help menu.

Before you start on the exercises in this section, make sure that you have correctly copied the Lessons folder from the CD in the back of this book onto your computer's hard disk as detailed in "Copying the Classroom in a Book files" on page 2, and created the LR4CIB Library Catalog file to manage the lesson files as described in "Creating a catalog file for working with this book" on page 3.

1 Start Lightroom. In the Adobe Photoshop Lightroom - Select Catalog dialog box, make sure that the file LR4CIB Library Catalog.lrcat is selected under Select A Recent Catalog To Open, and then click Open.

▶ **Tip:** If you can't see the Module Picker, choose Window > Panels > Show Module Picker, or press the F5 key. Note that on Mac OS the function keys are assigned to specific operating system functions by default and may not work as expected in Lightroom. If you find this to be the case, either press the fn key (not available on all keyboard layouts) together with the F5 key, or change the keyboard behavior in the system preferences.

2 Lightroom will open in the screen mode and workspace module that were active when you last quit. If necessary, switch to the Library module by clicking Library in the Module Picker at the top of the workspace.

Importing images into the library

The first step is to import the images for this lesson into the Lightroom library.

1 Choose File > Import Photos And Video. If the Import dialog box appears in compact mode, click the Show More Options button at the lower left of the dialog box to see all the options in the expanded Import dialog box.

2 Under Source at the left of the expanded Import dialog box, navigate to the Lessons folder that you copied into the LR4CIB folder on your hard disk. Select the Lesson 2 folder and ensure that all seven images in the Lesson 2 folder are checked for import.

3 In the import options just above the thumbnail previews, select Add so that the imported photos will be added to your catalog without being moved or copied.

4 Under File Handling at the right of the expanded Import dialog box, choose Minimal from the Render Previews menu and ensure that the Don't Import Suspected Duplicates option is activated.

5 Under Apply During Import, choose None from both the Develop Settings menu and the Metadata menu and type **Lesson 2** in the Keywords text box. Make sure that your import is set up as shown in the illustration below, and then click Import.

6 If necessary, press the F6 key to show the Filmstrip across the bottom of the Lightroom workspace.

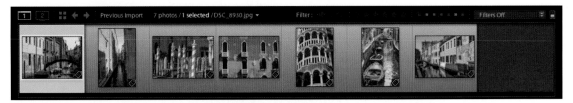

Thumbnails of the seven Lesson 2 images appear in the Grid view of the Library module and in the Filmstrip. You're now ready to start the exercises in this lesson.

Toggling screen modes

Note: Whether you are running Lightroom on Windows or Mac OS, the workspace looks almost identical—any variations are simply due to the different user interface conventions on each platform.

Lightroom can operate in any of three *screen modes*. In the default mode the workspace appears inside a regular document window that you can resize and position as you like on your screen. In the other two modes, the workspace expands to fill the entire screen—either with or without a menu bar—maximizing the space available for working with images. You can switch between screen modes at any time.

1   Choose Window > Screen Mode > Normal to ensure that you are in the default screen mode.

In Normal screen mode on Windows, the Lightroom workspace appears inside an application window with the menu bar just below the window's title bar.

Normal screen mode on Windows.

In Normal screen mode on Mac OS, the Lightroom workspace appears inside a document window with the menu bar across the top of the screen.

Normal screen mode on Mac OS.

2 Choose Window > Screen Mode > Full Screen With Menubar.

In Full Screen With Menubar screen mode on Windows, the Lightroom workspace expands to fill the screen with the menu bar across the top of the screen and the Windows task bar across the bottom.

Full Screen With Menubar screen mode on Windows.

In Full Screen With Menubar screen mode on Mac OS, Lightroom expands to fill the screen with the menu bar across the top of the screen and the Dock, if it's not currently hidden, at the bottom.

Full Screen With Menubar screen mode on Mac OS.

3 Choose Window > Screen Mode > Full Screen.

In Full Screen mode on Windows, the Lightroom workspace fills the entire screen with both the menu bar and the Windows task bar hidden.

In Full Screen mode on Mac OS, the Lightroom workspace fills the entire screen with both the menu bar and the Dock hidden.

4 Press Alt+Ctrl+F / Option+Command+F to return to Normal screen mode.

▶ **Tip:** In Full Screen mode, the menu bar appears when you move the pointer to the top edge of the screen, allowing access to menu commands.

5 Choose Window > Screen Mode > Full Screen And Hide Panels, or use the keyboard shortcut Shift+Ctrl+F / Shift+Command+F.

6 In the Grid view, double-click any of the thumbnails to enter Loupe view.

A variant of the Full Screen mode, Full Screen And Hide Panels is ideal for viewing an image as large as possible in Loupe view. By pressing T on your keyboard you can even hide the Toolbar below the work area, so that you see nothing but your photo. You'll learn more about showing and hiding panels later in this lesson.

7 Press F on your keyboard—the keyboard shortcut for Window > Screen Mode > Next Screen Mode. Press F repeatedly to cycle through the three screen modes. As you switch between the screen modes, you'll notice that the panels around the work area remain hidden.

8 To reveal all hidden panels, press Shift+Tab once or twice. If the Toolbar is hidden, press T to show it.

9 Press Alt+Ctrl+F / Option+Command+F to return to Normal screen mode.

Adjusting the workspace layout

Working with the application window on Windows

In Normal screen mode on Windows, you can resize and reposition the application window just as you are used to doing with other applications.

1   Move the pointer to any edge of the window. When the pointer changes to a horizontal or vertical double-arrow icon, you can drag the window's edge.

2   Move the pointer to any corner of the application window. When the pointer changes to a diagonal double-arrow (↗), you can drag the corner.

3   Click the Maximize button (▣), located beside the Close button (x) at the right of the title bar; the application window expands to fill the entire screen, though you are still in Normal screen mode with both the title bar and the menu visible. While the window is maximized, it's no longer possible to resize it as you did in steps 1 and 2, or reposition it by dragging the title bar.

4   Click the Restore Down button (▣) to return to the previous window size.

Working with the application window on Mac OS

1   In Normal screen mode on Mac OS, resize the application window by dragging its lower right corner.

2   Click the green Zoom button (◯), located beside the Close and Minimize buttons at the left of the title bar. The application window expands to fill the screen. Click the Zoom button again to return to the previous window size.

3   Reposition the application window on your screen by dragging the title bar.

Using a secondary display

If you have a second monitor connected to your computer, you can use it to display an additional view that is independent of the module and view mode currently active on your main monitor. You can choose between Grid, Loupe, Compare, and Survey views for your secondary display. You can choose to have the secondary view displayed in its own window that can be resized and repositioned, rather than have it fill your second screen.

If you have only one monitor connected to your computer, you can open the additional display in a floating window that you can resize and reposition as you work.

1   To open a separate window—whether you're using one or two monitors—click the Use Second Monitor / Show Second Window button (■2■), located at the upper left of the Filmstrip.

▶ **Tip:** You can use keyboard shortcuts to change the view in the secondary display—Shift+G for Grid, Shift+E for Loupe, Shift+C for Compare, and Shift+N for Survey. If the second window is not already open, you can use these keyboard shortcuts to quickly open it in the desired viewing mode.

2   In the top panel of the secondary display, click Grid or press Shift+G.

3   Use the Thumbnails slider in the lower right corner of the secondary display to change the size of the thumbnail images. Use the scrollbar on the right side, if necessary, to scroll to the end of the Grid view.

The Grid view in the secondary display shows the same images as the Grid view and the Filmstrip in the main application window. The source indicator and menu on the left side of the lower panel work the same way as they do in the Filmstrip, and the top and bottom panels can be hidden and shown, just as they can in the main window. You'll learn more about working with panels later in this lesson.

4 In the secondary display, select an image from the grid, and then click Loupe in the top panel. Make sure that Normal is selected in the view mode picker at the right of the top panel.

When the secondary display is in Normal mode, the Loupe view displays the active image from the Grid view and Filmstrip in the main display.

● **Note:** If your secondary display is open in a window rather than on a second screen, you may need to click inside the main window or on its title bar to change the focus of any keyboard input.

5 Use the left and right arrow keys on your keyboard to select either the previous or next photo in the Filmstrip. The new selection becomes the active image and the secondary display is updated accordingly.

6 In the secondary display, click Live in the view mode picker at the right of the top panel.

In Live mode, the secondary display shows the image that is currently under your pointer in either the Filmstrip, Grid, Loupe, Compare, or Survey view in the main window. You can set a different zoom level for the secondary display by choosing from the picker at the lower right of the secondary window.

7 Select an image in the Filmstrip, and then click Locked in the view mode picker in the top panel of the secondary window. The current image will now remain fixed in the secondary display until you switch back to Normal or Live mode—regardless of the image displayed in the main window.

8 Change the zoom level for the secondary display by choosing from the picker at the right of the lower panel: click Fit, Fill, or 1:1, or choose a zoom ratio from the menu at the far right.

9 Drag the zoomed image to reposition it in the secondary window, and then click the image to return to the previous zoom level.

10 (Optional) Right-click / Control-click the image to choose a different background color or texture from the context menu. These settings will apply to the secondary display independently of the options chosen for the main window.

11 Choose Compare from the view picker in the top panel of the secondary window. In the main window, select two or more images—either in the Grid view or in the Filmstrip.

The image in the left pane of the Compare view is the *Select* image; the image in the right pane is the *Candidate*. You can change the candidate image by clicking the Select Previous Photo button (⬅) or the Select Next Photo button (➡). If you selected more than two images, only images from the selection are considered as candidates. To replace the Select image with the current Candidate, click the Make Select button (✖▼).

12 In the main window, select three or more images—either in the Grid view or in the Filmstrip, and then click Survey in the top panel of the second window. Use the Survey view to compare more than two images at the same time (*See illustration on next page*). To remove an image from the Survey view, move the pointer over the unwanted image and click the Close button (x) that appears in the lower right corner of the image. You'll learn more about the Compare and Survey views later in this book.

13 Close the secondary display by disabling the menu option Window > Secondary Display > Show, or by clicking the Close button (x) (Windows) / (⊝) (Mac OS).

Resizing panels

You can customize the layout of the Lightroom workspace to suit the way you work or make more space for the task at hand by adjusting the width of the side panel groups and the height of the Filmstrip panel, or by hiding any of these elements.

1 Move the pointer over the right edge of the left panel group; the pointer changes to a horizontal double-arrow cursor. Drag to the right and release the mouse button when the panel group has reached its maximum width.

The central work area contracts to accommodate the expanded panel group. You might use this arrangement to maximize the Navigator preview.

2 Click Develop in the Module Picker to switch to the Develop module. You'll notice that the left panel group returns to the width it was when you last used the Develop module.

Lightroom remembers your customized workspace layout for each module independently, so that the workspace is automatically rearranged to suit the way you like to work for each stage in your workflow as you move between modules.

3 Press Alt+Ctrl+Up Arrow / Option+Command+Up Arrow to return quickly to the previous module.

4 In the Library module, drag the right edge of the left panel group to return the group to its minimum width.

5 Move the pointer over the top edge of the Filmstrip panel; the pointer changes to a vertical double-arrow cursor. Drag the top edge down until the Filmstrip reaches its minimum height.

The work area expands to fill the available space. This arrangement increases the screen space available for the Grid view when you're selecting photos, or for reviewing images in the Loupe, Compare and Survey views.

Note: For the side panel groups, double-clicking the border will produce a different result. This is discussed in the next section, "Showing and hiding panels or panel groups."

6 Switch to the Develop module. The Filmstrip remains unchanged as you move between modules. Whichever module you switch to, the Filmstrip will remain at its current height until you resize it.

7 Move the pointer over the top edge of the Filmstrip panel; the pointer changes to a vertical double-arrow cursor. Double-click the top edge of the Filmstrip to reset the panel to its previous height; then switch back to the Library module.

8 Drag the top border of the Filmstrip to its maximum height. The thumbnails in the Filmstrip are enlarged and, if necessary, a scrollbar appears along the bottom of the Filmstrip. Scroll to view all the thumbnails.

9 Double-click the top edge of the Filmstrip with the vertical double-arrow cursor to reset the panel to its previous height.

● **Note:** You can't change the height of the top panel, but you can hide or reveal it as you wish.

Showing and hiding panels or panel groups

As you've seen, one way of making more space for your work area is to resize the side panel groups and the Filmstrip. Another way is to completely hide panels from view. You can hide any of the panels surrounding the work area in the workspace. In some screen modes Lightroom even hides the title bar, the menu bar, and the Windows task bar or the Mac OS Dock.

1 To hide the left panel group, click the Show / Hide Panel Group icon (◀) in the left margin of the workspace window. The panel group disappears and the arrow icon is reversed.

2 Click the reversed Show / Hide Panel Group icon (▶) to reveal the left panel group.

▶ **Tip:** You don't need to be accurate when you click the Show / Hide Panel Group icons. In fact, you can click anywhere in the workspace margins to hide and show panels.

You can use the arrows in the top, right, and bottom margins of the workspace to show and hide the top panel, the right panel group, and the Filmstrip.

3 Disable the menu option Window > Panels > Show Left Module Panels or press the F7 key to hide the left panel group. To show the group again, press F7 or choose Window > Panels > Show Left Module Panels. Disable the menu option Window > Panels > Show Right Module Panels or press the F8 key to hide the right panel group. To show the group again, press F8 or choose Window > Panels > Show Right Module Panels.

4 Disable the menu option Window > Panels > Show Module Picker or press the F5 key to hide the top panel. To show it again, press F5 or choose Window > Panels > Show Module Picker. To hide the Filmstrip, press the F6 key or disable the menu option Window > Panels > Show Filmstrip. To show it again, press F6 or choose Window > Panels > Show Filmstrip.

5 To hide or show both side panel groups together, press the Tab key or choose Window > Panels > Toggle Side Panels. To hide or show the side panel groups, the top panel, and the Filmstrip together, press Shift+Tab, or choose Window > Panels > Toggle All Panels.

▶ **Tip:** On Mac OS, some function keys are assigned to specific operating system functions by default. If pressing a function key in Lightroom does not work as expected, either press the fn key (not available on all keyboard layouts) together with the respective function key, or change the keyboard behavior in the system preferences.

Lightroom offers even more options for showing and hiding panels or panel groups; you can have them show and hide automatically in response to the movements of the pointer.

6 Right-click / Control-click the Show / Hide Panel Group icon (◀) in the left margin of the workspace window. Choose Auto Hide & Show from the context menu.

7 Hide the left panel group by clicking the Show / Hide Panel Group icon (◀). Move the pointer over the icon, or anywhere in the left margin of the work-space. The left panel group automatically slides into view, partly covering the work area. You can click to select catalogs, folders, and collections; the left panel group will remain visible as long as the pointer remains over it. Move the pointer outside the left panel group and it will disappear again. To show or hide the left panel group regardless of the current panel settings, press the F7 key.

8 Right-click / Control-click the Show / Hide Panel Group icon (◀) in the left margin of the workspace window and choose Auto Hide from the context menu. Now the panel group disappears when you are done with it and does not reappear when you move the pointer into the workspace margin. To show the left panel group again, click in the workspace margin, or press the F7 key.

9 To turn off automatic show and hide, right-click / Control-click the Show / Hide Panel Group icon (◀) in the left margin of the workspace and choose Manual from the context menu.

10 To reset the left panel group to its default settings, activate Auto Hide & Show in the context menu. If necessary, press the F7 key or the F8 key to show the left and right panel groups.

Keep it in mind that Lightroom remembers your customized panel layout for each module independently, including your preferred show and hide options, so you can set these options differently to suit the way you like to work in each module. The options you choose for the Filmstrip and the top panel, however, remain unchanged as you move between modules.

Working with the left and right panel groups

Up to this point in our lesson, we've dealt with the left and right panels only as groups. Now you'll learn to work with the individual panels within the groups.

Expanding and collapsing panels

1   If you are not already in the Library module, switch to it now. Create more space to work with the side panel groups by hiding both the top panel and the Filmstrip. *(See step 4 in the previous exercise.)*

In the Library module, the left panel group contains the Navigator, Catalog, Folders, Collections, and Publish Services panels. Each panel within a group can be *expanded* to show its content or *collapsed* so that only the panel header is visible. A triangle next to the panel name indicates whether a panel is expanded or collapsed.

2   To expand a collapsed panel, click the triangle next to its name; the triangle turns downward and the panel expands to show its content. Click the triangle again to collapse the panel.

> **Tip:** You don't need to be accurate when you click the triangle. Clicking anywhere in the panel header will do, as long as you don't click any other control that might be located in the header, such as the Plus icon (+) in the header of the Collections panel.

Folders within a panel—such as the Smart Collections folder in the Collections panel—can be expanded and collapsed by clicking the triangle next to the folder name, or by double-clicking the folder header.

3   Panels that are currently expanded and fully visible in the panel group show a check mark in front of their names in the Window > Panels menu. Choose a panel from that menu and toggle its display status.

4 In the Window > Panels menu, look at the keyboard shortcuts for expanding and collapsing the individual panels. For the panels in the left group, the keyboard shortcuts begin with Ctrl+Shift / Control+Command followed by a number. The panels are numbered from the top down, so you press Ctrl+Shift+0 / Control+Command+0 for the Navigator panel, Ctrl+Shift+1 / Control+Command+1 for the Catalog panel, and so on. For the panels in the right group, the keyboard shortcuts begin with Ctrl / Command followed by a number. Press Ctrl+0 / Command+0 to collapse the Histogram panel. Press the same keyboard shortcut again to expand it. These keyboard shortcuts may be assigned to different panels in another workspace module, but this should not be too confusing if you remember that the panels are always numbered from the top of the group, starting at 0.

You can expand and collapse all panels (except the topmost in each group) with one command, or have all the panels other than the one you're working with (and the top panel in the group) close automatically. The top panel in each group has a special role and is not affected by these commands.

> **Tip:** Another way to access the panels context menu is to right-click / Control-click the empty area below the bottom panel.

5 To collapse all panels in either of the side groups, right-click / Control-click the header of any panel other than the top panel in the group, and then choose Collapse All from the context menu. The top panel remains unaffected.

6 To expand all panels in either side group, right-click / Control-click the header of any panel—other than the top panel in each group—and choose Expand All from the context menu. Once again, the top panel remains unaffected.

> **Tip:** Alt-click or Option-click the header of any panel to quickly activate or disable the Solo mode.

7 To collapse all the panels in a group other than the one you're working with, right-click / Control-click the header of any panel—other than the top panel in the group—and choose Solo mode from the context menu. Only one panel will remain expanded. The triangles beside the panel names change from solid to dotted when Solo mode is activated. Click the header of a collapsed panel to expand it. The previously expanded panel collapses automatically.

Hiding and showing panels

If you use some panels in a group less often than others, you can hide them from view to create more space to expand the panels you use most frequently.

1 To hide all the panels in a group other than the topmost, right-click / Control-click the header of any panel and choose Hide All from the context menu. All the panels in the group are now hidden, except the Navigator panel at the top.

2 To show all panels, right-click / Control-click inside the empty space below the visible panels and choose Show All from the context menu.

3 To show or hide an individual panel, choose it from the same context menu. Panels that are currently visible have a checkmark in front of their names.

Customizing the appearance of the panel groups

By default, Lightroom displays an ornament—the panel end mark—below the bottom panel in each group. You can select any of the designs that come preinstalled in Lightroom, change the panel end mark to one of your own design, or choose not to display a panel end mark at all.

1 Right-click / Control-click inside the empty space below the panels. Choose an ornament from the Panel End Mark submenu in the context menu, or select None.

The same panel end mark is used for both side panel groups in all the modules. To use your own PDF, JPEG, GIF, PNG, TIFF, or PSD image, place it in the Panel End Marks Folder. To find the Panel End Marks Folder, choose Go To Panel End Marks Folder from the Panel End Mark submenu in the panel context menu. The names of any images you place in the Panel End Marks folder will appear grouped below the pre-installed end marks in the menu. The panel end marks that come pre-installed in Lightroom are no more than 56 pixels high, but you can use a taller image if you wish. If your image is too wide, Lightroom will automatically scale it to the width of the panel. Your custom end mark design may contain transparent pixels.

You can also change the panel end mark—and the size of the font used in the panels—in the Preferences dialog box.

2 Choose Edit > Preferences / Lightroom > Preferences. In the Preferences dialog box, click the Interface tab.

You'll find the End Marks and Font Size menus in the Panels options. The End Marks menu offers the same options you saw in step 1. From the Panel Font Size menu you can choose either Small (the default) or Large, although the difference is subtle. Changes to the font size will take effect next time you launch Lightroom.

3 Without making any changes, click Cancel / the Close button (⊗) to close the Preferences dialog box.

Working with the main display area

The main display area—the work area—in the center of the application window is where you select, sort, and compare the images in your library, and preview the work in process as you make adjustments and create presentations. The work area serves different purposes in each of the Lightroom workspace modules. The Library and Develop modules offer a choice of view modes to suit a range of tasks, from organizing and sharing your collections to editing the individual photos. In the Slideshow, Print, and Web modules, the work area presents a working preview of your projects and presentations.

View modes

Depending on your workspace setup in the Library module, you may see the Filter bar across the top of the work area. You can use filters to limit the photos that are displayed in the Grid view and the Filmstrip to those that have been assigned a specified rating or flag status, or contain particular metadata content. You'll learn more about using the Filter bar controls in Lesson 5, "Organizing and Selecting."

Across the bottom of the work area is the Toolbar. The Toolbar is common to all the workspace modules but contains different tools and controls for each.

1 If you're not already in the Library module, switch to it now.

2 If the Filter bar is not already visible at the top of the work area, show it by pressing the backslash character (\) on your keyboard or by activating the menu option View > Show Filter Bar. Press backslash again or disable the menu option View > Show Filter Bar to hide it.

3 If the Toolbar is not already visible, press T to show it. Press T again to hide it.

4   Switch to the Develop module. If the Toolbar is not already visible, press T to show it. Switch back to the Library Module. In the Library module the Toolbar is still hidden from step 3; Lightroom remembers your Toolbar setting for each module independently. Press T to show the Toolbar in the Library module.

5   Double-click an image in Grid view to switch to Loupe view. The Loupe view is available in both the Library and Develop modules, but the controls available in the Loupe view Toolbar differ for each of these modules.

6   You can hide or show individual tools by choosing their names from the menu at the right end of the Toolbar. Tools that are currently visible in the Toolbar have a checkmark in front of their names.

Tip: If you have selected more tools than can be displayed in the width of the Toolbar, you can hide either of the side panel groups to increase the Toolbar's width, or disable tools that you don't need at the moment.

In Loupe view, you can view your images at different levels of magnification. The zoom controls in the top right corner of the Navigator panel in the left panel group enable you to switch quickly between preset magnification levels. You can choose from Fit, Fill, 1:1, or choose another option from a menu of ten zoom ratios.

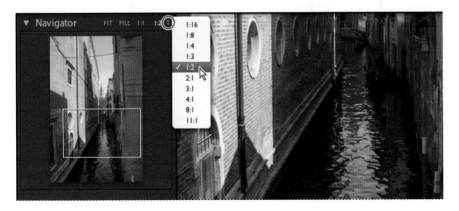

You can toggle between zoom levels by choosing View > Toggle Zoom View, or pressing Z on your keyboard. To better understand the Toggle Zoom View command, you should be aware that the magnification controls in the Navigator panel are organized into two groups: Fit and Fill are in one group, and the zoom ratio settings are in the other. The Toggle Zoom View command toggles between the magnification levels last used in each group.

7 Click Fit in the zoom controls in the top right corner of the Navigator panel. Now click the 1:1 control. Choose View > Toggle Zoom View, or press Z. The zoom setting reverts to Fit. Press the Z key; the zoom setting reverts to 1:1.

8 Click Fill in the zoom controls in the top right corner of the Navigator panel. Now choose a zoom ratio from the menu at the far right of the Navigator panel header; we used 2:1. Click the image in the Loupe view. The zoom setting reverts to Fill. In Loupe view, clicking the image is equivalent to pressing the Z key, or choosing View > Toggle Zoom View, except that the zoomed view of the image will be centered on the area you clicked.

9 While the view is magnified, drag the zoom rectangle in the Navigator preview, or drag in the Loupe view to change the area currently visible in the work area. At higher zoom levels you may find using the Navigator panel more convenient; dragging in the Loupe view is better suited to working at lower zoom levels.

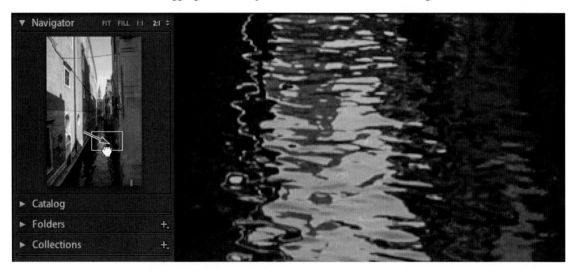

10 Press the Home key, or fn+Left Arrow, to position the zoom rectangle in the top left corner of the image; then press the Page Down key (fn+Down Arrow) repeatedly to scroll through the magnified image one section at a time. When you reach the bottom of the image the zoom rectangle jumps to the top of the next column. To start in the lower right corner of the image, press the End key (fn+Right Arrow); then use the Page Up key (fn+Up Arrow). This feature can be very helpful when you wish to inspect the entire image in close detail.

The zoom controls and the Navigator panel work the same way for the Loupe view in both the Library and Develop modules.

The other two view modes, Compare view and Survey view, will be covered in Lesson 4, "Reviewing," and Lesson 6, "Developing and Editing."

Grid and Loupe view options

You can customize the information Lightroom displays for each image in the Grid and Loupe views. Choose your preferences from the many options in the Library View Options dialog box. For Loupe view and the thumbnail tooltips you can activate two sets of options, and then use a keyboard shortcut to switch between them.

1 Press G to switch to Grid view in the Library module.

2 Choose View > View Options. The Library View Options dialog box will appear with the Grid View tab already selected. Position the Library View Options dialog box so you can see some of the images in the Grid view.

3 Disable the Show Grid Extras option in the top left corner of the Grid View tab. This will disable most of the other options.

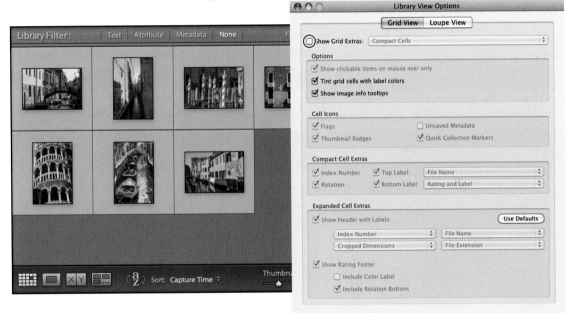

4 The only options still available are Tint Grid Cells With Label Colors and Show Image Info Tooltips. If they are not already activated, click the checkboxes for both of these options. As the images have not yet been assigned color labels, activating the first option has no visible effect in the Grid view. Right-click / Control-click any thumbnail in the Grid view—you can do this while the Library View Options dialog box is open—and choose a color from the Set Color Label

menu. A color-labeled image that is currently selected will show a thin colored frame around the thumbnail; a color-labeled image that is not selected has a tinted cell background.

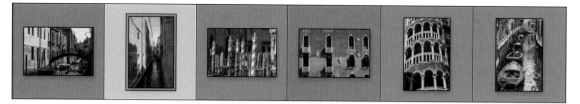

5   Position the pointer over a thumbnail in the Grid view or the Filmstrip; a tooltip appears. In Mac OS you'll need to click anywhere in the Lightroom workspace window to bring it to the front before you can see the tooltips. By default, the tooltip will display the file name, capture date and time, and the cropped dimensions. You can specify the information to be displayed in the tooltip by choosing from the Loupe View options.

6   On Mac OS, if the Library View Options dialog box is now hidden behind the main application window, press Command+J to bring it back to the front.

7   Activate the Show Grid Extras option and choose Compact Cells from the menu beside it. Experiment with each setting to see its effect in the Grid view display. Activate and disable the settings for Options, Cell Icons, and Compact Cell Extras. Position the pointer over the various icons in the image cells to see tooltips with additional information.

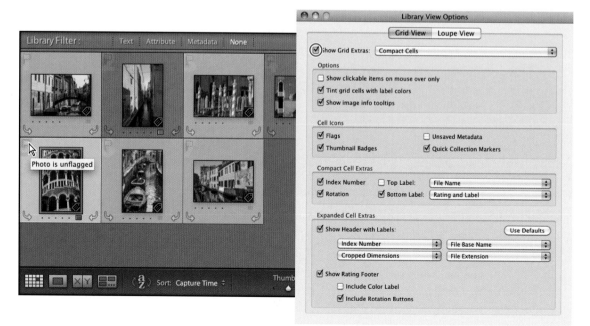

8 Under Compact Cell Extras, click the Top Label menu to see the long list of choices available. For some choices, such as Title or Caption, nothing will be displayed until you add the relevant information to the image's metadata.

9 Now choose Expanded Cells from the Show Grid Extras menu. Experiment with the options under Expanded Cell Extras to see the effects in the Grid view. Click any of the Show Header With Labels menus to see the many choices available to customize the information that is displayed in the cell headers.

10 Click the Loupe View tab. The work area switches from Grid to Loupe view so you can preview the effects of the changes you'll make in the Library View Options dialog box.

For the Loupe view, you can activate the Show Info Overlay option to display image information in the top left corner of the view. Choose items from the menus in Loupe Info 1 and Loupe Info 2 to create two different sets of information, and then choose either set from the Show Info Overlay menu. When you choose an information item such as Capture Date And Time, Lightroom extracts those details from the image metadata. If the image's metadata does not contain the specified information, nothing will be displayed for that item. For both the Grid and Loupe view options you can choose the information item Common Attributes, which will display the flagged status, star rating and color label for each image.

You can reset either group to its default state by clicking the Use Defaults button. Activate the Show Briefly When Photo Changes option to show the info overlay for only a few seconds when a new image is displayed in the Loupe view. Activate the Show Message When Loading Or Rendering Photos option to display a notification in the lower part of the view while the image preview is updated. It is recommended that you keep this option activated so that you don't inadvertently make judgments about the quality of an image before the update is complete.

11 Click the Close button (x) / (⬤) to close the Library View Options dialog box.

12 You can choose which of the two information sets will be displayed by choosing an option from the View > Loupe Info menu, or by pressing the I key to cycle the info overlay through Loupe Info 1, Loupe Info 2, and its disabled state.

13 Switch to the Grid view. From the View > Grid View Style menu you can choose whether or not to display additional information, using either the Compact Cells layout or the Expanded Cells layout. Press the J key to cycle through the Compact Cells layout, with and without additional information, and the Expanded Cells layout.

Dimming lights

Lightroom gives you the option to darken the workspace so that you can focus on the image or images with which you're working. In the Library and Develop modules, everything is dimmed or darkened except your selected photos. In the other three modules, everything except the presentation preview in the work area is dimmed or darkened. All tools and controls will still work in the Lights Dim or Lights Off modes—if you can find them! You could pick up the crop tool for example, and then switch to either the Lights Dim or Lights Off mode to help you concentrate on achieving the best result.

1 To dim the lights, press the L key or choose Window > Lights Out > Lights Dim.

2 If you're in the Grid view, double-click an image to switch to Loupe view. Click the image to switch between zoom levels. If you can see the Filmstrip, click to select a different image. Switch to a different module. If you remember the keyboard shortcuts they can really come in handy now.

3 To darken the workspace around the image completely, press the L key again or choose Window > Lights Out > Lights Off—if you can still see the menu bar. To return to the normal display mode, press the L key a third time, or choose Window > Lights Out > Lights On.

Lightroom achieves the dimming and darkening effects by means of a black overlay applied to the interface—at a default opacity of 80% for Lights Dim and 100% for Lights Off. You can choose instead to have the workspace fade to white or a shade of grey. This might be useful, for example, if your images contain a lot of black or dark colors. You can also adjust the level of opacity for the Lights Dim mode so that you can still see the controls if necessary.

4 To change the Lights Out screen color or to adjust the opacity for the Lights Dim mode, choose Edit > Preferences / Lightroom > Preferences. In the Preferences dialog box, click the Interface tab and choose a new opacity value from the Dim Level menu in the Lights Out options. From the Screen Color menu, choose white or a shade of grey.

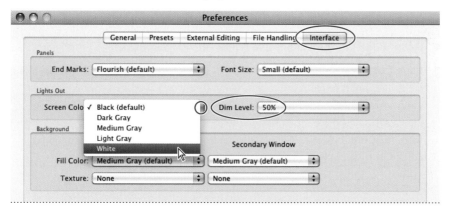

5 Click OK / the Close button ( ) to close the Preferences dialog box, and press the L key repeatedly to see your new settings in effect. Return to step 4 to modify your settings or reinstate the defaults.

Personalizing the identity plate

If you're using Lightroom to make presentations to clients on your computer, or if you'd simply like to personalize the workspace, you can change the graphic that is displayed as an identity plate in the top panel.

1 If the top panel is not currently visible, press the F5 key on your keyboard, or choose Window > Panels > Show Module Picker.

2 Choose Edit > Identity Plate Setup / Lightroom > Identity Plate Setup. Position the Identity Plate Editor dialog box so you can see both the dialog box and the identity plate in the top panel.

3 If not already selected, activate the Use A Styled Text Identity Plate option. Then activate the Enable Identity Plate option. You'll notice an immediate change in the appearance of the identity plate.

Note: If your Identity Plate Editor dialog box differs from the one shown in the illustration—other than the text in the text box on the left—click the Show Details button in the lower left corner.

To personalize the identity plate, you can either use styled text or place a graphic of your choice. If you wish, you can also change the typeface and text color used for the Module Picker at the other end of the top panel to better suit your design.

4 Select the text in the text box and replace it with your own.

5 Press Ctrl+A / Command+A to select your new text, and choose a typeface, font style, and font size from the menus beneath the text box. Use your company's corporate typeface or your own favorite—not necessarily mutually exclusive choices. Click the color box beside the font size menu and choose a new color from the Colors palette. Keep an eye on how your choices look in the top panel. Click OK to apply your changes or Cancel to reject them.

Tip: You can use more than one typeface, font style, size, or color in your identity plate text. Simply select a portion of your text and make the desired changes.

Tip: If your text is too long to be fully visible in the text box, either resize the dialog box or reduce the font size until you've finished editing.

6 (Optional) You can also change the typeface, font style, and font size used for the text in the Module Picker to better suit your new identity plate design. There is a second set of controls in the Identity Plate Editor dialog box for this purpose. Click the first color box to change the color used to highlight the name of the active module and the second to change the color used for the others.

7 To use an image as your identity plate, Choose Edit > Identity Plate Setup / Lightroom > Identity Plate Setup. In the Identity Plate Editor dialog box, activate the Use A Graphical Identity Plate option, and then click Locate File. In the Locate File dialog box, navigate to your Lesson 2 folder, select the file Identityplate.png, and click Choose.

Note: On Windows, you can choose a JPEG, PNG, GIF, BMP, or TIFF image for your graphical identity plate. The image can contain transparent pixels and should not be more than 48 pixels in height. On Mac OS, images in PSD or PDF format are also supported and the image height can be up to 57 pixels.

8 (Optional) You can save several identity plate setups as presets that can be easily accessed for different situations. Choose Save As from the Enable Identity Plate menu, enter a name for your identity plate preset and click Save. Your identity plate presets will appear in the Enable Identity Plate menu.

9 Disable the Enable Identity Plate option, and then click OK to close the Identity Plate Editor dialog box.

Keyboard shortcuts

Press Ctrl+/ (Windows) / Command+/ (Mac OS) to see a list of keyboard shortcuts for the currently active module. When you're done reviewing the keyboard shortcuts, click to dismiss the list.

This concludes your introduction to the Lightroom workspace. You've learned how to switch between the different screen and view modes and how to arrange the workspace layout to suit the way you work in each module. You know how to hide, show, collapse, or expand panels and panel groups, how to customize the Toolbar, and how to use a secondary display. Finally, you have personalized the Lightroom workspace with your own identity plate. Before you move on to the next lesson, take a minute or two to read through the review questions and answers on the following pages.

Review questions

1 How would you view an image at the largest size possible on your screen?

2 How do you adjust the size of the thumbnail images in the Grid view, the Navigator panel, and the Filmstrip?

3 What are the keyboard shorcuts to show or hide the four panels that surround the Lightroom workspace?

4 What do you do if you can't see the tool you're looking for in the Toolbar?

5 How can you personalize the Lightroom interface?

Review answers

1 In the Grid view, double-click the image thumbnail to enter the Loupe view. Choose Window > Screen Mode > Full Screen And Hide Panels, or use the keyboard shortcut Shift+Ctrl+F / Shift+Command+F. A variant of Full Screen mode, Full Screen And Hide Panels is ideal for viewing an image at the largest size possible on your display. Press the T key to hide the Toolbar, leaving nothing on screen but your photo.

2 To change the size of the Grid view thumbnails on your main screen, use the Thumbnails slider in the Toolbar. In Grid view on a secondary display use the slider in the lower right corner of the window. The thumbnail images in the Navigator panel and the Filmstrip are resized automatically as you resize the left panel group or the Filmstrip.

3 The keyboard shortcuts to show or hide the top panel, the Filmstrip, the left panel group, and the right panel group are F5, F6, F7, and F8, respectively.

4 Check what module and view mode you are in. The Toolbar contains different tools for different views and modules. Click the triangle at the right of the Toolbar and activate the missing tool in the tools menu. If the tool is activated and you still can't see it, there may be too many active tools to fit across the Toolbar. Disable tools you are not using in the tools menu and they will be removed from the Toolbar.

5 Lightroom offers several options to personalize the interface:

- You can change the identity plate, the graphic that is displayed at the left corner of the top panel. You can either use styled text or place your own graphic.

- It's also possible to change the typeface and text color used for the Module Picker at the other end of the top panel to better suit your new identity plate.

- You can customize the panel end mark displayed in the left and right panel groups. Choose from the preinstalled designs or use one of your own.

- You can set the color and texture of the background that shows behind the images in many of the working views.

- Set the level of opacity for the Lights Dim modes in the Preferences dialog box.

- Show or hide different workspace panels to suit different tasks. Set panels to show and hide automatically. You can arrange the workspace differently in each of the Lightroom modules so that when you switch between modules, your tools are always set out the way you like them.

3 IMPORTING

Lesson overview

Lightroom allows a great deal of flexibility in importing your photos; you can download images directly from a camera, import them from your hard disk or external storage media, or transfer them between catalogs on different computers. During the import process you can organize your folders, add keywords and metadata to make your photos easy to find, make backup copies, and even apply editing presets.

This lesson will familiarize you with the many options available to you as you add more photos to your Lightroom library:

- Importing images from a camera or card reader
- Importing images from a hard disk or removable media
- Choosing file handling options
- Evaluating images before importing
- Organizing, renaming, and processing images automatically
- Applying keywords and metadata as part of the import process
- Initiating backup strategies
- Setting up automatic importing and creating import presets
- Transferring images from other applications and between different computers and catalogs

 You'll probably need between one and two hours to complete this lesson.

Lightroom starts helping you to organize and manage your growing photo library from the moment you click the Import button; you can make backups, organize folders, inspect images at high magnification, apply editing presets, and add keyword tags and other info that will save you hours of work sorting and searching your image library later—all before your photos even reach your catalog!

Getting started

Tip: The first time you enter any of the Lightroom modules, you'll see module tips that will help you get started by identifying the components of the Lightroom workspace and stepping you through the workflow. Dismiss the tips by clicking the Close button. To reactivate the tips for any module, choose [*Module name*] Tips from the Help menu.

Before you begin, make sure that you have correctly copied the Lessons folder from the CD in the back of this book onto your computer's hard disk as detailed in "Copying the Classroom in a Book files" on page 2, and created the LR4CIB Library Catalog file to manage the lesson files as described in "Creating a catalog file for working with this book" on page 3.

1 Start Lightroom. In the Adobe Photoshop Lightroom - Select Catalog dialog box, make sure the file LR4CIB Library Catalog.lrcat is selected under Select A Recent Catalog To Open, and then click Open.

2 Lightroom will open in the screen mode and workspace module that were active when you last quit. If necessary, switch to the Library module by clicking Library in the Module Picker at the top of the workspace.

Tip: If you can't see the Module Picker, choose Window > Panels > Show Module Picker, or press the F5 key. If you're working on Mac OS, you may need to press the fn key together with the F5 key, or change the function key behavior in the system preferences.

The import process

Lightroom allows a great deal of flexibility in the import process. You can download images directly from a digital camera or card reader, import them from your hard disk or external storage media, and transfer them from another Lightroom catalog or from other applications.

Import at the click of a button, use a menu command, or simply drag and drop. You can have Lightroom launch the import process when you connect your camera or even import automatically when you move files into a watched folder.

Whether you're downloading photos from a camera or importing them from a hard disk or DVD, you'll be working with the Import dialog box, so we'll begin there.

You have the option to use the Import dialog box in either a compact or expanded mode, providing flexibility in the process from the very beginning. The top panel of the Import dialog box, common to both modes, presents the basic steps in the import process, arranged from left to right: choose an import source, specify how Lightroom is to handle the files you're importing, and then—if you choose to copy or move the source files—set up an import destination.

In expanded mode, the Import dialog box works very much like the Lightroom workspace modules. The Source panel at the left provides easy access to your files on any available drive. The Preview pane displays images from the source selection as thumbnails in Grid view or enlarged in Loupe view. Depending on the type of import, the right panel group offers a Destination panel that mirrors the Source panel, and a suite of controls for processing your images as they're imported.

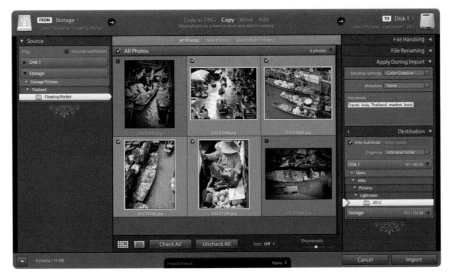

Importing photos from a digital camera

If you have a digital camera or a memory card reader at hand, you can step through this exercise using your own photos. If not, you can simply read through the steps and study the illustrations—most of the information in this exercise is equally applicable to importing from other sources.

To begin with, you'll configure the Lightroom preferences so that the import process is triggered automatically when you connect your camera or a memory card to your computer.

1 Choose Edit > Preferences (Windows) / Lightroom > Preferences (Mac OS). In the Preferences dialog box, click the General tab. Under Import Options, activate the option Show Import Dialog When A Memory Card Is Detected by clicking the checkbox.

Some cameras generate folder names on the memory card. If you don't find these folder names helpful for organizing your images, activate the option Ignore Camera-Generated Folder Names When Naming Folders. You'll learn more about folder naming options later in this lesson.

If your camera records Raw images, it may also generate a JPEG version of each photo. If you wish to import both files, activate the option Treat JPEG Files Next To Raw Files As Separate Photos; otherwise, Lightroom will display only the Raw images in the Import Photos dialog box.

2 Click OK / the Close button (⬤) to close the Preferences dialog box.

3 Connect your digital camera or card reader to your computer, following the manufacturer's instructions.

4 This step may vary depending on your operating system and the image management software on your computer:

• On Windows, if the AutoPlay dialog box shown in the illustration at the right appears, click the Close button (×) at the right of the header bar to dismiss it.

• If you have more than one Adobe image management application—such as Adobe Bridge—installed on your computer and the Adobe Downloader dialog box appears, click Cancel.

● **Note:** You'll find more options relating to the creation of DNG files during import on the File Handling preferences tab, but for this exercise, you can ignore those settings. For information on DNG files, see "About file formats" on page 91.

- If the Import dialog box appears, continue to step 5.

- If the Import dialog box does not appear, choose File > Import Photos, or click the Import button below the left panel group.

5 If the Import dialog box appears in compact mode, click the Show More Options button at the lower left of the dialog box to see all the options in the expanded Import dialog box.

The top panel of the Import dialog box—which is visible in both the compact and expanded modes—presents the three basic steps in the import process, arranged from left to right:

- Select the source location of the images you wish to add to your catalog.

- Specify the way you want Lightroom to handle the files you're importing.

- Choose the destination to which the image files will be copied and any develop presets, keywords, or other metadata that you would like applied to your photos as they are added to your catalog.

Your camera or memory card is now shown as the import source in the FROM area at the left of the top panel and under Devices in the Source panel at the left of the Import dialog box.

Depending on your computer setup, it's possible that your camera's memory card will be recognized as a removable storage disk. If this is the case, you may see some differences in the options available in the Import dialog box, but these differences will not affect the actions you'll take in the remainder of this exercise.

6 If your memory card is listed as a removable disk—rather than a device—in the Source panel, click to select it from the Files list and make sure that the Include Subfolders option is activated.

7 From the import type options in the center of the top panel, choose Copy, so that the photos will be copied from your camera to your hard disk, and then added to your catalog, leaving the original files on your camera's memory card.

Note: If your memory card has been recognized as a removable disk, the Move and Add options may not be disabled as illustrated at the right and below; these import options will be discussed later in this lesson.

Lightroom displays a brief description of the action that will be taken for whichever option is currently selected, as shown in the illustration below.

8 Move your pointer over each of the options shown in the bar across the top of the Preview pane to see a tool tip describing the option. For this exercise, leave the default All Photos option selected. Don't click the Import button yet.

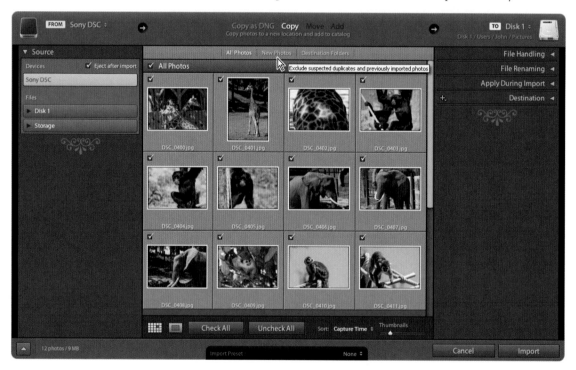

Tip: Use the slider below the preview pane to change the size of the thumbnails.

A check mark in the top left corner of an image cell indicates that the photo will be imported. By default, all the photos on your memory card will be check-marked for import; you can exclude an image from the selection to be imported by clicking its checkbox to remove the check mark.

You can select multiple images and then change all their check marks simultaneously. To select a contiguous range of images, select the first image in the range by clicking the thumbnail or the surrounding image cell, then hold down the Shift key and select the last image in the range. Select individual additional photos by Ctrl-clicking / Command-clicking their thumbnails. Click the check mark of any image in a multiple selection to change the import status for the entire selection.

When you import photos from your hard disk or from external storage media, the Import dialog box offers you the option to add them to your catalog without moving them from their current locations. This is possible because Lightroom does not actually import the image files themselves; it only adds entries to the library catalog to record their locations. However, because memory cards are expected to be erased and reused, images on your camera don't have very permanent addresses. For this reason, you're not offered the Add or Move options when you import from a camera—Lightroom expects to copy your photos from your camera to a more permanent location before it adds their addresses to the library catalog.

Therefore, the next step in the process of importing from a camera is to specify a destination folder to which your photos should be copied. This is the time to give some thought to how you are going to organize your photos on your computer hard disk. For now, leave the Import Photos dialog box open; you'll choose a destination folder and deal with the rest of the import options in the following exercises.

Organizing your copied photos in folders

Although there's no technical reason why you can't choose a different destination folder for each import, it will be much easier to keep your hard disk organized if you create a single folder to contain all the images that are associated with a particular catalog. Within this folder you can create a new subfolder for each batch of images downloaded from your camera or copied from other external media.

Before beginning the lessons in this book, you created a folder named LR4CIB inside your *[username]*/My Documents (Windows) or *[username]*/Documents (Mac OS) folder on your computer. This folder already contains subfolders for your LR4CIB Library Catalog file and for the image files used for the lessons in this book. For the purposes of this exercise, you'll create a subfolder inside the LR4CIB folder as the destination for the images that you import from your camera's memory card:

1 In the right panel group of the Import dialog box, collapse the File Handling, File Renaming, and Apply During Import panels; then, expand the Destination panel.

2 In the Destination panel, navigate to your LR4CIB folder. With the LR4CIB folder selected, click the Create New Folder button (⊕) at the left of the Destination panel header and choose Create New Folder from the menu.

3 In the Browse For Folder / Create New Folder dialog box, navigate to and select your LR4CIB folder, if it's not already selected. Click the Make New Folder / New Folder button, type **Imported From Camera** as the name for your new folder, and then press Enter (Windows) / click Create (Mac OS).

4 Make sure the new Imported From Camera folder is selected in the Browse For Folder / Create New Folder dialog box, and then click OK / Choose. Note that the new folder is now listed, and already selected, in the Destination panel.

The name of the new destination folder also appears in the TO area at the right of the top panel of the Import dialog box.

The Organize menu, near the top of the Destination panel, offers various options to help you organize your photos into folders as you copy them onto your hard disk:

- **Into One Folder** With the current settings, the images would be copied into the new Imported From Camera folder. You could then use the Into Subfolder option to create a new subfolder for each import.

Note: If your memory card has been recognized as a removable disk, you may also see the Organize option By Original Folders; this option will be discussed later in this lesson.

- **By Date:** *[Date Format]* The remaining options are all variations on organizing your photos by capture date. Your images would be copied into the Imported From Camera folder and placed into one or more subfolders, depending on your choice of date format. Choosing the date format "2012/01/03," for example, would result in one folder per year, containing one folder per month, containing one folder per day for each capture date, as shown in the illustration at the right.

You should think about which system of folder organization best suits your needs before you begin to import photos from your camera for your own purposes and maintain that system for all your camera imports.

5 For the purposes of this exercise, choose the option Into One Folder from the Organize menu.

6 Click the Put Into Subfolder checkbox and type **Lesson 3 Import** in the adjacent text box as the name for the new subfolder.

About file formats

Camera raw formats Camera raw file formats contain unprocessed data from a digital camera's sensor. Most camera manufacturers save image data in a proprietary camera format. Lightroom reads the data from most cameras and processes it into a full-color photo. You can use the controls in the Develop module to process and interpret the raw image data for your photo. For a list of supported cameras and camera raw formats, see www.adobe.com/go/learn_ps_cameraraw.

Digital Negative format (DNG) The Digital Negative (DNG) file format is a publicly available archival format for raw files generated by digital cameras. DNG addresses the lack of an open standard for the raw files created by individual camera models, helping ensure that photographers will be able to access their files in the future. You can convert proprietary raw files to DNG from within Lightroom. For more information about the Digital Negative (DNG) file format, visit www.adobe.com/dng.

TIFF format Tagged-Image File Format (TIFF, TIF) is used to exchange files between applications and computer platforms. TIFF is a flexible bitmap image format supported by virtually all paint, image-editing, and page-layout applications. Also, virtually all desktop scanners can produce TIFF images. Lightroom supports large documents saved in TIFF format (up to 65,000 pixels per side). However, most other applications, including older versions of Photoshop (pre-Photoshop CS), do not support documents with file sizes greater than 2 GB. The TIFF format provides greater compression and industry compatibility than Photoshop format (PSD), and is the recommended format for exchanging files between Lightroom and Photoshop. In Lightroom, you can export TIFF image files with a bit depth of 8 bits or 16 bits per channel.

JPEG format Joint Photographic Experts Group (JPEG) format is commonly used to display photographs and other continuous-tone images in web photo galleries, slide shows, presentations, and other online services. JPEG retains all color information in an RGB image but compresses file size by selectively discarding data. A JPEG image is automatically decompressed when opened. In most cases, the Best Quality setting produces a result indistinguishable from the original.

Photoshop format (PSD) Photoshop format (PSD) is the standard Photoshop file format. To import and work with a multi-layered PSD file in Lightroom, the file must be saved in Photoshop with the Maximize PSD and PSB File Compatibility preference turned on. You'll find the option in the Photoshop file handling preferences. Lightroom saves PSD files with a bit depth or 8 bits or 16 bits per channel.

CMYK files Lightroom imports CMYK files but adjustments and output are performed in the RGB color space.

Video files Lightroom 3 will import video files from most digital cameras. You can tag, rate, filter and include video files in collections, but editing is not supported. Click the camera icon on the thumbnail of a video file to launch an external viewer such as QuickTime or Windows Media Player.

File format exceptions Lightroom does not support the following types of files: PNG files; Adobe Illustrator® files; Nikon scanner NEF files; files with dimensions greater than 65,000 pixels per side or larger than 512 megapixels.

Note: To import photos from a scanner, use your scanner's software to scan to TIFF or DNG format, and then import those files into Lightroom.

Creating import presets

When you import photos on a regular basis, you'll probably find that you're setting up the same configurations of options over and over. Lightroom enables you to streamline your import workflow by saving your preferred settings as import presets. To create an import preset, set up your import in the expanded Import dialog box, and then choose Save Current Settings As New Preset from the Import Preset menu below the Preview pane.

Type a descriptive name for your new preset, and then click Create.

Your new preset will include all of your current settings: the source, import type (Copy as DNG, Copy, Move, or Add), file handling and renaming options, develop and metadata presets, keywords, and destination. You might set up one preset to move photos from a single folder on your hard disk into dated subfolders, and another to create a single folder of renamed black-and-white copies. Create separate import presets tailored to the characteristics of different cameras, so you can quickly apply your favorite noise reduction, lens correction and camera calibration settings during the import process, saving yourself time in the Develop module later.

Using the Import dialog box in compact mode

Once you've created the presets you need, you can speed up the process even more by using the Import dialog box in compact mode, where you can use your import preset as a starting point, and then change the source, metadata, keywords, and destination settings as required.

Backup strategies

Your next choice is whether or not to make backup copies of the images from your camera at the same time as Lightroom creates primary copies in the location you've just specified and adds them to the library catalog. It's a good idea to create backup copies on a separate hard disk or on external storage media so you don't lose your images should your hard disk fail or in case you accidentally delete them.

1   In the right panel group of the Import Photos dialog box, expand the File Handling panel and activate the option Make A Second Copy To by clicking the checkbox.

2   Click the small triangle to the right and select Choose Folder to specify a destination for your backup copies.

3   In the Browse For Folder / Choose Folder dialog box, navigate to the folder in which you wish to store the backup copies of your images, and then click OK / Choose.

The purpose of this backup is mainly as a precaution against loss of data due to disk failure or human error during the import process; it's not meant to replace the standard backup procedure you have in place—or should have in place—for the files on your hard disk.

It's worthwhile to archive each photo shoot by burning your images to a DVD, which you can store separately. This will also help you organize your image library in Lightroom because you'll feel more secure trimming your collection down to the best images knowing that you have a backup before you press the Delete key.

Renaming files as they are imported

The cryptic file names created by digital cameras are not particularly helpful when it comes to sorting and searching your photo library. Lightroom can help by renaming your images for you as they are imported. You can choose from a list of predefined naming options, or create your own customized naming templates.

1   In the right panel group of the Import Photos dialog box, expand the File Renaming panel and activate Rename Files. Choose Custom Name - Sequence from the Template menu and type a descriptive name in the Custom Text box (we used Zoo), and then press the Tab key on your keyboard. A sample name at the bottom of the File Renaming panel shows how your settings will be applied for the first image imported.

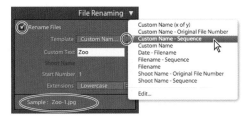

Tip: An option you should consider, if it's supported by your camera, is to set the camera to generate file names with unique sequence numbers. When you clear your memory card, or change memory cards, your camera will continue to generate unique sequence numbers rather than start counting from one again. This way, the images you import into your library will always have unique file names.

You can enter a number other than 1 in the Start Number text box; this is useful if you're importing more than one batch of images from the same series.

2 Click the small triangle to the right of the Custom Text box; your new text has been added to a list of recently entered names. You can choose from this list if you import another batch of files that belong in the same series. This not only saves time and effort but helps you ensure that subsequent batches are named identically. Should you wish to clear the list, choose Clear List from the menu.

3 Choose Custom Name (x of y) from the Template menu. Note that the sample name at the bottom of the File Renaming panel is updated to reflect the change.

4 Choose Edit from the Template menu to open the Filename Template Editor.

In the Filename Template Editor dialog box you can set up a filename template that makes use of metadata information stored in your image files—such as file names, capture dates, or ISO settings—adding automatically generated sequence numbers and any custom text you specify. A filename template includes placeholders—or *tokens*—that will be replaced by actual values during the renaming process.

You could rename your photos Zoo-January 03, 2012-01, Zoo-January 03, 2012-02, and so on, by setting up a filename template with a custom text token, a date token, and a 2-digit sequence number token, separated by typed hyphens, as shown in the illustration at the right. After closing the Filename Template Editor you could type **Animals** over the word Zoo in the Custom Text box; "Animals" would then replace the custom text token in the filename. The capture date from the images' metadata and the sequence number will be added automatically.

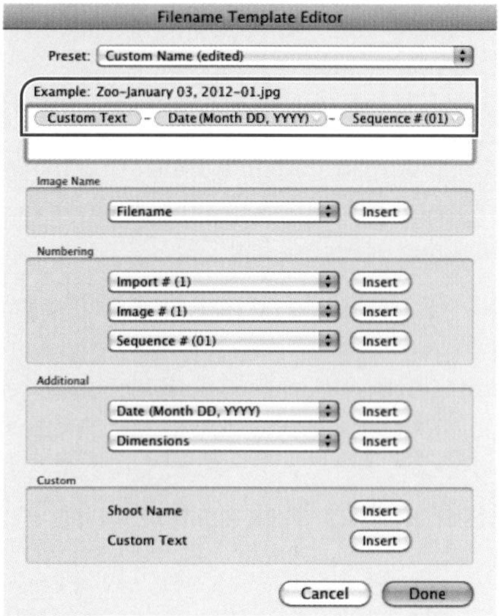

Tip: For more information on using the Filename Template Editor please refer to Lightroom Help.

5 Click Cancel to close the Filename Template Editor without making any changes.

Despite all of the options available for renaming your images during the import process, there's only so much information you can squeeze into a single file name. It might be better to take a minimal approach to renaming your photos and instead take advantage of the other file management capabilities of Lightroom. Metadata and keyword tags are far more powerful and versatile tools for organizing and searching your image library.

You'll learn about using metadata and keyword tags in the following exercises and in Lesson 5, "Organizing and Selecting."

You have now completed this exercise on importing photos from a digital camera or a memory card. You'll learn about the other options that are available in the Import dialog box in the exercises to follow.

6 For now, click Import if you wish to bring your photos into the LR4CIB catalog, or Cancel to close the Import dialog box without actually importing any images.

Importing images from a hard disk

When you import photos from your hard disk or from external storage media, Lightroom offers you more options for organizing your image files than are available when importing from a camera.

If you wish, you can still choose to copy your images to a new location during the import process as you did in the previous exercise, but you also have the option to add them to your catalog without moving them from their current locations. You might choose to do this if the images you wish to import are already well organized in a folder hierarchy.

For images that are already located on your hard disk you have an extra option: to *move* them to a new location, removing them from the original location at the same time. This option might appeal if the images on your hard disk are not already organized in a satisfactory manner.

1 To import images from your computer hard disk—or from a CD, DVD, or other external storage media—either choose File > Import Photos And Video, press Ctrl+Shift+I / Command+Shift+I, or simply click the Import button below the left panel group in the Library module.

2 In the Source panel at the left of the Import dialog box, navigate to the Lessons folder you've already copied into the LR4CIB folder on your hard disk. Select the Lesson 3 folder and click the checkbox at the top right of the Source panel to activate the Include Subfolders option.

An image count in the lower left corner of the Import dialog box shows that the Lesson 3 folder and its subfolders contain a total of 28 photos with a combined file size of 32 MB.

3 From the import type options in the center of the top panel, choose Add so that your photos will be added to your catalog without being moved—an option that is not available when importing images from a camera. Do not click Import yet!

4 Use the scrollbar at the right of the Preview pane to view all of the images in the Lesson 3 folder and its subfolders. Drag the Thumbnail slider below the Preview pane to the left to reduce the size of the thumbnails so that you can see as many of the images as possible in the Preview pane.

5 In the Source panel, disable the Include Subfolders option. The Preview pane now displays only the nine images in the Lesson 3 folder and the image count in the lower left corner of the Import dialog box reads: 9 photos / 10 MB.

In the next exercise, you'll apply keywords and other metadata to these images to make them easier to organize once you've added them to your catalog. For now, you can review the import type options above the Preview pane.

6 Click each of the import type options in turn, from left to right:

- Choose the option Copy As DNG to have Lightroom make copies of your images in DNG (Digital Negative) file format, which will be stored in a new location, and then added to your catalog. Collapse all of the panels in the right panel group. For the Copy As DNG, Copy, and Move options, the right panel group offers the same suite of panels—File Handling, File Renaming, Apply During Import, and Destination.

- Choose the option Copy to have Lightroom create copies of your images in a new location, and then add them to your catalog, leaving the originals in their current locations. You can set a destination for your copies in the Destination panel, as you did in the previous exercise. Expand the Destination panel and click the Organize menu. When you use either the Copy As DNG, Copy, or Move options to import images from your hard disk or from external storage media, the Organize menu offers you the option to copy your photos into a single folder, into subfolders based on the capture dates, or into a folder structure that replicates the original arrangement.

- Choose the option Move to have the images moved to a new location on your hard disk, arranged in whatever folder structure you choose from the Organize menu, and then deleted from their original locations..

- Choose Add to have Lightroom add the images to your catalog without moving or copying them from their current locations, or altering the folder structure in which they are stored. Note that for the Add option, the right panel group offers only the File Handling and Apply During Import panels; you cannot rename the original source images during import, and there's no need to specify a destination because the files will remain where they are. Expand the File Handling and Apply During Import panels to see the options available.

Applying metadata

Lightroom uses the metadata information attached to image files to enable you to quickly find and organize your photos. You can search your image library and filter the results by keyword, creation date, flag status, color label, shooting settings, or any combination of a wide range of other criteria. You can also choose specific information about your images from this metadata and have Lightroom display it as a text overlay applied to each image in a slideshow, web gallery, or print layout. Some metadata is automatically generated by your camera when you take a photo. You can also add your own information as part of the import process, making it even easier to locate and organize your images on your own terms.

1 In the Apply During Import panel, choose New from the Metadata menu.

2 In the New Metadata Preset dialog box, type a descriptive name for these nine photos in the Preset Name box (we used "Street Typography"); then, enter metadata information that is applicable to the images as a group, such as copyright information. You can customize the metadata for each individual image in Lightroom later, adding information such as titles and captions.

3 Click Create to close the New Metadata Preset dialog box, and then confirm that your new metadata preset is selected in the Metadata menu.

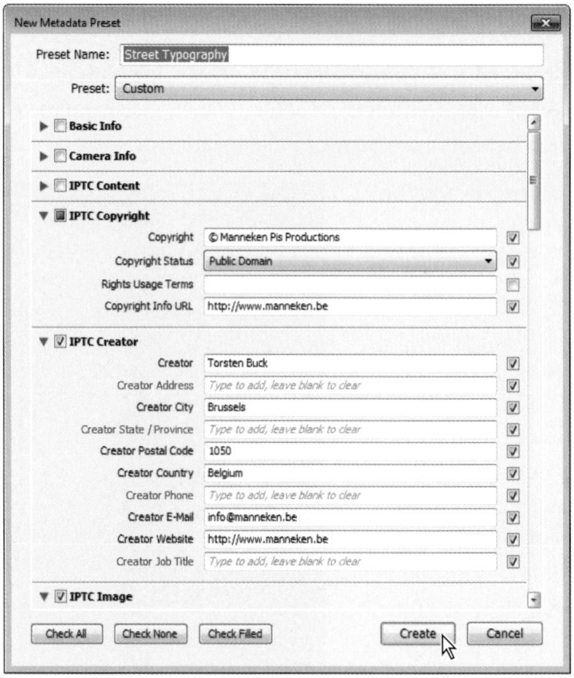

You can edit your metadata presets by choosing Edit Presets from the Metadata menu in the Apply During Import panel. In the Edit Metadata Presets dialog box you can edit, rename, or delete presets, or save modified settings as a new preset.

4 In the Apply During Import panel, choose None from the Develop Settings menu, and then type **Lesson 3, Typography, Signs** in the Keywords text box.

5 In the File Handling panel, choose Minimal from the Render Previews menu. Check that your settings are the same as those shown in the illustration below, and then click Import.

The nine photos from the Lesson 3 folder are imported into your library catalog and thumbnails of the images appear in the Grid view and the Filmstrip in the Library module.

6 Right-click / Control-click any of the images in the Grid view and choose Go To Folder In Library from the context menu. In the Folders panel in the left panel group, the Lesson 3 folder is highlighted and the image count indicates that it contains 9 photos.

7 Right-click / Control-click the Lesson 3 folder in the Folders panel, and then choose Show In Explorer / Show In Finder from the context menu.

8 The Lessons folder opens in a Windows Explorer / Finder window, with the Lesson 3 folder highlighted. Leave the Windows Explorer / Finder window open for use in the next exercise.

Importing via drag and drop

Perhaps the easiest way to add photos to your image library is to simply drag a selection of files—or even an entire folder—directly into Lightroom.

1 The Windows Explorer / Finder window showing your Lesson 3 folder should still be open from the previous exercise. Position the window so that you can see the Grid view in the Lightroom workspace beside it.

2 Open your Lesson 3 folder, if necessary, and drag the Batch1 folder from the Windows Explorer / Finder window onto the Grid view.

In the Import dialog box, the Batch1 subfolder is now selected in the Source panel and the seven photos it contains are displayed in the Preview pane.

3 In the Apply During Import panel, choose None from the Metadata menu and type **Lesson 3, Animals** in the Keywords box. Don't click Import just yet.

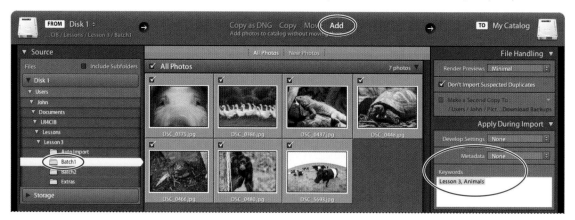

Evaluating photos before importing

Lightroom 4 makes it easier to decide which of your photos you wish to import by providing an enlarged Loupe view in the Import dialog box; you can examine each image in detail so that you can choose between similar images or exclude a photo that is out of focus.

1 Double-click any of the thumbnails to see the photo in Loupe view, or select the thumbnail and click the Loupe view button (▣) below the preview pane; the image is enlarged to fit the preview area and the pointer becomes a magnifying glass cursor (⊕).

2 Click the image again to further magnify the image to a zoom ratio of 1:1. Use the Zoom slider below the preview pane to see even more detail. Drag the enlarged image in the preview pane to inspect portions of the photo that are not currently visible.

While you're examining the photo in Loupe view, you can check mark the image for import or un-check it to exclude it by clicking the Include In Import check box below the preview pane. Alternatively, press the P key to check-mark the photo, the X key to un-check it, or the Tilde key (~) to toggle between the two states.

Note: The P, X, and Tilde (~) keyboard shortcuts are disabled at magnification levels higher than 1:1.

3 Drag the Zoom slider all the way to the left to return to the Fit view where the entire image is visible. Double-click the image, or click either the Loupe view button or the Grid view button beside it to return to the thumbnail display.

4 For the purposes of this exercise, un-check one of the images to exclude it, and then click Import.

5 In the Folders panel, click the triangle beside the Lesson 3 folder, if necessary, to see the listing for the Batch1 subfolder inside it.

Both the Batch1 subfolder and the Previous Import listing in the Catalog panel show an image count of 6 and the six recently imported photos are displayed in the Grid view and the Filmstrip.

6 Switch back to Windows Explorer / the Finder and drag the Batch1 folder onto the Grid view in the Library module again.

In the Import dialog box, the six photos that are already registered in the catalog are dimmed and unavailable for import. Clicking New Photos above the Preview pane would remove them from view entirely.

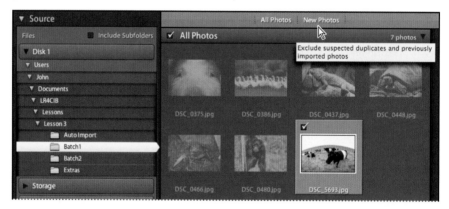

7 Type **Lesson 3, Animals** in the Keywords box, and then click Import to add the remaining Batch1 photo to your library catalog.

8 In the Folders panel, the Batch1 folder now shows an image count of 7; click the Batch1 folder to see all seven photos in the Grid view and the Filmstrip.

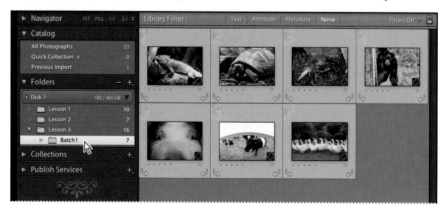

Importing and viewing video

Lightroom will import many common digital video files from digital still cameras, including AVI, MOV, MP4, and AVCHD. Choose File > Import Photos And Video or click the Import button in the Library module; then, set up your import in the Import dialog box, just as you would for photos.

In the Library module Grid view, you can scrub backwards and forwards in your video clips by simply moving the mouse over the thumbnails, making it easy to select the clip you want. Double-click a thumbnail to preview the video in Loupe view; drag the circular current time indicator in the playback control bar to scrub through the video manually.

Setting distinctive thumbnail images (poster frames) for your videos can make it easier to find the clip you want in the Grid view. Move the current time indicator to the frame you want; then, click the Frame button (▣) in the control bar and choose Set Poster Frame. Choose Capture Frame from the same menu to convert the current frame to a JPEG image that will be stacked with the clip.

To shorten a video clip, click the Trim Video button (⚙). The playback control bar expands to display a time-line view of the clip where you can drag the start and end markers to trim the clip as desired.

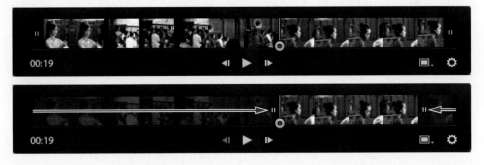

Importing to a specific folder

From within the Library module, you can import photos directly to a folder in the Folders panel without needing to specify a destination in the Import dialog box.

1   In the Folders panel, right-click / Control-click the Batch1 folder and choose Import To This Folder from the context menu.

2   In the Import dialog box, click Select A Source at the left of the top panel, just above the Source panel, and then choose the path to the Lesson 3 folder from the list of recent sources in the menu.

3   Expand the Source panel; then expand the Lesson 3 folder so that you can see the subfolders inside it. Select the folder Extras, which contains two photos. In the top panel, choose Move from the import type options to move the photos from the Extras folder to the destination folder and add them to your catalog. Check that your previous settings are still active in the Apply During Import panel. You may need to re-type **Lesson 3, Animals** in the Keywords box.

4   Expand the Destination panel, if necessary. You can see that the Batch1 folder has been automatically selected as the destination to which the photos will be moved from the Extras folder. At the top of the Destination panel, choose Into One Folder from the Organize menu; then, click Import. Thumbnails of the two new images appear in the Grid view and the Filmstrip in the Library module.

5   In the Folders panel, the Batch1 folder now shows an image count of 9. Click the Batch1 folder to see all nine images together in the Grid view and the Filmstrip.

6   In the Folders panel, right-click / Control-click the Lesson 3 folder and choose Show In Explorer / Show In Finder from the context menu. In the Windows Explorer / Finder window, open the Extras folder inside the Lesson 3 folder; the two image files have been removed and the Extras folder is now empty.

Importing from other catalogs

If you work on a laptop while you're on location and need to merge your new photos with the Lightroom library on your desktop computer, or if you work in a situation where more than one person will be using the same images in Lightroom on different computers, you can move photos from one computer to another using the Export As Catalog and Import From Catalog commands. Your images will be transferred with all of your edits, adjustments, and settings in place—including any keywords or other metadata you may have added.

Lesson 11, "Making Backups and Exporting Photos," will discuss exporting photos as a catalog; for this lesson you'll import photos from a catalog you'll find in the Batch2 subfolder inside the Lesson 3 folder on your hard disk.

1 Choose File > Import From Another Catalog.

2 In the Import From Lightroom Catalog dialog box, navigate to and open your Lesson 3 > Batch2 folder, select the file Batch2 Catalog.lrcat and click Choose.

3 In the Import From Catalog dialog box, click the Show Preview check box in the lower left corner. Choose Add New Photos To Catalog Without Moving from the File Handling menu, and then click Import.

Tip: The option Don't Import New Photos in the File Handling menu is useful when you've exported images from one computer, modified the files on a different computer, and then wish to re-import them without importing any new images.

4 If you see the Photo Is Missing icon (⊞?) in the top right corner of the image cells in the Grid view, click the icon on the first image, and then click Locate in the Confirm dialog box. Navigate to the Images folder inside the Batch2 folder, select the missing photo, activate the Find Nearby Missing Photos option, and then click Select.

5 The Batch2 subfolder is now listed in the Folders panel and three newly imported photos are displayed in the Grid view and the Filmstrip.

When you import images from a Lightroom catalog, you don't have the option to apply develop settings or to add keywords and other metadata during the import process as you do when you import from your camera or hard disk. Lightroom preserves the keywords and other metadata that were exported in the catalog with the images; once the photos have been added to your catalog, you can modify the metadata as you wish.

6 Select one of the images in the Grid view.

In the Keywording panel in the right panel group, you can see that the keyword tags Lesson 3, Signs, and Typography have already been applied. If you wished, you could add keywords to the images individually.

7 Expand the Metadata panel in the right panel group. If necessary, collapse the other panels in the group or scroll down so that you can see the contents of the Metadata panel. Note that these images already include the metadata from the Street Typography preset. You can edit the metadata to your liking.

The imported images have also been edited. Lightroom records every editing operation performed on an image in the library catalog file. When images are exported in a catalog their entire edit history is exported with them.

8 Select one of the images in the Grid view, and then switch to the Develop module. If necessary, scroll down in the left panel group so that you can see the contents of the History panel. Click the Import entry at the bottom of the History panel to see how the image looked originally. Then, choose Edit > Undo to return to the edited version.

9 Switch back to the Library module in readiness for the next exercise.

Importing photos from Photoshop Elements

Lightroom makes it easy to import photographs and video from Photoshop Elements. The media files from your Photoshop Elements catalog are imported complete with keyword tags, ratings, and labels—even your stacks are preserved. Version sets from Photoshop Elements are converted to stacks in Lightroom, and your albums become collections.

If you're migrating from Photoshop Elements to Lightroom, or if you intend to work with both applications, you might like to watch to the tutorial videos in "Going from Photoshop Elements to Lightroom" on Adobe TV (http://tv.adobe.com/show/going-from-photoshop-elements-to-lightroom/) for tips on making the transition, understanding the differences between the way Lightroom and Photoshop Elements work, and using the two applications together.

Upgrading a Photoshop Elements catalog

Lightroom 4 can import photos and library catalog information from Photoshop Elements 6 through Elements 10 on Windows, and from Photoshop Elements 9 and 10 on Mac OS, but first you'll need to upgrade your Photoshop Elements catalog.

1   In the Library module, choose File > Upgrade Photoshop Elements Catalog.

Lightroom searches your computer for Photoshop Elements catalogs and displays the most recently opened catalog in the Upgrade Photoshop Elements Catalog dialog box.

2   To choose a different Photoshop Elements catalog, click the Photoshop Elements menu. To specify a different destination for the new Lightroom catalog, click Change at the right of the Lightroom Catalog Destination path and navigate to the desired folder.

3   Click Upgrade to import the photos and catalog information from your Photoshop Elements library catalog into a new Lightroom catalog.

4   To combine a converted Photoshop Elements library with an existing Lightroom catalog, open the destination catalog and use the File > Import From Another Catalog command.

Importing from a watched folder

Designating a folder on your hard disk as a *watched folder* can be a very convenient way to automate the import process. Once you've nominated a folder that is to be watched, Lightroom will detect any photos that are placed or saved into it, then automatically move them to a specified location and add them to the catalog. You can even have Lightroom rename the files and add metadata in the process.

1 Choose File > Auto Import > Auto Import Settings.

2 In the Auto Import Settings dialog box, click the first Choose button to designate a watched folder.

3 In the Browse For Folder / Auto-Import From Folder dialog box, navigate to the Lesson 3 folder. Open the Auto Import folder and select the subfolder named Watched Folder; then, click OK / Choose.

> **Tip:** Once you've set a watched folder, you can activate or disable Auto Import at any time, without opening the Auto Import Settings dialog box, by choosing File > Auto Import > Enable Auto Import. A check mark beside this menu command indicates that the Auto Import feature is currently enabled.

4 Now that you have designated a watched folder, you can click the checkbox at the top of the Auto Import Settings dialog box to enable Auto Import.

5 Click the second Choose button under Destination to specify a folder to which Lightroom will move your photos in the process of adding them to the library catalog.

6 In the Browse For Folder / Choose Folder dialog box, navigate to the Lessons folder. Select the Lesson 3 folder (you'll set up a subfolder inside the Lesson 3 folder in the next step), and then click OK / Choose.

7 Still in the Destination section in the Auto Import Settings dialog box, type **Batch3** in the Subfolder Name text box. Lightroom will create this subfolder inside the Lesson 3 folder.

8 Choose Filename from the File Naming menu.

9 Under Information, choose the metadata preset you created earlier in this lesson from the Metadata menu and type **Lesson 3, Colors** in the Keywords text box. Choose None from the Develop Settings menu and Minimal from the Initial Previews menu. Click OK to close the Auto Import Settings dialog box.

10 Switch to Windows Explorer / the Finder and navigate to the Lesson 3 folder. Note that as yet there is no Batch3 folder inside the Lesson 3 folder. Open the folder Auto Import and drag the seven image files inside it to the Watched Folder. When Lightroom has finished importing, you'll see the newly created Batch3 folder inside the Lesson 3 folder. The Watched Folder is empty once more and the seven lesson images have been moved into the Batch3 folder.

11 Return to Lightroom; the Batch3 folder is now listed in the Folders panel and the newly imported photos are displayed in the Grid view and the Filmstrip.

You can now import images into your Lightroom library by simply dragging them onto the watched folder. This makes importing photos directly from a camera or memory card reader even easier; there's no need to attend to a dialog box and yet your images can be renamed and have custom metadata added automatically.

Specifying initial previews when importing

As photos are imported, Lightroom can immediately display a photo's embedded preview, or display higher-quality previews as the program renders them. You can choose the rendered size and quality for previews using the Standard Preview Size and Preview Quality menus in File Handling tab of the Catalog Settings (choose Edit > Catalog Settings / Lightroom > Catalog Settings). Please keep in mind that embedded previews are created on-the-fly by cameras and are not color managed therefore they don't match the interpretation of the camera raw files made by Lightroom. Previews rendered by Lightroom are color managed.

In the Import Photos dialog box, do one of the following:

- To immediately display images using the smallest previews embedded in the photos, choose Initial Previews > Minimal. Lightroom renders standard-size previews when needed.

- To display the largest possible preview available from the camera, choose Initial Previews > Embedded & Sidecar. This may take longer to display than a Minimal preview but is still faster than rendering a standard-size preview.

- To display previews as Lightroom renders them, choose Initial Previews > Standard. Standard-size previews use the ProPhoto RGB color space.

- To display previews that are a 1 to 1 view of the actual pixels, as in the Develop module, choose Initial Previews > 1:1.

—From Lightroom Help

Tethered shooting

Many modern digital cameras support tethered shooting, a process where you connect—or tether—your digital camera to your computer and save images to the computer's hard disk rather than to the camera's memory card. With tethered shooting you can view a photo on your computer screen immediately after you shoot it—a vastly different experience from seeing it on your camera's LCD screen.

▶ **Tip:** To see a list of cameras for which integrated tethered shooting is currently supported, please refer to Lightroom Help.

For a range of DSLR cameras including many models from Canon and Nikon, you can capture photographs directly into Lightroom 4 without the need for any third-party software. If your camera allows tethered shooting, but is not on the list of models supported by Lightroom, you can still capture images into your Lightroom library using either the image capture software associated with the camera or any of a number of third-party software solutions.

You can have Lightroom name the photos, add metadata, apply developing settings, and organize them in your library then and there. If necessary, you can adjust your camera settings (white balance, exposure, focus, depth of field, and others), or even change cameras, before taking the next shot. The better the quality of the captured image the less time you'll need to spend adjusting it later.

Tethered shooting with a supported camera

● **Note:** Depending on your camera model and the operating system your computer uses, you may also need to install the necessary drivers for your camera.

1 Connect your camera to the computer.

2 In the Library module, choose File > Tethered Capture > Start Tethered Capture.

3 In the Tethered Capture Settings dialog box, type a name for your shooting session. Lightroom will create a folder with this name inside the destination folder of your choice; this session folder will appear in the Folders panel.

4 Chose a naming scheme for your shots, select a destination folder, and specify any metadata or keywords that you want Lightroom to apply as the newly captured images are imported.

5 Click OK to close the Tethered Capture Settings dialog box. The tethered capture control bar appears.

The control bar displays the model name of the connected camera, the name you entered for the shooting session, and the current camera settings. You can choose from a wide range of Develop presets in the Develop Settings menu at the right. Trigger the shot either with the shutter button on your camera or by clicking the large circular button at the right of the control bar.

As you shoot, the images captured will appear in both the Grid view and the Filmstrip. To see each captured photo as large as possible, use the Loupe view and hide unwanted panels—as shown in the illustration below—or chose Window > Screen Mode > Full Screen And Hide Panels.

> **Tip:** To collapse the control bar to just the shutter button, hold down the Alt / Option key and click the close button at the upper right. Repeat to expand the control bar again.

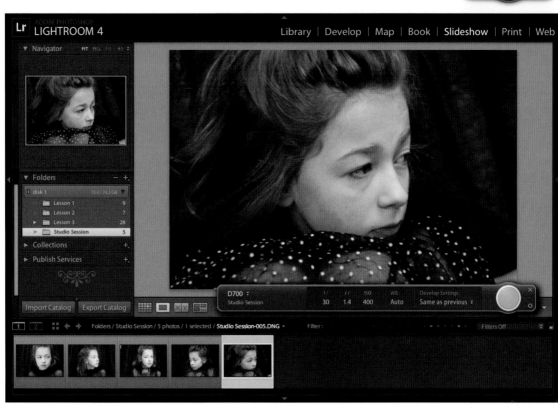

Tethered shooting with other cameras

▶ **Tip:** To find out about third-party image capture software compatible with your camera, search "tethered shooting" on the Internet or in Adobe Community Help.

If your camera allows tethered shooting, but is not on the list of models for which the process is integrated in Lightroom, you can still capture images into your Lightroom library by using the image capture software associated with your camera—or a third-party software solution—to save your photos to a watched folder. Lightroom will remove the images from the watched folder and add them to your catalog as soon as it detects them.

1   Choose File > Auto Import > Auto Import Settings. In the Auto Import Settings dialog box, click the first Choose button to choose a watched folder. Once you've designated a folder to be watched, you can click the checkbox at the top of the Auto Import Settings dialog box to enable Auto Import.

2   Click the second Choose button under Destination to specify a folder to which Lightroom will save your photos in the process of adding them to the library catalog. Type a name for your photo shoot in the Subfolder Name text box; Lightroom will create this subfolder inside the designated destination folder.

3   Choose a naming option for your images from the File Naming menu. Under Information, you can choose a metadata preset and enter any keywords that you wish Lightroom to apply as your newly captured images are imported. If you wish, you can also choose a developing preset and specify a preview option. Click OK to close the Auto Import Settings dialog box.

4   Use your camera's image capture software to designate your new watched folder as the destination to which the camera will save your photos.

By way of an example, this illustration shows the download and metadata options from the Camera Control component of Nikon's Capture NX software.

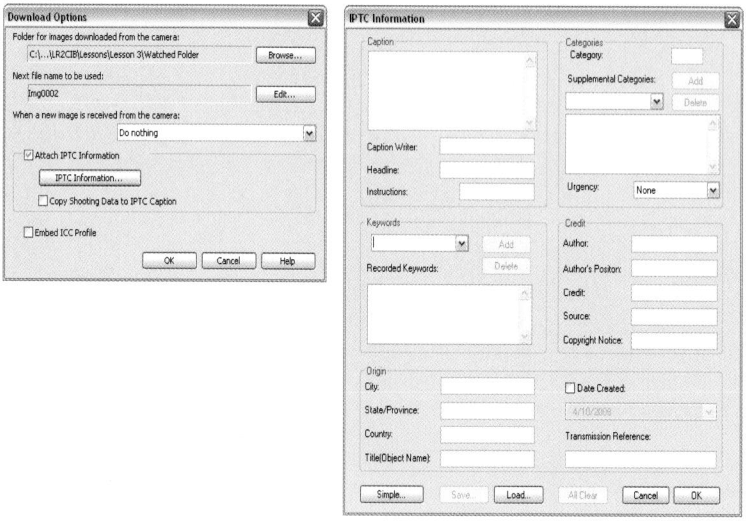

5   Before you begin shooting, make sure that you are in the Library module. In the Folders panel, select the subfolder you created for your tethered shoot in step 2, so that your newly captured photos will be displayed as they are imported.

Review questions

1   When would you choose to copy imported images to a new location on your hard disk and when would you want to add them to your library catalog without moving them?

2   Which file formats are supported by Lightroom?

3   What is DNG?

4   When would you use the Import dialog box in compact mode?

5   How can you transfer photos between Lightroom libraries on separate computers?

Review answers

1   You don't have the option to import photos from a camera at their current location; Lightroom needs to record a location for each file in the library catalog, and as memory cards are expected to be erased and reused the images need first to be copied to a more permanent location. Copying or moving images might also be useful when you want Lightroom to organize the files into a more ordered folder hierarchy during the import process. Images that are already arranged in a useful way on the hard disk or removable media can be added to the library catalog in their current locations.

2   Lightroom supports the following file formats: most camera raw formats, Digital Negative (DNG), TIFF, JPEG, Photoshop PSD, and CMYK files. Lightroom does not support PNG files, Adobe Illustrator® files, Nikon scanner NEF files, or files with dimensions greater than 65,000 pixels per side or larger than 512 megapixels.

3   The Digital Negative (DNG) file format is a publicly available archival format intended to address the lack of an open standard for raw files generated by cameras. Converting raw files to DNG in Lightroom will help ensure that you'll be able to access your raw files in the future even if the original proprietary format is no longer supported.

4   Once you've created import presets to suit your workflow, you can speed up the import process by using the Import dialog box in compact mode. Use your import preset as a starting point, and then modify the settings as required.

5   On one computer, export the images from Lightroom as a catalog file. On the other computer, choose File > Import From Catalog to import the photos into the Lightroom library together with their develop settings and metadata.

4 REVIEWING

Lesson overview

It's a good policy to spend some time reviewing, sorting, and marking your newly imported images. A little time spent organizing and grouping photos at this stage will make it much easier to find exactly the images you want when you need them.

In this lesson you'll become familiar with using a variety of viewing modes, tools, and techniques for reviewing your images and navigating through your Lightroom catalog:

- Working in the different Library module views

- Navigating through your catalog

- Using the Navigator panel

- Comparing photos

- Flagging rejects and deleting images

- Using the Quick Collection

- Converting and clearing the Quick Collection

- Designating a target collection

- Hiding the Filmstrip and adjusting its size

- Applying the Filmstrip Source Filters

- Rearranging photos in the Grid view or the Filmstrip

 You'll probably need between one and two hours to complete this lesson.

The Lightroom Library module offers you a variety of ways to review, evaluate, mark, and label your photos after you import them, making it easier to organize and manage your growing image library. You can sort and group thumbnails in the Grid view, examine a single photo up close in Loupe view, assess images side by side in Compare view, or refine a multiple selection of shots in Survey view.

Getting started

Tip: The first time you enter any of the Lightroom modules, you'll see module tips that will help you get started by identifying the components of the Lightroom workspace and stepping you through the workflow. Dismiss the tips by clicking the Close button. To reactivate the tips for any module, choose [*Module name*] Tips from the Help menu.

This lesson assumes that you are already familiar with the Lightroom workspace and with moving between the different modules. If you find that you need more background information as you go, refer to Lightroom Help, or review the previous lessons in this book.

Before you start on the exercises in this section, make sure that you have correctly copied the Lessons folder from the CD in the back of this book onto your computer's hard disk as detailed in "Copying the Classroom in a Book files" on page 2, and created the LR4CIB Library Catalog file to manage the lesson files as described in "Creating a catalog file for working with this book" on page 3.

1 Start Lightroom.

2 In the Adobe Photoshop Lightroom - Select Catalog dialog box, make sure that the file LR4CIB Library Catalog.lrcat is selected under Select A Recent Catalog To Open, and then click Open.

Tip: If you can't see the Module Picker, choose Window > Panels > Show Module Picker, or press the F5 key. If you're working on Mac OS, you may need to press the fn key together with the F5 key, or change the function key behavior in the system preferences.

3 Lightroom will open in the screen mode and workspace module that were active when you last quit. If necessary, switch to the Library module by clicking Library in the Module Picker at the top of the workspace.

Importing images into the library

The first step is to import the images for this lesson into the Lightroom library.

1 In the Library module, click the Import button below the left panel group.

2 If the Import dialog box appears in compact mode, click the Show More Options button at the lower left of the dialog box to see all the options in the expanded Import dialog box.

3 Under Source at the left of the expanded Import dialog box, navigate to and select the LR4CIB > Lessons > Lesson 4 folder. Ensure that all twelve images in the Lesson 4 folder are checked for import.

4 In the import options above the thumbnail previews, select Add so that the imported photos will be added to your catalog without being moved or copied. Under File Handling at the right of the expanded Import dialog box, choose Minimal from the Render Previews menu and ensure that the Don't Import Suspected Duplicates option is activated. Under Apply During Import, choose None from both the Develop Settings menu and the Metadata menu and type **Lesson 4, New York** in the Keywords text box. Make sure that your import is set up as shown in the illustration below, and then click Import.

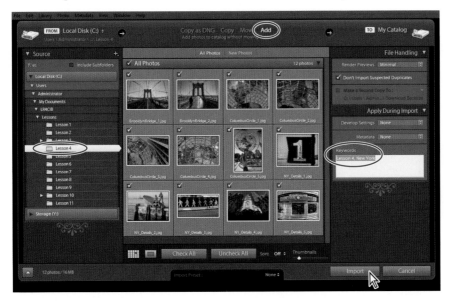

The twelve images are imported from the Lesson 4 folder and now appear in both the Grid view of the Library module and in the Filmstrip across the bottom of the Lightroom workspace.

Viewing and managing your images

The Library module offers a range of viewing modes and a variety of tools and controls to help you evaluate, compare, sort, mark, and group your images. During the import process you applied common metadata in the form of keyword tags to the selection of images as a whole. As you review your photos in the Library module you can add another layer of organization to your catalog, flagging images as picks or rejects, assigning ratings, and applying tags and labels.

The Library module also provides sophisticated search functions and customizable filters that enable you to leverage the metadata you attach to your photos. You can search and sort the images in your library by category, subject, or any other association, and then create Collections to group them—making it easy to retrieve exactly the photos you want quickly, no matter how extensive your catalog.

In the left panel group of the Library module are panels where you can access and work with the folders and collections containing your photos. The right panel group contains panels for adjusting your images and working with keywords and metadata. At the top of the work area is the Filter bar, where you can set the criteria for a customized search of your catalog. The Toolbar, immediately below the work area, provides easy access to your choice of tools and controls.

Switching views

In the Library module you can move between four viewing modes to suit different phases of your workflow. Press the G key or click the Grid view button (▦) in the Toolbar to see thumbnails of your images while you search, apply flags, ratings and labels, or create collections. Use the keyboard shortcut E or click the Loupe view button (▣) to inspect a single photo at a range of magnifications. Press C or click the Compare view button (⊠Y) to see two images side by side. Click the Survey view button (▤▪) in the Toolbar or use the keyboard shortcut N to evaluate several images at once. The Toolbar displays a different set of controls for each view mode.

The Grid view

By default your images will be displayed in Grid view after they've been imported.

1   Click the triangle at the right end of the Toolbar and ensure that View Modes is activated in the tools menu. If you're working on a small screen, you can disable all the other options except Thumbnail size for this lesson.

Tools and controls that are currently visible in the Toolbar have a check mark beside their names in the menu. The order of the tools and controls from top to bottom in the menu corresponds to their order from left to right in the Toolbar.

2   If Grid view is not already selected, click the Grid view button (▦). Adjust the size of the thumbnails by dragging the Thumbnails slider so that you can see at least two rows of thumbnails in the Grid view without having to scroll down.

3   To specify how your photos will be displayed in the Grid view image cells, choose View > View Options. The Library View Options dialog box appears.

4   Activate the Show Grid Extras option and choose Compact Cells from the menu beside it. Customize the Options, Cell Icons, Compact Cell Extras, and Expanded Cell Extras settings to your liking. As a guide to the options available, please refer to "View Options for the Grid view" on the facing page.

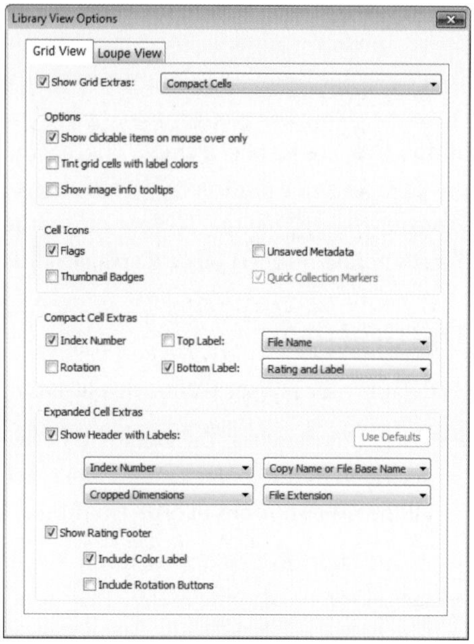

5   From the Show Grid Extras menu at the top of the Library View Options dialog box, choose Expanded Cells. Examine the options available and make whatever changes you wish. When you're done, choose Compact Cells from the Show Grid Extras menu and close the Library View Options dialog box.

▶ **Tip:** To conveniently cycle through the different Grid view styles, press the J key on your keyboard repeatedly, or choose View > Grid View Style > Cycle View Style.

To switch quickly between the two groups of options that you just set in the Library View Options dialog box, choose from the Grid View Style options on the View menu.

6   Switch to the Expanded Cell mode by choosing the Expanded Cells option from the View > Grid View Style menu. Make sure that the Show Extras option is activated in the same menu.

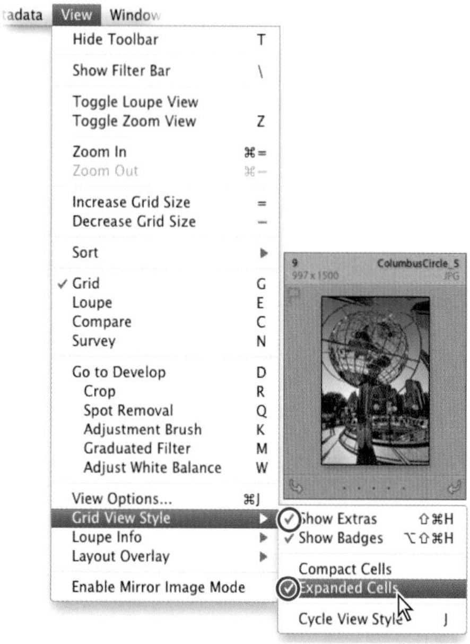

View options for the Grid view

Depending on the way you like to work, you can choose from a wide range of options that affect the way your photos are displayed in the Grid view image cells—from simplified cells containing nothing but the image thumbnails to expanded cells that display your choice of image information, status indicators, labels, and clickable (interactive) controls.

Show Grid Extras Displays your choice of labels, markers, and controls in each image cell. If this option is disabled, most of the other Grid view options are unavailable.

Compact Cells Shows simple cells with less information so more thumbnails are visible in the grid.

Expanded Cells Expands the image cells to include more information in cell headers and footers.

Show Clickable Items On Mouse Over Only Displays rotation controls, flags, and labels only when you move the pointer over an image cell. Disable this option to show these controls at all times.

Tint Grid Cells With Color Labels Tints the image cell around a photo to indicate its color label.

Show Image Info Tooltips Displays a brief description of an item when you hold the pointer over it, including image info and the names of the controls, status badges, and indicators in the image cell.

Flags Activates clickable flag status indicators in the upper left corner of the image cells. Click the indictor to change the flag status.

Quick Collection Markers Shows a clickable Quick Collection marker in the upper right corner of each thumbnail. Images with a solid grey dot are part of the Quick Collection. Click the marker to add an image to, or remove it from, the Quick Collection.

Thumbnail Badges Displays indicator badges on the thumbnail images indicating which photos have keywords attached and which have been adjusted or cropped.

Unsaved Metadata An icon with a down arrow in the upper right of a cell indicates that an image has changes in its metadata that have not yet been saved to file. An up arrow icon shows that the image file's metadata has been changed in an external application and an exclamation mark icon indicates that a photo's metadata has unsaved changes made in both Lightroom and an external application.

Index Number Shows image cell numbers indicating the order of the photos in the Grid view.

Rotation Displays Rotation buttons in the lower corners of the image cells.

Top Label and **Bottom Label** Displays your choice of image information and attributes above and below the thumbnail in a compact image cell.

Show Header With Labels Displays up to four labels in the headers of expanded image cells, showing whatever information you specify. For each label, you can choose from a menu of image information and attributes.

Use Defaults Restores the Header Label options to their default settings.

Show Rating Footer Shows the rating stars, and optionally the color label and rotation buttons, below the thumbnail in expanded image cells.

Zooming with the Navigator in Loupe view

In Loupe view you can look closely at one photo at a time at a wide range of zoom levels. Use the Loupe view to help you to evaluate your images as you sort them in the Library module and to inspect and adjust them in the Develop module. In the Navigator panel you can set the level of magnification for the Loupe view and find your way around a zoomed image with ease. Like the Loupe view, the Navigator is common to both the Library and Develop modules.

1 In the Grid view or the Filmstrip, select the image of the diner, NY_Details_5.jpg, and then click the Loupe view button (■) in the Toolbar. Alternatively, press the E key or double-click the thumbnail in the Grid view or the Filmstrip.

2 If necessary, expand the Navigator panel at the top of the left panel group. The zoom controls for the Loupe view are in upper right corner of the Navigator panel. Click 1:1 to see this photo at 100% (or "actual pixels") magnification.

3 Click the small triangle at the right of the Navigator panel header and choose the zoom ratio 3:1 from the menu.

4 When you're working at such a high level of magnification, the Navigator helps you to move around in the image quickly and easily. Click anywhere in the Navigator preview and the zoomed view will be centered on that point. Drag in the Navigator preview to reposition the view. The white rectangle indicates the area currently displayed in the Loupe view. Click in the Loupe view to move back and forth between the last two zoom levels used; when zooming in, the view will be centered on the point you click. Double-click the image to switch quickly back and forth between the Loupe and Grid views.

▶ **Tip:** The Show Grid Extras option on the Grid View tab of the Library View Options dialog box enables you to display a range of information about your photos in their image cells. In the Loupe View options, activate Show Info Overlay to display the same kind of information overlaid on your enlarged image in the Loupe view. By default, the Loupe view info overlay in disabled.

5 In the header of the Navigator panel, click each of the four zoom levels in turn (Fit, Fill, 1:1, and 3:1—the option you chose from the menu). Press the Ctrl key (Windows) / Command key (Mac OS) together with the Minus key (-) repeatedly to zoom out through the last four zoom levels used and to finally switch to Grid view; press the Ctrl key / Command key together with the Equal key (=) repeatedly to switch back to Loupe view and to progressively zoom in. Finally, set the zoom level to Fit.

Comparing photos

As the name suggests, the Compare view is ideal for examining and evaluating images side by side.

1 Press the Tab key to hide the side panels. In the Filmstrip, click to select the photo BrooklynBridge_1.jpg, and then Ctrl-click / Command-click its neighbor, BrooklynBridge_2.jpg. Click the Compare View button (⊠Ⓨ) in the Toolbar.

The first image selected becomes the *Select* image, which is displayed in the left pane of the Compare view; the image displayed in the right pane is the *Candidate*. In the Filmstrip, the Select image is marked with a white diamond in the upper right corner, and the Candidate image with a black diamond.

To use the Compare view to make a choice from a group of more than two photos, select your favored choice first to place it as the Select image, and then add the other photos to the selection. Click the Select Previous Photo and Select Next Photo buttons (⬅⮕) in the Toolbar or press the left and right arrow keys on your keyboard to move between the selected candidates. Should you decide that the current Candidate is better than the Select image, you can reverse their positions by clicking the Swap button (⊠Ⓨ) in the Toolbar.

2 To compare fine detail in the images, zoom in by dragging the Zoom slider in the Toolbar. You'll notice that the images are zoomed together. Drag either of the images in the Compare view and the images move in unison. The closed lock icon to the left of the Zoom slider indicates that the view focus of the two images is locked.

3 If you wish to zoom and move the Select and Candidate images independently, you need to click the view focus lock icon to unlink them.

A thin white line surrounds whichever of the two images in the Compare view is currently the active image: the image that will be affected by the Zoom slider, the controls in the right panel group, or any menu command you may apply.

4 Press Tab to show the side panels. Click the lock icon to link the focus for the two views, and then choose Fit from the zoom picker at the top of the Navigator.

5 Click the Select photo to make it the active image; then expand the Quick Develop panel, if necessary. From the Saved Preset menu at the top of the panel, choose Lightroom B&W Toned Presets > Cyanotype. Under Tone Control, click the single arrow at the right of the Exposure control once, and the double arrow at the right of the Clarity control twice.

Using the controls in the Quick Develop panel while you're working in Compare view can be a helpful aid in making a choice between images. Although the candidate image in our example contains more detail and is sharper, the Select image is more graphically striking and—with the Cyanotype preset applied—more atmospheric. Applying a develop preset or making other adjustments in the Quick Develop panel can help you to make a judgement on how a candidate image will look once it's edited and adjusted. You can then either undo your Quick Develop operations and move to the Develop module to edit the image with greater precision, or keep the modifications you've made as a starting point.

Using Survey view to narrow a selection

The last of the four viewing modes in the Library module, the Survey View lets you see multiple images together on one screen, and then refine your selection by dropping one photo after another from the view.

1   In the Filmstrip, select the five images of the Trump Globe at Columbus Circle. Click the Survey view button (▦) in the Toolbar, or press the N key on your keyboard. Press the F8 key on your keyboard to hide the right panel group.

2   Navigate between the images by pressing the arrow keys on your keyboard or click the Select Previous Photo and Select Next Photo buttons (⇦⇨) in the Toolbar. The active image is surrounded by a thin white border.

▶ **Tip:** If you have eliminated a photo accidentally, choose Edit > Undo to return it to the selection, or simply Ctrl-click / Command-click its thumbnail in the Filmstrip. You can easily add a photo to the selection in the Survey view in the same way.

3   Position the pointer over the second photo; then, click the Deselect Photo icon (✖) in the lower right corner of the thumbnail to drop this image from the selection in the Survey view.

As you eliminate candidates the remaining photos are progressively resized and shuffled to fill the space available in the work area.

4 Continue to eliminate photos from the Survey view. For the purposes of this exercise, deselect all but one favorite (we chose the active photo—the one in the center, marked with a white border—in the illustration below).

Dropping a photo from the Survey view doesn't delete it from its folder or remove it from the catalog; the dropped image is still visible in the Filmstrip—it has simply been deselected. You can see that the images that are still displayed in the Survey view are also the only ones that remain selected in the Filmstrip.

Flagging and deleting images

Now that you have narrowed down a selection of images to one favorite in the Survey view, you can mark your choice with a flag.

Flagging images as either picks or rejects as you review them is an effective way to quickly sort your work; flag status is one of the criteria by which you can filter your photo library. You can also quickly remove images flagged as rejects from your catalog using a menu command or keyboard shortcut.

A white flag denotes a pick (⬜), a black one with an x marks a reject (🏴), and a neutral grey flag indicates that an image has not been flagged (⬜).

▶ **Tip:** Press the P key on your keyboard to flag a selected image as a pick (⬜), the X key to flag it as a reject (🏴), or the U key to remove any flags.

1 Still in the Survey view, move the pointer over the remaining photo to see the flag icons just below the lower left corner. The grayed icons indicate that the image is not yet flagged. Click the flag to the left. The flag turns white, which marks this image as a pick. In the Filmstrip, you can see that the thumbnail now displays a white flag in the upper left of the image cell.

2 Select a different image in the Filmstrip, and then press the X key. The black reject flag icon appears at the lower left corner of the image in the Survey view and at the upper left of the thumbnail in the Filmstrip. The thumbnail of the rejected image is dimmed in the Filmstrip.

3 Choose Photo > Delete Rejected Photos or press Ctrl+Backspace / Command+Delete. Click Remove to remove the rejected photo from your catalog without deleting the master file from your hard disk.

Having been removed from the Lightroom library catalog file, the rejected image is no longer visible in the Filmstrip.

4 Press the G key or click the Grid view icon in the Toolbar to see all the remaining images as thumbnails in the Grid view.

Grouping images in the Quick Collection

A collection is a convenient way to keep a group of photos together in your catalog, even when the image files are actually located in different folders on your hard disk. You can create a new collection for a particular presentation or use collections to group your images by category or any other association. Your collections are always available from the Collections panel where you can access them quickly.

The Quick Collection is a temporary holding collection: a convenient place to group images as you review and sort your new imports, or while you assemble a selection of photos drawn from different folders in your catalog.

In the Grid view or the Filmstrip, you can add images to the Quick Collection with a single click—and remove them just as easily. Your images will stay in the Quick Collection until you're ready to convert it to a more permanent grouping that will be listed in the Collections panel. You can access the Quick Collection from the Catalog panel so that you can return to work with the same selection of images at any time.

Moving images into or out of the Quick Collection

1   Expand the Catalog panel in the left panel group, if necessary, to see the listing for the Quick Collection.

2   Choose View > Sort > File Name, or choose File Name from the Sort menu in the Toolbar; then, select the five NY_Details images by Ctrl-clicking / Command-clicking their thumbnails in the Grid view or the Filmstrip.

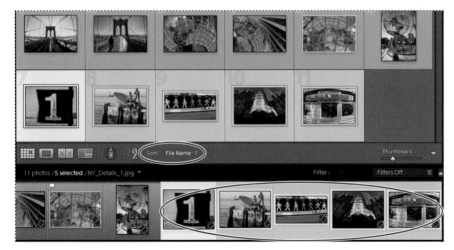

3   To add the selected photos to the Quick Collection, press the B key or choose Photo > Add To Quick Collection.

The image count beside the Quick Collection in the Catalog panel indicates that the Quick Collection now contains five images. If you have activated the option Show Quick Collection Markers in the Library View Options dialog box, each image in the Quick Collection is marked with a gray dot in the upper right corner of its thumbnail in the Grid view. The same markers are also shown in the Filmstrip unless the thumbnail size is too small.

▶ **Tip:** If you don't see the Quick Collection marker when you move your pointer over a thumbnail, make sure that Show Extras is activated in the View > Grid View Style menu. Choose View > View Options and activate Quick Collection Markers under Cell Icons in the Library View Options dialog box.

You can remove all of the selected photos from the Quick Collection by simply clicking the marker on one of the thumbnails or by pressing the B key.

4   For this exercise, you'll remove only the last image, NY_Details_5.jpg, from the Quick Collection. First, deselect the other four images, and then, with only the image NY_Details_5.jpg selected, press the B key. Your Quick Collection is reduced to four images.

Converting and clearing the Quick Collection

1   Click the Quick Collection entry in the Catalog panel. The Grid view now displays only four images. Until you clear the Quick Collection, you can easily return to this group of images to review your selection.

Now that you've refined your selection you can move your grouped images to a more permanent Collection.

2 Choose File > Save Quick Collection.

3 In the Save Quick Collection dialog box, type **New York Collection** in the Collection Name box. Activate the option Clear Quick Collection After Saving, and then click Save.

4 In the Catalog panel, you can see that the Quick Collection has been cleared; it now has an image count of 0. If necessary, expand the Collections panel so that you can see the listing for your new collection, which displays an image count of 4.

5 In the Folders panel, click the Lesson 4 folder. The grid view once more shows all the lesson images, including those in your new collection.

Designating a target collection

By default, the Quick Collection is designated as the *target collection;* this status is indicated by the plus sign (+) that follows the Quick Collection's name in the Catalog panel. The target collection is that collection to which a selected image is moved when you press the B key or click the circular marker in the upper right corner of the thumbnail, as you did in the previous exercise.

You can designate a collection of your own as the target collection so that you can use the same convenient techniques to add and remove photos quickly and easily.

1 Right-click / Control-click the entry for your new New York Collection in the Collections panel, and then choose Set As Target Collection from the context menu. The name of your collection is now followed by a plus sign (+).

2 Click the Previous Import folder in the Catalog panel, and then select the image NY_Details_5.jpg in the Grid view or the Filmstrip.

3 Open the Collections panel and watch as you press the B key on your keyboard; the image count for the New York Collection increases to 5 as the selected image is added to the collection.

4 Right-click / Control-click the Quick Collection in the Catalog panel and choose Set As Target Collection from the context menu. The Quick Collection once again displays the plus sign (+).

Working with the Filmstrip

No matter which module or view you're working in, the Filmstrip across the bottom of the Lightroom workspace provides constant access to the images in your selected folder or collection.

As with the Grid view, you can quickly navigate through your images in the Filmstrip using the arrow keys on your keyboard. If there are more images than will fit in the Filmstrip you can either use the scroll bar below the thumbnails, drag the Filmstrip by the top edge of the thumbnail frame, or click the shaded thumbnails at either end to access photos that are currently out of view.

Across the top of the Filmstrip, Lightroom provides a convenient set of controls to help streamline your workflow.

At the far left you'll find buttons for working with two displays, with pop-up menus that enable you to set the viewing mode for each display independently.

To the right of these buttons is the Grid view button, and arrow buttons for navigating between the different folders and collections you've recently been viewing.

Next is the Filmstrip Source Indicator, where you can see at a glance which folder or collection you're viewing, how many photos it contains, which images are currently selected, and the name of the image currently under your pointer. Click the Source Indicator to see a menu with all the image sources you've recently accessed.

At the far right of the Filmstrip header are the Filter controls, which we'll look at later in this lesson.

Hiding the Filmstrip and adjusting its size

You can show and hide the Filmstrip and adjust its size, as you can with the side panel groups, to make more screen space available for the image you're working on.

1   Click the triangle in the lower border of the workspace window to hide and show the Filmstrip. Right-click / Control-click the triangle to set the automatic show and hide options.

2   Position the pointer over the top edge of the Filmstrip; the cursor becomes a double arrow. Drag the top edge of the Filmstrip up or down to enlarge or reduce the thumbnails. The narrower you make the Filmstrip the more thumbnails it can display.

Using filters in the Filmstrip

With so few photos in the Lesson 4 folder it's not difficult to see all the images at once in the Filmstrip. However, when you're working with a folder containing many images it can be inconvenient to scroll the Filmstrip looking for the photos you want to work with. You can use the Filmstrip filters to narrow down the images displayed in the Filmstrip to only those that share a specified flag status, rating, color label, or any combination of these attributes.

1   In the Filmstrip you can see that one of the images in the Lesson 4 folder displays the white Pick flag that you assigned in a previous exercise. If you don't see the flag, right-click / Control-click anywhere in the Filmstrip and activate the context menu option View Options > Show Ratings And Picks. Examine the other options available in the Filmstrip context menu. Many of the commands apply to the image or images currently selected in the Filmstrip; others affect the Filmstrip itself.

2   From the Filter menu at the top right of the Filmstrip, choose Flagged. Only the image with the white flag is displayed in the Filmstrip.

3 The white flag icon is now highlighted among the Filter controls in the top bar of the Filmstrip. Click the word Filter at the left of the flag icons to see the attribute filter options displayed as buttons in the Filmstrip header.

You can activate or disable any of the filters you saw in the Filter menu by clicking the respective Filter buttons. You can set up a combination of filters and save it as a custom preset by choosing Save Current Settings As New Preset from the menu.

4 Click the white flag button to deactivate the active filter or choose Filters Off from the menu to disable all filters. The Filmstrip once more displays all the images in the folder. Click the word Filter again to hide the filter buttons.

You'll learn more about using filters in Lesson 5, "Organizing and Selecting."

Changing the sorting order of the thumbnails

Use the Sort Direction control and the Sort Criteria menu in the Toolbar to change the display order of the thumbnails images in the Grid view and the Filmstrip.

1 If the sorting controls are not currently visible in the Toolbar, choose Sorting from the tools menu at the right of the Toolbar.

2 Choose Pick from the Sort Criteria menu.

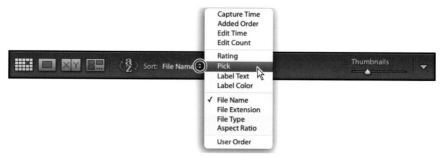

The thumbnails are rearranged in both the Grid view and the Filmstrip to display the image with the white Pick flag first.

3 Click the Sort Direction control ( ) to reverse the sorting direction of the thumbnails. The image with the white Pick flag now appears last in the order.

When you've grouped images in a Collection, you can manually rearrange their order however you wish. This can be particularly useful when you're creating a presentation such as a slideshow or web gallery, or putting together a print layout, as the images will be placed in the template according to their sort order.

4 Expand the Collections panel and click the New York Collection that you created earlier in this lesson. Choose File Name from the Sort Criteria menu.

5 In the Filmstrip, drag the second image to the right and release the mouse button when you see a black insertion bar appear between the third and fourth thumbnails.

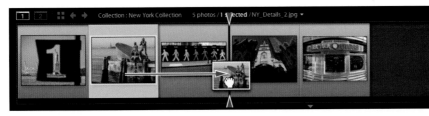

▶ **Tip:** You can also change the order of the photos in a collection by dragging the thumbnail images in the Grid view.

The image snaps to its new location in both the Filmstrip and the Grid view. The new sorting order is also apparent in the Toolbar; your manual sorting order has been saved and is now listed as User Order in the Sort Criteria menu.

6 Choose File Name from the Sort menu; then return to your manual sorting by choosing User Order.

Congratulations; you've finished another lesson. You've gained confidence navigating through your library and learned techniques for reviewing, sorting, filtering, and grouping your images as collections. You'll learn more about structuring and organizing your photo library in the next lesson.

Review questions

1   How would you use each of the views in the Library module?

2   What is the Navigator?

3   How do you use the Quick Collection?

4   What is the target collection?

Review answers

1   Press the G key or click the Grid view button (▦) in the Toolbar to see thumbnails of your images while you search, apply flags, ratings and labels, or create collections. Use the keyboard shortcut E or click the Loupe view button (▣) to inspect a single photo at a range of magnifications. Press C or click the Compare view button (⊠Y) to see two images side by side. Click the Survey view button (▤▤) in the Toolbar or use the keyboard shortcut N to evaluate several images at once or refine a selection.

2   The Navigator is an interactive full image preview that helps you move around easily within a zoomed image in Loupe view. Click or drag in the Navigator preview to reposition the view while a white rectangle indicates the portion of the magnified image that is currently visible in the workspace. The Navigator panel also contains controls for setting the zoom levels for the Loupe view. Click the image in Loupe view to switch between the last two zoom levels set in the Navigator panel.

3   To create a Quick Collection, select one or more images and then press the B key or choose Photo > Add To Quick Collection. The Quick Collection is a temporary holding area; you can continue to add—or remove—images until you are ready to save the grouping as a more permanent Collection. You'll find the Quick Collection listed in the Catalog panel.

4   The target collection is the collection to which a selected image will be moved when you press the B key or click the circular marker in the upper right corner of the thumbnail. By default, the Quick Collection is designated as the target collection; this status is indicated by the plus sign (+) that follows the Quick Collection's name in the Catalog panel. You can designate a collection of your own as the target collection so that you can use the same convenient techniques to add and remove photos quickly.

5 ORGANIZING AND SELECTING

Lesson overview

As your photo library grows larger it will become increasingly important that you're able to locate your images quickly. Lightroom offers a range of options for organizing your image files before you even click the Import button—and even more once you've added them to your catalog. You can manage and synchronize your folders or move files between them without leaving the Library module; then apply keyword tags, flags, ratings, and labels, and group your photos in easy-to-access collections, regardless of where they're stored.

This lesson will familiarize you with the tools and techniques you'll use to organize, manage, and search your photo library:

- Creating a folder structure

- Moving files and synchronizing folders

- Understanding Collections

- Working with keywords and keyword sets

- Using Flags, Ratings, and Color Labels

- Adding and editing Metadata

- Using the Painter tool

- Finding and filtering files

- Reconnecting renamed and missing files

 You'll probably need between one and two hours to complete this lesson.

Lightroom delivers powerful, versatile tools to help you organize your image library. Use keywords, flags, labels, and ratings to sort your images, and group them into virtual collections by any association you choose. You can easily configure fast, sophisticated searches, based on practically limitless combinations of criteria, that will put exactly the photos you want at your fingertips, right when you need them.

Getting started

This lesson assumes that you are already familiar with the Lightroom workspace and with moving between the different modules. If you find that you need more background information, refer to Lightroom Help, or review the previous lessons.

Before you begin, make sure that you have correctly copied the Lessons folder from the CD in the back of this book onto your computer's hard disk as detailed in "Copying the Classroom in a Book files" on page 2, and created the LR4CIB Library Catalog file to manage the lesson files as described in "Creating a catalog file for working with this book" on page 3.

1 Start Lightroom.

2 In the Adobe Photoshop Lightroom - Select Catalog dialog box, make sure the file LR4CIB Library Catalog.lrcat is selected under Select A Recent Catalog To Open, and then click Open.

Tip: The first time you enter any of the Lightroom modules, you'll see module tips that will help you get started by identifying the components of the Lightroom workspace and stepping you through the workflow. Dismiss the tips by clicking the Close button. To reactivate the tips for any module, choose [*Module name*] Tips from the Help menu.

3 Lightroom will open in the screen mode and workspace module that were active when you last quit. If necessary, switch to the Library module by clicking Library in the Module Picker at the top of the workspace.

Importing images into the library

The first step is to import the images for this lesson into the Lightroom library.

1 In the Library module, click the Import button below the left panel group.

2 If the Import dialog box appears in compact mode, click the Show More Options button at the lower left of the dialog box to see all the options in the expanded Import dialog box.

3 Under Source at the left of the expanded Import dialog box, navigate to and select the LR4CIB > Lessons > Lesson 5 folder. Ensure that all twelve images in the Lesson 5 folder are checked for import.

4 In the import options picker above the thumbnail previews, select Add so that the imported photos will be added to your catalog without being moved or copied. Under File Handling at the right of the Import dialog box, choose Minimal from the Render Previews menu and ensure that the Don't Import Suspected Duplicates option is activated. Under Apply During Import, choose None from both the Develop Settings menu and the Metadata menu, and type **Lesson 5, Europe** in the Keywords text box. Make sure that your import is set up as shown in the illustration below, and then click Import.

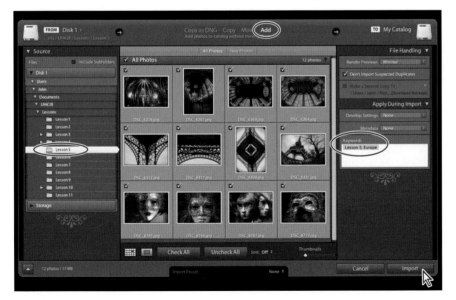

The twelve images are imported from the Lesson 5 folder and now appear in both the Grid view of the Library module and in the Filmstrip across the bottom of the Lightroom workspace.

Organizing folders

Each time you import an image, Lightroom creates a new catalog entry to record the file's address and lists the folder in which it is stored—and the volume that contains that folder—in the Folders panel in the left panel group.

In the Folders panel, you can organize your photo library at the most basic level by rearranging files and folders on your hard disk without ever leaving the Lightroom workspace; you can create or delete folders at the click of a button and move files and folders by simply dragging them. When you use the Folders panel to move a photo between folders, Lightroom will delete the image file from its original location and update the library catalog with the file's new address. Lightroom maintains a single catalog entry for each photo you import, so a master image cannot be duplicated in separate folders or added to the catalog twice.

Creating subfolders

In this exercise you'll use the Folders panel to begin organizing the photos in the Lesson 5 folder into categories by separating them into subfolders. You'll use two methods of creating a subfolder.

1   Click the Lesson 5 folder in the Folders panel; then, Ctrl-click / Command-click to select the four images of masks in the Grid view.

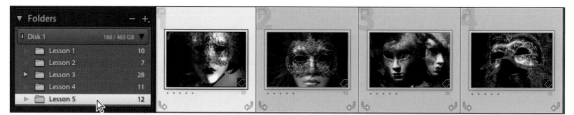

2   In the Folders panel header, click the Create New Folder button (➕) and choose Add Subfolder from the menu. Make sure the Show Photos In Subfolders option is activated.

3   In the Create Folder dialog box, type **Masks** as the folder name, activate the Include Selected Photos option, and then click Create.

4 In the Folders panel, expand the Lesson 5 folder to see the Masks folder nested inside it. The image count for the new subfolder shows that it contains the four images that you selected in step 1.

5 With the Lesson 5 folder still selected in the Folders panel, select the remaining eight images.

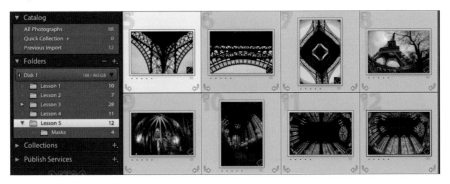

6 Right-click / Control-click the Lesson 5 folder and choose Create Folder Inside "Lesson 5" from the context menu. Type **Architecture** as the folder name, activate the Include Selected Photos option, and then click Create. Click the Architecture subfolder to see the eight images you selected in step 5.

Making changes to a folder's content

When you rearrange files and folders in the Folders panel the changes are also made on your hard disk. Inversely, the Folders panel needs to be updated to reflect any changes you make to the location, name, or contents of a folder from outside the Lightroom workspace. In this exercise you'll experience this first hand by deleting an image in Windows Explorer / the Finder.

1 Click the Lesson 5 folder in the Folders panel. Right-click / Ctrl-click any of the photos of masks in the Grid view and choose Show In Explorer / Show In Finder from the context menu.

▶ **Tip:** To rename a folder in the Folders panel, right-click / Control-click its name and choose Rename from the context menu. Be aware that when you rename a folder in the Folders panel, the change affects the folder on the hard disk.

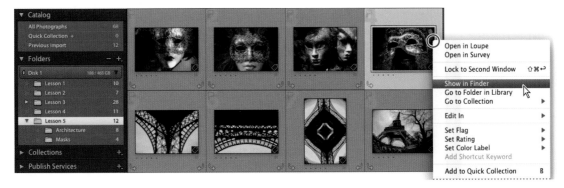

2 The Explorer / Finder window opens. Note the Architecture and Masks subfolders inside the Lesson 5 folder. Right-click / Ctrl-click the image file DSC_8733.jpg inside the Lesson 5 folder and choose Delete / Move To Trash from the context menu.

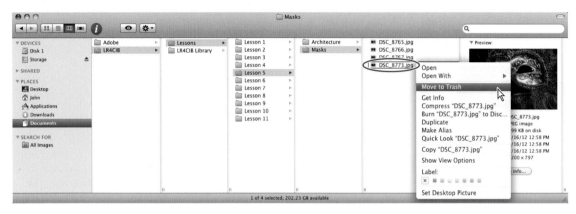

3 Switch back to Lightroom. In the Grid view, note that the thumbnail of the image that you just deleted in the Explorer / Finder window now has a question mark badge in the upper right corner of its grid cell. This indicates that Lightroom still has an entry for the image in its library catalog but the link to the original file has been broken.

4 Click the question mark badge. A dialog box opens offering you the option to locate the missing file and reestablish its link to the catalog. Click Cancel.

As you deleted the file intentionally you should now remove it from the library catalog. You can remove a missing photo from your catalog by selecting its thumbnail in the Grid view or the Filmstrip and pressing Alt+Backspace / Option+Delete or by choosing Photo > Remove Photos From Catalog. Don't remove the photo from the catalog yet—if you've done so already, choose Edit > Undo Remove Images. In the next exercise you'll learn a different technique for updating the catalog by synchronizing folders.

Synchronizing folders

When you synchronize the folders in the Lightroom catalog with the folders on your hard disk you have the option to remove catalog entries for files that have been deleted, import photos that have been added to your folders, or scan for files with updated metadata.

You can specify which folders and subfolders will be synchronized and which new images you want added to your library.

1　Make sure that the Lesson 5 folder is still selected in the Folders panel.

2　Choose Library > Synchronize Folder.

3　In the Synchronize Folder "Lesson 5" dialog box, the import options are unavailable, indicating that there have been no new photos added to the Lesson 5 folder. Activate the option Remove Missing Photos From Catalog (1), disable Scan For Metadata Updates, and then click Synchronize.

Tip: The Import New Photos option in the Synchronize Folders dialog box automatically imports any files that have been added to a folder without yet having been added to your image library. Optionally, activate Show Import Dialog Before Importing to choose which of those files you wish to import. Activate the Scan For Metadata Updates option to check for files with metadata modified in another application.

The missing image is removed from your catalog and its thumbnail is no longer displayed in the Grid view; all the links between your library catalog and the Lesson 5 folder on your hard disk have been restored.

Using collections to organize images

Although an organized system of folders provides a good foundation for your photo library, grouping images into collections is a far more efficient and flexible way to classify your images—and offers many more options when you need to access them.

A collection is like a virtual folder: a grouping of photos from your library based on your own associations rather than on the actual location of the files. A collection may contain images drawn from any number of separate folders on your hard disk. Inversely, a single master image can be included in any number of collections; the same photo might appear in a collection of images with architectural content and also in a compilation of shots with an Autumn theme; it may be part of a collection you've assembled for a client presentation and in another created for a family vacation slideshow. Grouping images as collections in your library doesn't affect the arrangement of the files and folders on your hard disk, and removing a photo from a collection won't remove it from the library catalog or delete it from the hard disk.

There are three basic types of collection: Collections, Smart Collections and the Quick Collection. Any collection can also be part of an Output Collection—a listing in the Collections that is created automatically when you save a print layout or a creative project such as a photo book or web gallery. An Output Collection links a set of images to a particular project template and records all of your customized settings. Any collection or selection of images can also become a Publish collection, which automatically keeps track of images that you've shared online.

Note: Once you've grouped a selection of photos as a collection you can rearrange them in the Grid view or the Filmstrip, changing the order in which they will appear in a presentation or a print layout. Your customized sorting order will be saved with the collection.

Tip: You'll learn more about Publish collections in Lesson 10, "Publishing Your Photos."

The Quick Collection

● **Note:** If the Thumb-nail Badges option is activated in the Library View Options, a photo that is included in a collection of any kind displays the collection badge () in the lower right of its thumbnail.

The Quick Collection is a temporary holding collection; a convenient place to group images while you gather photos from different folders. You can access the Quick Collection from the Catalog panel so that you can easily return to work with the same selection of images at any time. Your images will stay in the Quick Collection until you are ready to convert your selection to a permanent collection that will then be listed in the Collections panel.

You can create as many collections and smart collections as you wish, but there is only one Quick Collection; if there is already a selection of images in the Quick Collection, you'll need to convert it to a standard collection, and then clear the Quick Collection before you can use it to assemble a new a new grouping. To create a new collection for images that are currently in the Quick Collection, right-click / Control-click the Quick Collection folder in the Catalog panel and choose Save Quick Collection from the context menu.

If the Quick Collection Markers option is enabled in the View Options for the Grid view, a circular marker appears in the top right corner of a thumbnail in the Grid view or the Filmstrip when you move your pointer over the image cell. You can add the image to the Quick Collection by clicking this marker.

Click the badge to see a menu listing the collections in which the image is included. Select a collection from the list to switch to that collection as the image source folder.

Once the photo is added to the Quick Collection the marker becomes a solid grey circle. Click the solid marker to remove the image from the Quick Collection. You can perform the same operations for a multiple selection of images by clicking the Quick Collection marker on any of the selected thumbnails.

You can also add a selected image or group of images to the Quick Collection by pressing the B key or choosing Photo > Add To Quick Collection, or remove a selected image or group of images from the Quick Collection by pressing the B key again or choosing Photo > Remove From Quick Collection.

Collections

You can create as many permanent collections as you wish. Use a collection to collate the images you need for a particular project or to group photos by subject or any other another association.

When you create a collection of images for a slideshow or a web page, all the work you do on your presentation will be saved with the collection in the catalog file. In fact, the catalog entry for a single collection can incorporate your settings from the Develop module, a slide layout and playback options from the Slideshow module, designs you set up in the Book and Web modules, and a page layout modified in the Print module. Output collections for print jobs that will also include your color management and printer settings.

Note: Remember that a single photo can be included in any number of collections, although the master image file is located in only one folder in your library. For this reason, grouping your images in collections is a far more versatile organizational method than sorting them into categorized folders.

To create a collection, choose Library > New Collection. Alternatively, you can click the New Collection button (⊕) in the header of the Collections panel and choose Create Collection from the menu. Enter a name in the Create Collection dialog box and click Create. Your new collection will be added to the list in the Collections panel. You can then simply drag photos onto the listing in the Collections panel to add them to the collection.

Smart collections

A smart collection searches the metadata attached to your photos and gathers together all those images in your library that meet a specified set of criteria. Any newly imported photo that matches the criteria you've set up for a smart collection will be added to that collection automatically.

You can create a Smart Collection by choosing Library > New Smart Collection, and then specify the search criteria for your smart collection by choosing options from the menus in the Create Smart Collection dialog box.

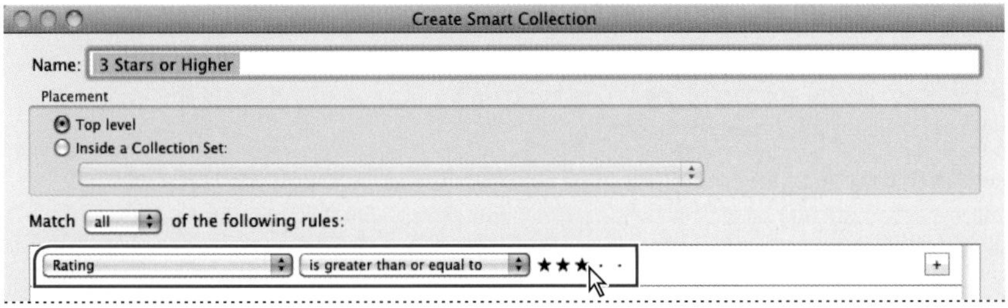

You can add more search criteria by clicking the + button to the right of any of the rules. Hold down the Alt / Option key and click the Plus button (+) to refine a rule. In the illustration below a second rule has been added to search for images containing "Europe" in any searchable text, and then a refined rule has been added to search for images which were either captured or edited this year.

Stacking images

Another effective way of organizing images within a folder or collection is by creating stacks.

Stacks are ideal for reducing clutter in the Grid view—and the number of thumbnails you need to scroll through in the Filmstrip—by grouping similar or related photos so that only the top image in each stack is displayed. You can stack a selection of images of the same subject, a series of photos shot to test different camera settings, or action shots taken using burst mode or auto-bracketing.

A stack can be identified in the Grid view and the Filmstrip by an icon representing a stack of photos, together with an image count, in the upper left corner of the thumbnail.

You can expand or collapse the stack by clicking the stack icon; rearrange the order of the photos within the stack or specify which image appears at the top either by choosing commands from the Photo > Stacking menu or by using keyboard shortcuts.

When you're working with a folder containing hundreds of photos from the same shoot, you can have Lightroom stack the images automatically based on capture time; you can specify the time interval between stacks so that your shots are grouped in a way that reflects the flow of the shoot.

To create a stack, select two or more images in the Grid view or the Filmstrip, and then choose Photo > Stacking > Group Into Stack.

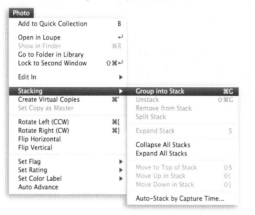

To learn more about Stacks, please refer to Lightroom Help.

Applying keyword tags

Perhaps the most direct way to mark your photos so that they're easier to find later is by tagging them with keywords—text metadata attached to the image files to categorize them by subject or association.

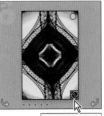

For example, the image in the illustration at the right could be tagged with the keywords Architecture and Paris, and could therefore be located by searching for either or both of those tags. If the Thumbnail Badges option is activated in the Library View Options dialog box, photos with keyword tags are identified by a keywords badge (⊠) in the lower right corner of the thumbnail.

Photo has keywords

You can apply keywords to your photos individually or tag an entire series of images with shared metadata in one operation, thereby linking them by association and making them easier to access amongst all the photos that make up your library. Keywords added to images in Lightroom can be read by Adobe applications such as Bridge, Photoshop, and Photoshop Elements, and by other applications that support XMP metadata.

Viewing keyword tags

Because you applied keyword tags to the images for this lesson during the import process, the thumbnails in the Grid view and the Filmstrip are all marked with the keywords badge. Let's review the keywords you already attached to these photos.

1   Make sure that you are still in the Grid view, and then select the Lesson 5 folder in the Folders panel.

2   Show the right panel group, if necessary; then, expand the Keywording panel. Expand the Keyword Tags pane at the top of the panel. By selecting each thumbnail in the Grid view in turn you can confirm that all the images in the Lesson 5 folder share the keywords "Lesson 5" and "Europe."

▶ **Tip:** Clicking the thumbnail badge of an image in Grid view will automatically expand the Keywording panel.

3   Select any one of the photos in the Lesson 5 folder. In the Keyword Tags pane at the top of the Keywording pane, select the text "Lesson 5" and press the Backspace key on your keyboard to delete it.

4   Click anywhere in the Grid view, and then choose Edit > Select All or press Ctrl+A / Command+A to select all the Lesson 5 photos. In the Keyword Tags pane, the keyword "Lesson 5" is now marked with an asterisk to indicate that this tag is not shared by every image in the selection.

5   Expand the Keyword List panel.

▶ Tip: You can apply an existing keyword tag to selected images by clicking the tag in the Keyword Suggestions pane in the Keywording panel. To remove a tag from a selected photo or photos, either delete the word from the Keyword Tags pane in the Keywording panel, or click the checkbox to disable that keyword in the Keyword List panel.

In the Keyword List, a check mark in front of the keyword "Europe" indicates that this tag is shared by every image in the selection, while the tag "Lesson 5" is marked with a dash—indicating that it attached to some, but not all, of the selected images. The image count to the right of the Lesson 5 tag shows that it is shared by only ten of the eleven images.

6   With all eleven images still selected, click the dash mark in front of the Lesson 5 tag to reinstate the deleted tag; a check mark replaces the dash and the image count for the Lesson 5 keyword increases to 11.

Adding keyword tags

You already added keywords to your images during the process of importing them into your Lightroom library. Once the images have been added to your Lightroom library, you can add more keywords by using the Keywording panel.

1   In the Folders panel, select the Architecture subfolder inside the Lesson 5 folder, and then choose Edit > Select All or press Ctrl+A / Command+A.

2   In the Keywording panel, click the grey text "Click Here To Add Keywords" below the Keyword Tags pane and type **Paris, France**. Make sure to separate the words with a comma as shown in the illustration at the right, below.

Always use a comma to separate keywords. Using a space or period will not work; Lightroom would treat both "Paris France" and "Paris. France" as a single keyword.

3   Press Enter / Return. The new keywords are listed in alphabetical order in the Keyword Tags panel and in the Keyword List panel.

4   In the Folders panel, select the Lesson 5 folder, and then choose Edit > Invert Selection to select all the images other than the eight in the Architecture folder.

5   In the Keywording panel, click in the text box below the Keyword Tags pane and type **Italy**. Press Enter / Return.

6   Choose Edit > Select None or press Ctrl+D / Command+D on your keyboard.

Working with keyword sets and nesting keywords

You can use the Keyword Set pane of the Keywording panel to work with *keyword sets*; groups of keyword tags compiled for a particular purpose. You could create a set of keywords for a specific project, another set for a special occasion, and one for your friends and family. Lightroom provides three basic keyword set presets. You can use these sets as they are or as starting points for creating sets of your own.

1 Expand the Keyword Set pane in the Keywording panel, if necessary, and then choose Wedding Photography from the Keyword Set menu. You can see that the keywords in the set would indeed be helpful in organizing the shots from a big event. Look at the categories covered by the other Lightroom keyword sets. You can use these as templates for your own keyword sets by editing them to suit your needs and saving your changes as a new preset.

Grouping your keywords in Keyword Sets is one way to keep your keywords organized; another handy technique is to nest related tags in a keywords hierarchy.

▶ **Tip:** Keyword sets are a convenient way to have the keywords you need at hand as you work on different collections in your library. A single keyword tag may be included in any number of keyword sets. If you don't see the Lightroom presets in the Keyword Set menu, open the Lightroom Preferences and click the Presets tab. In the Lightroom Defaults options, click Restore Keyword Set Presets.

2 Ctrl-click / Command-click to select the keywords "France" and "Italy" in the Keyword List panel; then, drag the selected tags onto the keyword "Europe." Click the triangle at the left of the Europe tag to see the France and Italy tags nested inside it.

3 In the keyword list, drag the Paris tag from its alphabetical position on the keyword list onto the keyword "France," and then expand the France tag.

4 Right-click / Control-click the keyword "Italy" and choose Create Keyword Tag Inside "Italy" from the context menu.

5 In the Keyword Tag text box, type **Venice**. In the Synonyms text box just below, type **Venezia**. Make sure all the Keyword Tag Options are activated as shown in the illustration below, and then click Create.

Include On Export Includes the keyword tag when your photos are exported.

Export Containing Keywords Includes the parent tag when your photos are exported.

Export Synonyms Includes any synonyms associated with the keyword tag when your photos are exported.

6 Right-click / Control-click the keyword "Venice" and choose Create Keyword Tag Inside "Venice" from the context menu. Type **Carnival**, and then click Create. Expand the Venice tag so that you can see all the tags in the hierarchy.

7 In the Folders panel, select the Masks subfolder inside the Lesson 5 folder, and then choose Edit > Select All or press Ctrl+A / Command+A. Drag the Venice and Carnival tags from the Keyword List panel onto any of the three selected images in the Grid view.

The check marks in front of the new Venice and Carnival tags in the keyword list, and the image counts to the right of each entry, indicate that both keyword tags have been applied to all three of the photos in the selection.

8 In the Folders panel, select the Lesson 2 folder. and then choose Edit > Select All or press Ctrl+A / Command+A.

9 Move the pointer over the Europe tag in the Keyword List panel, and then click the empty check box at the left. Repeat the process to apply the Italy and Venice keyword tags to the selected images.

Searching by keywords

Once you've taken the time to organize your images by adding keywords and other metadata such as ratings, flags, and labels, it will be easy to set up sophisticated and detailed filters to find exactly the photo you're looking for.

For now, we'll look at some techniques for searching the photos in your library by keywords alone.

> **Tip:** If you find that you cannot open two panels in one of the side panel groups at the same time, right-click / Control-click the header of any panel in the group and disable the Solo Mode option in the context menu

1 In the left panel group, collapse the Navigator, Collections, and Publish Services panels if necessary, so that you can clearly see the contents of the Catalog and Folders Panels. In the Folders panel, select the Lesson 5 folder, and then choose Edit > Select None or press Ctrl+D / Command+D.

2 Use the Thumbnails slider in the Toolbar to reduce the size of the thumbnails to the minimum, so that you'll be able to see as many images as possible in the Grid view. If the Filter Bar is not already visible above the Grid view, choose View > Show Filter Bar, or press the Backslash key (\).

3   In the right panel group, collapse the Histogram, Quick Develop, and Keywording panels, if necessary, so that you can clearly see the whole of the expanded Keyword List panel.

4   In the Keyword list panel, move your pointer over the entry for the keyword "Europe," and then click the white arrow that appears to the right of the image count.

In the left panel group, All Photographs is now selected in the Catalog panel, indicating that your entire catalog has been searched for photos with the Europe tag.

The Metadata filter has been activated in the Filter bar at the top of the work area, and the Grid view now displays only those images in your library that are tagged with the keyword "Europe."

5   In the Keyword column at the left of the Metadata filter pane, expand the Europe entry; then, expand the nested Italy tag and click Venice.

▶ **Tip:** To transfer lists of keywords between computers or share them with colleagues who are also working in Lightroom, use the Export Keywords and Import Keywords commands, which you'll find in the Metadata menu.

The images in the Grid view are filtered so that only the ten photos with the Venice tag are still visible. Now you'll use a different technique to narrow the search further.

6 Click Text in the Filter Picker in the Filter bar at the top of the work area.

7 In the Text filter bar, choose Any Searchable Field from the first menu and Contains from the second menu, noting the options available in each menu; then type **carnival** in the text box at the right and press Enter.

Tip: You can use the lock button at the right end of the Filter bar to keep your current filter settings active when you choose a different image source from the Catalog, Folders, or Collections panels.

Only the three photos of Venetian masks are still displayed in the Grid view. Of course, the true power of the Library filters only comes into play when you set up more complex filters based on a combination of criteria—but this exercise should have given you at least a glimpse of the possibilities.

8 Disable the combined Text and Metadata filter by clicking None in the picker in the center of the Filter bar. In the Folders panel, select the Lesson 5 folder, and then choose Edit > Select None or press Ctrl+D / Command+D.

Using flags and ratings

The Attribute filters in the Filter bar allow you to search and sort your images according to attributes such as flags and ratings.

When you choose Attribute from the Library Filter options in the Filter bar, the Filter bar expands to display controls for sorting your images by flag status, star rating, color label, copy status, or any combination of these attributes.

Flagging images

Assigning flags to sort the good images from the rejects can be a good way to begin organizing a group of photos. An image can be flagged as a pick (🚩), a reject (🚩), or left unflagged (🚩).

1 Choose Attribute from the picker in the Filter bar. The Filter bar expands to show the Attribute filter controls.

2   If the Toolbar is not already visible below the Grid view, press the T key. Click the triangle at the right side of the Toolbar and activate the Flagging tool in the menu to show the Flag As Pick and Set As Rejected buttons in the Toolbar.

▶ **Tip:** In the Grid and Loupe views, you'll find tools for adding ratings, flags, and color labels in the Toolbar. In the Compare and Survey views you can change these attributes using the controls beneath the images. You can also flag, rate, or color label a selected image by using the Set Flag, Set Rating, or Set Color Label commands in the Photo menu.

3   In the Folders panel, select the Architecture subfolder inside the Lesson 5 folder.

4   In the Grid view, select DSC_6264.jpg, a photo of the stained glass windows and vaulted roof of La Sainte-Chapelle (The Holy Chapel) in Paris. If the Flags option is activated in the Library View Options dialog box, a grey flag icon in the upper left corner of the image cell indicates that this photo is unflagged. If necessary, hold the pointer over the image cell to see the flag, or disable Show Clickable Items On Mouse Over Only in the Library View Options dialog box.

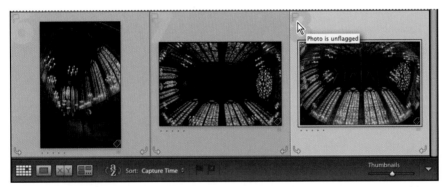

5   To change the flag status to Flagged, you can either click the flag badge in the image cell or the Flag As Pick button (⚑) in the Toolbar. Note that the photo is now marked with a white flag icon in the upper left corner of the image cell.

6   Click the white flag button in the Attribute Filter bar. The Grid view displays only the image that you just flagged. The view is now filtered to display only flagged images from the Architecture folder.

Tip: You can use the Library > Refine Photos command to sort your photos quickly on the basis of their flagging status. Choose Library > Refine Photos, and then click Refine in the Refine Photos dialog box; any unflagged photos are flagged as rejects and the picks are reset to unflagged status.

Lightroom offers a variety of ways to flag a photo. To flag a photo as a pick, choose Photo > Set Flag > Flagged or press the P key on your keyboard. Click the flag icon at the top left corner of the image cell to toggle between Unflagged and Pick status. To flag an image as a reject, choose Photo > Set Flag > Rejected, press the X key, or Alt-click / Option-click the flag icon in the corner of the image cell. To remove a flag from an image, choose Photo > Set Flag > Unflagged or press the U key. To set any flag status for an image, right-click / Control-click the flag icon in the corner of the image cell and choose Flagged, Unflagged, or Rejected from the context menu.

7 Click the grey flag button (the flag in the center) in the Attribute Filter bar. The Grid view now displays any photos flagged as Picks and all unflagged photos, so once again we see all of the images in the Architecture folder.

8 In the Filter bar, click None to disable the Attribute filters.

Assigning ratings

A quick and easy way to sort your images as you review and evaluate them is to assign each photo a rating on a scale from one to five stars.

1 In the Grid view, select the image DSC_6312.jpg: a detail from the Eiffel Tower.

2 Press the 3 key on your keyboard. The message "Set Rating to 3" appears briefly and the photo is now marked with three stars in the lower left of its image cell.

Tip: If you don't see the star rating in the image cell, choose View > View Options and make sure Rating And Label is activated in the image cell display options.

3 If necessary, click the triangle at the right of the Toolbar and make sure that the Rating controls are activated in the menu. The stars in the Toolbar reflect the rating you just applied to the selected image.

It's easy to change the rating for a selected image; simply press another key between 1 and 5 to apply a new rating or press the 0 key to remove the rating altogether. Alternatively, you can click the stars in the Toolbar to change the rating, or click the highest star in the current rating to remove it.

You can also assign ratings in the Metadata panel, by choosing from the Photo > Set Rating menu, or by right-clicking / Control-clicking a thumbnail and choosing from the Set Rating submenu in the context menu.

Working with color labels

Color labeling can be a very versatile tool for organizing your workflow. Unlike flags and ratings, color labels have no predefined meanings; you can attach your own meaning to each color and customize separate label sets for specific tasks.

While setting up a print job you might assign the red label to images you wish to proof, a blue label to those that need retouching, or a green label to mark images as approved. For another project, you might use the different colors to indicate levels of urgency.

Applying Color Labels

You can use the colored buttons in the Toolbar to assign color labels to your images. If you don't see the color label buttons, click the triangle at the right of the Toolbar and choose Color Label from the menu. You can also click the color label icon displayed in a photo's image cell (a small grey rectangle, for an unlabeled image) and choose from the menu. Alternatively, choose Photo > Set Color Label and choose from the menu; you'll notice that four of the five color labels have keyboard shortcuts.

To see—and set—color labels in the Grid view image cells, choose View > View Options or right-click / Control-click any of the thumbnails and choose View Options from the context menu to open the Library View Options dialog box. On the Grid View tab in The Library View Options dialog box, activate Show Grid Extras. In the Compact Cell Extras options, you can choose Label or Rating And Label from either the Bottom Label or Top Label menus. In the Expanded Cell Extras options, activate the Include Color Label checkbox.

Editing Color Labels and using Color Label Sets

You can rename the color labels to suit your own purposes and create separate label sets tailored to different parts of your workflow. The Lightroom default options in the Photo > Set Color Label menu are Red, Yellow, Green, Blue, Purple, and None. You can change the color label set by choosing Metadata > Color Label Set, and then choosing either the Bridge or Lightroom default sets, or the Review Status set.

The Review Status label set gives you an idea of how you might assign your own label names to help you keep organized. The options in the Review Status set are To Delete, Color Correction Needed, Good To Use, Retouching Needed, To Print, and None.

You can use this label set as it is or as a starting point for creating your own sets. To open the Edit Color Label Set dialog box, choose Metadata > Color Label Set > Edit. You can enter your own name for each color, and then choose Save Current Settings As New Preset from the Presets menu.

Searching by color label

In the Filter bar, click Attribute to see the Attribute filter controls. You can limit your search to a single color label by clicking just one button, or activate more than one button at once. To disable an active color label button, simply click it again. You can use the color label search buttons together with other Attribute filters, or to refine a Text or Metadata search.

The Attribute filters, including the Color Label filters, are also available in the bar above the thumbnails in the Filmstrip.

Adding metadata

You can leverage the metadata information attached to the image files to help you organize and manage your photo library. Much of the metadata, such as capture date, exposure time, focal length and other camera settings, is generated by your camera, but you can also add your own metadata to make it easier to search and sort your catalog. In fact, you did just that when you applied keywords, ratings, and color labels to your images. In addition, Lightroom supports the information standards evolved by the International Press Telecommunications Council (IPTC), which includes entries for descriptions, keywords, categories, credits, and origins.

You can use the Metadata panel in the right panel group to inspect or edit the metadata attached to a selected image.

1   In the Folders panel, click the Masks folder; then, Select the image DSC_8766.jpg: the photo featuring a mask trimmed with orange feathers.

2   Expand the Metadata panel. If necessary, hide the Filmstrip or collapse the other panels in the right panel group so that you can see as much of the Metadata panel as possible. Choose Default from the Metadata Set menu in the header of the Metadata panel.

Even the default metadata set exposes a great deal of information about the image. Although most of this metadata was generated by the camera, some of it can be very useful in sorting your photos; you could filter images by capture date, search for shots taken with a particular lens, or easily separate photos taken on different cameras. However, the default set displays only a subset of an image's metadata.

3   Choose EXIF And IPTC from the Metadata Set menu in header of the Metadata panel. Scroll down in the Metadata panel to get an idea of the kinds of information that can be applied to an image.

4   For the purposes of this exercise, you can choose Quick Describe from the Metadata Set menu.

In the Quick Describe metadata set, the Metadata panel shows the File-name, Copy Name (if the image is a virtual copy), Folder, Rating, and some EXIF and IPTC metadata. You can use the Metadata panel to add a title and caption to a photo, attach a copyright notice, provide details about the photographer and the location where the photo was shot, and also change the star rating.

5   Click in the Metadata panel to assign the image a rating, and type **Carnival Mask 2** in the Title text box.

6   Control-click / Command-click either of the other two mask photos to add it to the selection. In the Metadata panel you can see that the folder name and the camera model are shared by both files; items not shared by both images now show the entry <mixed>. Changes made to any of the items in the metadata panel, even those with mixed values, will affect both of the selected images. This is a convenient way to edit items such as copyright details for a whole batch of selected images at the same time.

Storage of metadata

File information is stored using the Extensible Metadata Platform (XMP) standard. XMP is built on XML. In the case of camera raw files that have a proprietary file format, XMP isn't written into the original files. To avoid file corruption, XMP metadata is stored in a separate file called a sidecar file. For all other file formats supported by Lightroom (JPEG, TIFF, PSD, and DNG), XMP metadata is written into the files in the location specified for that data.

XMP facilitates the exchange of metadata between Adobe applications and across publishing workflows. For example, you can save metadata from one file as a template, and then import the metadata into other files. Metadata that is stored in other formats, such as EXIF, IPTC (IIM), and TIFF, is synchronized and described with XMP so that it can be more easily viewed and managed. To find out more about Metadata, please refer to Lightroom Help.

—From Lightroom Help

Organizing photos by location

Note: You need to be online to make use of the Map module.

Lightroom 4 introduces geotagging in the new Map module, where you can see exactly where your photos were captured on a Google map, and search and filter the images in your library by location.

Photos that were captured with a camera or phone that records GPS coordinates will appear on the map automatically. You can easily add location metadata to images captured without GPS information by dragging them directly onto the map from the Filmstrip, or by having Lightroom match their capture times to a tracklog exported from a mobile device.

1   In the Library module, click the Import button below the left panel group.

2   If the Import dialog box appears in compact mode, click the Show More Options button at the lower left of the dialog box to see more options.

Tip: If geocoding has been disabled for your catalog, you may see a dialog box asking you to authorize Lightroom to exchange GPS location information with Google Maps. Click Enable.

3   Under Source at the left of the Import dialog box, navigate to and select the LR4CIB > Lessons > LR4CIB GPS folder. Make sure that both of the images in the LR4CIB GPS folder are checked for import. In the import options picker above the thumbnail previews, click Add to add the imported photos to your catalog without moving or copying them. In the Apply During Import panel at the right, type **Lesson 5, GPS** in the Keywords text box, and then click Import.

4   In the Grid view or the Filmstrip, select the image Audreys_House.jpg, and then click Map in the module picker across the top of the workspace.

Working in the Map module

Lightroom has automatically plotted the photo's location by reading the GPS metadata embedded in the image file. The mapped location is marked by a colored pin.

Tip: If you don't see the Map Info overlay and the Map Key, which explains the different color-coded location pins, choose Show Map Info and Show Map Key from the View Menu.

Note: What you see on screen may differ from this illustration, depending on the map style and zoom depth set when you last used the Map module.

The Navigator panel at the left shows a thumbnail overview map, with a white-bordered rectangle indicating the area currently visible in the main map view.

The Toolbar below the map view offers a Map Style menu, a Zoom slider, and buttons for locking marker pins and accessing imported GPS tracklogs. You can add location details and other information in the Metadata panel at the right.

1   Dismiss the Map Key by clicking the Close button (x) in the upper right corner of the overlay, or by disabling the Show Map Key option in the View menu.

2   Experiment with changing the magnification of the map by dragging the Zoom slider in the Toolbar, or by clicking the Zoom In (+) and Zoom Out (-) buttons at either end of the slider. Hold down the Alt / Option key and drag a rectangle in the map to zoom into that area. Drag the map to reposition it in the view, or move the focus by dragging the white-bordered rectangle in the Navigator.

● **Note:** The maximum zoom depth available depends on your choice of map style.

3   In the Map Style menu at the left of the Toolbar, select each of the six styles in turn, then set the map to the look you prefer.

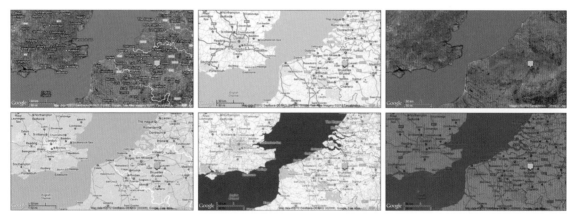

Map styles, clockwise from upper left: Hybrid, Road Map, Satellite, Dark, Light, Terrain.

The Location Filter bar above the map lets you highlight just those photos captured at locations currently visible on the map or filter for tagged or untagged shots.

4   Click each of the four options in the Location Filter bar in turn, noting the effect of the filters on which images are displayed in the Filmstrip.

In the Filmstrip and the Library module's Grid view, images that have been tagged with a GPS location are marked with a location marker badge (■).

▶ **Tip:** Click the location marker badge on a thumbnail in the Filmstrip or in the Library module's Grid view to zoom in to the image's map location.

Geotagging images captured without GPS data

Tip: To see whether a selected photo has GPS metadata, choose the Location preset in the Metadata panel; then, look for coordinates in the GPS field.

Even if your camera does not record GPS data, the Map module makes it easy to tag your photos by location.

1   In the header of the Filmstrip, click the white arrow to the right of the name of the currently selected image and choose Folder - Lesson 5 from the Recent Sources list in the menu.

2   In the Filter bar's text search box, type **Venice, Italy**; then, press Enter / Return.

The map is redrawn and the new location is marked with a Search Result marker, distinguished by a bold black spot.

3   Clear the Search Result marker by clicking the X button at the right of the text search box in the Location Filter bar.

4   Select the three photos of carnival masks, and then right-click / Control-click Venice on the map and choose Add GPS Coordinates To Selected Photos.

Tip: If geocoding has been disabled for your catalog, you may see a dialog box asking you to authorize Lightroom to exchange GPS information with Google Maps. Click Enable. You can also disable or activate this feature at any time on the Metadata tab of the Catalog Settings dialog box; choose Catalog Settings from the Edit / Lightroom menu.

5   Choose Edit > Select None. Move the pointer over the marker pin on the map to see a preview of the photos captured at that location. Click the marker pin to select the photos captured at that location. Click the white arrows at the sides of the preview thumbnail to see the other images at this location, and then click away from the preview to close it.

6   In the header of the Filmstrip, click the arrow to the right of the image source information and choose Previous Import from the source menu.

Adding locations using GPS tracklogs

Although your camera may not record GPS data, many mobile devices such as phones can export a tracklog that records your location over a given period of time. You can import this information, and then have Lightroom tag your photos automatically by matching their capture times to the locations recorded in the tracklog.

1 Click the GPS Tracklogs button () in the Toolbar and choose Load Tracklog, or choose Map > Tracklog > Load Tracklog. In the Import Track File dialog box, navigate to your LR4CIB > Lessons > LR4CIB GPS folder; then, select the file NY_Marathon.gpx and click Open / Choose.

The map is updated to a view of New York, with the recorded GPS track shown as either a blue or yellow line on the map, depending on your choice of map style.

This tracklog file was generated by a sports watch that was set to a different time zone than the camera used to capture our lesson photo, so you may need to offset the times recorded in the tracklog. The amount of offset you'll need to apply will depend on the time zone setting on your computer.

2 Click the GPS Tracklogs button ( ) in the Toolbar and choose Set Time Zone Offset, or choose the same command from the Map > Tracklog menu. Use the slider in the Offset Time Zone dialog box, or type a number in the adjacent text box, to shift the starting time for the tracklog to 11:27 AM; then, click OK.

> **Tip:** Lightroom can work with tracklogs exported in GPX format. If your device doesn't export in GPX format, you can use GPS Babel to convert its output.

3 Set the map to a style other than Satellite. Select the image NY_Marathon.jpg in the Filmstrip, and then choose Map > Tracklog > Auto-Tag 1 Selected Photo.

Lightroom matches the capture time of the selected image to the corresponding location on the marathon route recorded by the tracklog.

4 Move the pointer over the new marker pin on the map—or double-click the marker—to see a preview of the tagged image.

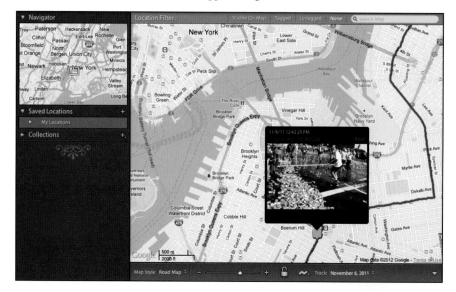

5 Zoom into the map close enough to read the street names around the new marker pin. As you can see, the photo was taken near the corner of 4th Avenue and Dean Street. Click Library in the module picker at the top of the workspace and double-click the New York marathon thumbnail in the Grid view to enter Loupe view. Zoom into the upper right corner of the image; the street sign confirms that the photo has been correctly placed.

6 Click Map in the module picker to return to the Map module.

Saving map locations

In the Saved Locations panel, you can save a list of your favorite places, making it easy to locate and organize a selection of related images. You could create a saved map location to encompass a cluster of places that you visited during a particular vacation, or to mark a single location that you used for a photo shoot for a client.

1 Zoom out in the map view until you can see all of the GPS track.

2 Expand the Saved Locations panel, if necessary; then, click the Create New Preset button (⊕) at the right of the header.

3 In the New Location dialog box, type **New York Marathon** as the location name; then, click Create.

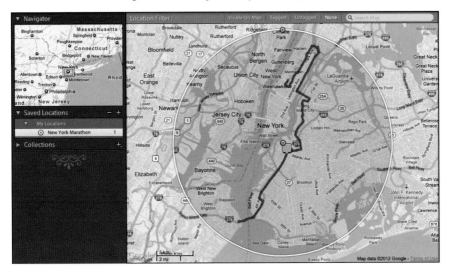

Your new listing appears in the Saved Locations panel; the image count at the right of the location name shows that there is just one tagged image that falls within the specified radius. On the map, the saved location has a center pin that can be repositioned, and a matching pin on the border for increasing or decreasing the target area by changing the radius.

▶ **Tip:** Marking a saved location as Private in the New Location and Edit Location dialog boxes ensures that the GPS information will always be removed when photos from that location are exported or shared, without deleting the location from the images in your catalog. This is useful for protecting your privacy at locations such as your home address. For photos that are not in a saved location, you can choose to omit GPS metadata when you set up an export. For more detail, see Lesson 11.

Selecting or deselecting a location in the Saved Locations panel shows and hides the circular location overlay, and makes the location active for editing. To add photos to a saved location, you can either drag them directly from the Filmstrip into the white circle on the map, or select the images in the Filmstrip and click the check box next to the location name in the Saved Locations panel.

Click the white arrow button that appears to the right of the location name when you move your pointer over the location in the Saved Locations panel to move to that saved location on the map. To edit a location, right-click / Control-click its entry in the Saved Locations panel and choose Location Options from the menu.

Once your photos are tagged with locations, you can search your library using the filter picker and search box in the Location Filter bar above the map, the Saved Locations panel, and the Library Metadata filters set to GPS Data or GPS Location.

4 Click Library in the module picker to return to the Library module.

Using the Painter tool

Of all the features Lightroom provides to help you organize your growing image library, the Painter tool () is the most flexible. By simply dragging the Painter tool across your images in the Grid view you can add metadata, assign keywords, labels, ratings, and flags—and even apply developing settings, rotate your photos, or add them to the Quick Collection.

When you pick the Painter tool up from its well in the Toolbar, the Paint menu appears beside the empty tool well. From the Paint menu you can choose which settings or attributes you wish to apply to your images.

The appearance of the Painter tool's spray can icon changes slightly, depending on which option you choose. The illustration below shows the different spray can icons that correspond to the Paint menu options. Reading from left to right, they are: Keywords, Labels, Flag, Rating, Metadata, Settings, Rotation, and Target Collection.

In this exercise you'll use the Painter tool to mark images with a color label.

1 Click the Architecture folder in the Folders panel and make sure that none of the images are selected in the Grid view. If you don't see the Painter tool in the Toolbar, click the triangle at the right side of the Toolbar and choose Painter from the tools menu.

2 Click the Painter tool to pick it up from its well in the Toolbar; then choose Label from the Paint menu, and click the red color label button.

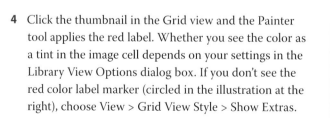

3 The Painter tool is now "loaded." Move the pointer over any of the thumbnails in the Grid view and a red spray can icon appears.

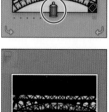

4 Click the thumbnail in the Grid view and the Painter tool applies the red label. Whether you see the color as a tint in the image cell depends on your settings in the Library View Options dialog box. If you don't see the red color label marker (circled in the illustration at the right), choose View > Grid View Style > Show Extras.

5 Move the pointer back over the same thumbnail, and then hold down the Alt / Option key and; the cursor changes from the Painter tool spray can to an eraser. Click the thumbnail with the eraser cursor and the red color label is removed.

6 Release the Alt / Option key and click the image once more—but this time drag the spray can across all three images. You've applied the red color tag to all the images with one stroke. Hold down the Alt / Option key again, and then remove the label from all but one of the photos.

7 Click Done at the right side of the Toolbar, or click the Painter tool's empty well, to drop the Painter tool and return the Toolbar to its normal state.

Finding and filtering files

Now that you're familiar with the different techniques for categorizing and marking your photos, it's time to see some results. Next you'll look at how easy it is to search and sort your images once they've been prepared in this way. You can now filter your images by rating or label or search for specific keywords, GPS locations and other metadata. There are numerous ways to find the images you need but one of the most convenient is to use the Filter bar across the top of the Grid view.

Using the Filter bar to find photos

1 If you don't see the Filter bar above the Grid view, press the backslash key (\) or choose View > Show Filter Bar. In the Folders panel, select the Lesson 5 folder. If you don't see all eleven photos, choose Library > Show Photos In Subfolders.

The Filter bar contains three filter groups: Text, Attribute, and Metadata filters. Click any of these options and the Filter bar will expand to display the settings and controls you'll use to set up a filtered search. You can use these filters separately or combine them for a more sophisticated search.

Use the Text filter to search any text attached to your images, including filenames, keywords, captions, and the EXIF and IPTC metadata. The Attribute filter searches your photos by flag status, star rating, color label, or copy status. The Metadata filter enables you to set up to eight columns of criteria to refine your search. Choose from the menu at the right end of a column header to add or remove a column.

Library Filter :		Text	Attribute	Metadata	None	No Filter	
Date		Keyword		Label		Aspect Ratio	
All (2 Dates)	11	All (2 Keywords)	11	All (2 Labels)	11	All (2 Aspect Ratio)	11	Add Column
2011-04-26	3	► Europe		Red	1	Portrait	2	Remove this Column
2012-01-16	8	Lesson 5	11	No Label	10	Landscape	9	

2 If the Text or Metadata filters are active, click None to disable them. Click Attribute to activate the Attribute filters. If any of the flag filters is still active from the previous exercise, click the highlighted flag to disable it, or choose Library > Filter By Flag > Reset This Filter.

3 In the Rating controls, click the second star to search for any image with a rating of one star or higher.

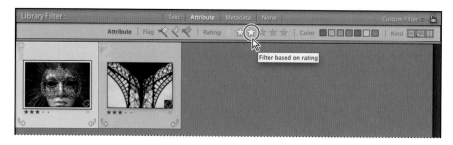

The grid view displays only the two images to which you've applied a star rating.

4 There are many options for refining your search. Click Text in the header of the Filter bar to add an additional filter. In the Text filter bar, open the first menu to see the search target options. You can narrow the search to Filename, Copy Name, Title, Caption, Keywords, or searchable IPTC and EXIF metadata, but for this exercise you can choose the search target Any Searchable Field. Click the second menu and choose Contains All.

5 In the search text box, type **Venice**. Your narrowed search returns only one image in the Grid view.

6 In the Rating controls, click the second star to disable the current Rating filter or choose Library > Filter By Rating > Reset This Filter. Click Attribute in the header of the Filter bar to close the Attribute filter controls.

7 In the Text filter bar, clear the search term "Venice" by clicking the x icon at the right of the text box, and then type **Europe**.

The Grid view now displays all eleven of the photos in the Lesson 5 folder.

8 In the Text filter bar, type a space after the word Europe, and then type **!Italy** (note the exclamation mark). The search is narrowed to find those images with searchable text that contains the word Europe, but does not contain the word Italy. The Grid view now displays eight photos. Leave the Text filters set as it is for the next exercise.

> **Tip:** In the search text box, add an exclamation mark (!) before any word to exclude it from the results. Add a plus sign (+) before any word to apply the "Starting With" rule only to that word. Add a plus sign (+) after a word to apply the "Ending With" rule only to that word.

Using the Metadata filter

1   Click Metadata in the header of the Filter bar to open the Metadata filter pane. Choose Default Columns from the menu at the far right of the Filter bar header.

2   Click Date in the header of the first column to see the wide range of search criteria from which you can choose for each of up to eight columns. Choose Aspect Ratio from the menu as the criteria for the first column, and then choose Landscape from the Aspect Ratio options in the column. The selection in the Grid view is narrowed to six images.

3   Click Text in the header of the Filter bar to disable the Text filter. This search returns nine photos from the Lesson 5 folder. In the Aspect Ratio column, click Portrait to find the remaining two Lesson 5 images.

4   Click the lock icon at the right of the Filter bar header. This will lock the current filter so that it remains active when you change the image source for the search.

5   Click the All Photographs listing in the Catalog panel. The Grid view now displays every portrait format image in your catalog.

As you can see, there are endless possibilities for combining filters to find just the image you're looking for.

6   Click None in the Filter bar to disable all filters. Click the Lesson 5 folder in the Folders panel

Using the filters in the Filmstrip

The Attribute filter controls are also available in the header of the Filmstrip. As in the Filter bar the Filter Presets menu lists filter presets and offers the option to save your filter settings as a custom preset, which will then be added to the menu.

The Default Columns preset opens the four default columns of the Metadata search options: Date, Camera, Lens, and Label. Choose Filters Off to turn off all filters and collapse the Filter bar. Select the Flagged preset to display photos with a Pick flag. Use the Location Columns preset to filter photos by their Country, State/Province, City, and Location metadata. The Rated filter preset displays any photos that match the current star rating criteria. Choose Unrated to see all the photos without a star rating or Used and Unused to see which pictures have been included in projects.

> **Tip:** If you don't see any filter presets in the presets menu, open Lightroom Preferences and click Restore Library Filter Presets under Lightroom Defaults on the Presets tab.

1 Choose Flagged from the Filter Presets menu at the top right of the Filmstrip. The Attribute filter bar opens above the Grid view. The Grid view and the Filmstrip show only one photo that you flagged as a pick in a previous exercise.

2 Click the white flag icon in the header of the Filmstrip to disable the current filter, and then click the red color label button. If you don't see the color label buttons in the header of the Filmstrip, click the word Filter to the left of the flag buttons. The Attribute filter settings change in the Filter bar above the Grid view and both the Grid view and the filmstrip display only the image that you labeled with the Painter tool.

▶ **Tip:** To save time and effort setting up searches, save your filter settings as a new preset. Specify criteria for any combination of Text, Attribute, and Metadata filters. Then choose Save Current Settings As New Preset from the Custom Filter menu in the Filter bar or the Filmstrip.

3 To disable all filters and display all the images in the Lesson 5 folder, choose Filters Off from the Filter Presets menu or click the switch at the far right of the Filmstrip's header.

Reconnecting missing files and folders

Remember that when you import a photo into your library, Lightroom adds the image file's name and address to the library catalog file, and displays an entry for the folder in which the photo is stored in the Folders panel.

If you rename or move a photo—or a folder—while you're outside the Lightroom workspace the link to the catalog will be broken and Lightroom may no longer be able to locate the image file.

Lightroom will alert you to the problem by marking the thumbnail of the missing photo—or the entry for the missing folder in the Folders panel—with a question mark icon.

1 In the Grid view, right-click / Control-click one of the photographs of Venetian Carnival masks and choose Show In Explorer / Show In Finder from the menu.

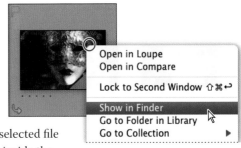

2 In the Explorer / Finder window, change the name of the selected file to **Mask.jpg**. Change the name of the Architecture folder inside the Lesson 5 folder to **Paris**.

3 Back in the Grid view in Lightroom, you'll notice the missing file icon in the upper right corner of the image cell. Click the icon, and then click Locate in the dialog box.

4 In the Locate file dialog box, select the renamed file and then click Select.

When you have merely moved, rather than renamed files, you can activate the Find Nearby Missing Photos option in the Locate file dialog box and Lightroom will find any other missing photos in the same folder automatically.

5 Click Confirm to verify that Mask.jpg is the correct file despite the changed name. You have now reestablished the link to your renamed file; the missing file icon no longer appears in its image cell.

6 In the Folders panel, the Architecture folder is now dimmed and marked with a question mark icon. Right-click / Control-click the Architecture folder; you *could* choose Find Missing Folder from the context menu, and then locate the renamed folder as you did for the missing file, but we'll take this opportunity to look at a different method instead.

7 Choose Library > Find Missing Photos. A new temporary collection named Missing Photographs is created in the Catalog panel. The new collection is automatically selected and the eight photos from the Architecture folder appear in the Grid view.

Select each image in turn; the missing photo icon appears on each image cell.

8 Click the missing photo icon on any of the images in the Grid view and follow the same steps you used previously. Navigating to the renamed folder and locate the selected file. This time, activate the Find Nearby Missing Photos option in the Locate file dialog box and Lightroom will find the other three missing photos in the renamed folder automatically. Click Select.

9 The renamed folder is now listed in the Folders panel. Although the missing Architecture folder is still listed in the Folders panel, it now shows an image count of 0. Right-click / Control-click the empty Architecture folder and choose Remove from the context menu.

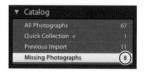

10 Right-click / Control-click the Missing Photographs folder in the Catalog panel and choose Remove This Temporary Collection from the context menu.

This concludes the lesson on organizing your image library. You've learned about structuring your folders, sorting and grouping images into collections, and a variety of methods for tagging and marking your photos to make them easier to find by applying a range of search filters.

However, it's worth discussing a final step that is invaluable in managing your growing library of photos: perform regular catalog backups. The library catalog contains not only your entire image database but also all the preview images and metadata, together with records of your collections and all your settings from the Develop, Slideshow, Web and Print modules. It is as important to make backups of your catalog as it is to keep copies of your image files. You'll learn more about backing-up your library in Lesson 10, "Creating Backups and Exporting Photos."

Before you move on to the next lesson, take a moment to refresh some of what you've learned by reading through the review on the next page.

Review questions

1 What is a Smart Collection?

2 Why would you create a Stack?

3 What are keyword tags?

4 What are the three modes in the Filter bar?

5 How can you search for images by location?

Review answers

1 A Smart collection can be configured to search the library for images that meet specified criteria. Smart collections stay up-to-date by automatically adding any newly imported photos that meet the criteria you've specified.

2 Stacks can be used to group similar photos and thereby reduce the number of thumbnails displayed at one time in the Grid view and the Filmstrip. Only the top image in a stack appears in the thumbnail display but the stack can be expanded and contracted by clicking the thumbnail.

3 Keyword tags are text added to the metadata of an image to describe its content or classify it in one way or another. Shared keywords link images by subject, date, or some other association. Keywords help to locate, identify, and sort photos in the catalog. Like other metadata, keyword tags are stored either in the photo file or (in the case of proprietary camera raw files) in XMP sidecar files. Keywords applied in Lightroom can be read by Adobe applications such as Bridge, Photoshop, or Photoshop Elements, and by other applications that support XMP metadata.

4 The Filter bar offers three filter groups: Text, Attribute, and Metadata filters. Using combinations of these filters you can search the image library for metadata text, filter searches by flag, copy status, rating, or label, and specify a broad range of customizable metadata search criteria.

5 Once your photos are tagged with locations, you can search your library from the Map module by using the Location Filter bar above the map and the Saved Locations panel. In the Library you can use the Metadata filters, set to GPS Data or GPS Location.

6 DEVELOPING AND EDITING

Lesson overview

Artificial light sources, unusual shooting conditions, and incorrect camera exposure settings can all cause faults in an image. In the Develop module Lightroom delivers a suite of powerful developing tools to quickly rectify these problems in your photos.

This lesson introduces you to editing options from easy-to-use presets and retouching tools to an array of specialized settings. Along the way you'll pick up a little computer graphics background knowledge as you become familiar with some basic techniques:

- Applying Develop presets
- Cropping and rotating images
- Working with video
- Using the History and Snapshots panels
- Removing blemishes
- Correcting color problems and adjusting the tonal range
- Sharpening images and removing noise
- Making discrete color adjustments
- Working with black and white and split tone effects
- Adjusting specific areas of an image

 You'll probably need between one and two hours to complete this lesson.

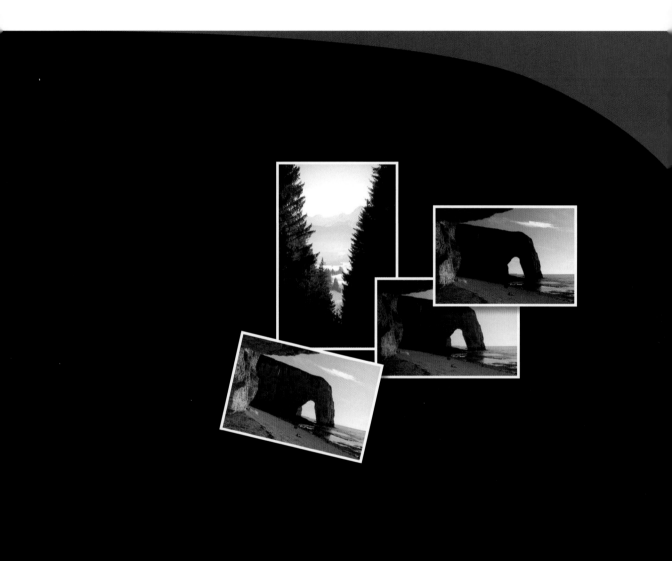

Fine-tune and polish your photographs—and your videos—with precise, easy-to-use tools, secure in the knowledge that the modifications you make in Lightroom won't alter your master file. Take your developing a step beyond just correcting your images; use the Develop module controls creatively to customize your own special effects, and then save them as develop presets.

Getting started

This lesson assumes that you are already familiar with the Lightroom workspace and with moving between the different modules. If you find that you need more background information as you go, refer to Lightroom Help, or review the previous lessons in this book.

Before you start on the exercises in this section, make sure that you have correctly copied the Lessons folder from the CD in the back of this book onto your computer's hard disk as detailed in "Copying the Classroom in a Book files" on page 2, and created the LR4CIB Library Catalog file to manage the lesson files as described in "Creating a catalog file for working with this book" on page 3.

1 Start Lightroom.

2 In the Adobe Photoshop Lightroom - Select Catalog dialog box, make sure that the file LR4CIB Library Catalog.lrcat is selected under Select A Recent Catalog To Open, and then click Open.

Tip: The first time you enter any of the Lightroom modules, you'll see module tips that will help you get started by identifying the components of the Lightroom workspace and stepping you through the workflow. Dismiss the tips by clicking the Close button. To reactivate the tips for any module, choose [*Module name*] Tips from the Help menu.

3 Lightroom will open in the screen mode and workspace module that were active when you last quit. If necessary, switch to the Library module by clicking Library in the Module Picker at the top of the workspace.

Importing images into the library

The first step is to import the images for this lesson into the Lightroom library.

1 In the Library module, click the Import button below the left panel group.

2   If the Import dialog box appears in compact mode, click the Show More
    Options button at the lower left of the dialog box to see all the options in the
    expanded Import dialog box.

3   At the top of the Source panel at the left of the Import dialog box, navigate to
    and select the LR4CIB > Lessons > Lesson 6 folder. Ensure that all six files in the
    folder are checked for import.

4   In the import options above the thumbnail previews, select Add so that the
    imported media will be added to your catalog without being moved or copied.
    Under File Handling at the right of the expanded Import dialog box, choose
    Minimal from the Render Previews menu and ensure that the Don't Import
    Suspected Duplicates option is activated. Under Apply During Import, choose
    None from both the Develop Settings menu and the Metadata menu and type
    Lesson 6 in the Keywords text box. Make sure that your import is set up as
    shown in the illustration below, and then click Import.

The six files in the Lesson 6 folder are added to the LR4CIB Library Catalog and
now appear in the Grid view of the Library module and also in the Filmstrip across
the bottom of the Lightroom workspace.

Quick developing in the Library module

The Library module's Quick Develop panel offers an array of simple controls that let you apply developing presets, correct tone and color, sharpen images, and even crop them—without ever switching to the Develop module.

▶ **Tip:** You can make multiple selections in the Grid view or the Filmstrip and apply a develop preset—or any of the Quick Develop adjustments—to all the selected photos at once.

1 In the Grid view, double-click the image DSC_6056.NEF (a photo of the famous cliffs of Etretat, in Normandy) to see it in Loupe view.

2 In the right panel group, expand the Quick Develop panel, if necessary.

3 From the Saved Preset menu, at the top of the Quick Develop panel, choose the preset B&W Look 4, from the category Lightroom B&W Presets. Examine the results in the Loupe view, and then choose the Yesteryear preset from the Lightroom Color Presets category.

▶ **Tip:** Although the Saved Preset menu is located at the top of the Quick Develop panel, it's sometimes preferable to apply a developing preset as a final step—after you've made any adjustments that are needed to correct tone and color.

Develop presets apply a combination of different developing settings to an image at the same time, enabling you to achieve dramatic results with a single click. You can choose from over fifty Lightroom presets, ranging from fine-tuned contrast settings to creative special effects. Apply a preset from the menu as is, or use it as a starting point and tweak the settings to suit your purpose; you can even save your own develop settings as custom presets, and then organize them in folders that will be listed as new categories in the Saved Preset menu.

4 To return the image to its original state, choose Default Settings from the Saved Preset menu.

5 Expand the White Balance pane in the Quick Develop panel. Try each of the White Balance presets. When you're done, choose the Daylight white balance preset.

6 Click twice on the second button of the four beside the Tint control (the button with a single, left-facing arrow) to reduce the pinkish color cast in the sky and around the reflected glare on the water.

Adjusting the white balance can mean making some very subjective choices. If you wish to stay fairly close to the original look of an image, start with the As Shot preset in the White Balance menu, and then fine-tune the Temperature and Tint settings. If you feel that the white balance was set incorrectly when an image was captured—perhaps as a result of artificial lighting—or if you wish to create a specific effect, use an appropriate preset from the menu as a starting point.

7 Expand the Tone Control pane and click the Auto Tone button.

As the original photo was too bright overall, Auto Tone darkens the entire image considerably—exposing much more detail in the sky and sea but effectively losing detail from the overly darkened beach and cliffs.

Tip: You can use the developing controls not only to correct image problems but also to create effects or moods. For this photo, a technically difficult image in terms of correction, the Auto Tone adjustment approaches the look of a night scene.

Next you can use the controls below the Auto Tone button to fine-tune the tonal balance of the image, recovering detail from the shadows and reducing the glare.

8 Click the fourth button beside Exposure to increase the setting by one stop. Click three times on the right-most Shadows button, and six times on the left-most Whites button. Adjust the Blacks control by clicking the first and second buttons once each. Finally, click the right-most Vibrance button twice.

Tip: If you lose track of your Quick Develop adjustments, you can reset any control to its original state by simply clicking the name of the control. Clicking the Reset All button located at the bottom of the Quick Develop panel will revert the image to its original state.

You've already improved this photo considerably without even leaving the Library module, but you could still do a lot more to enhance it in the Develop module.

Quick and easy video editing

Many digital cameras enable photographers to capture video as well as still images, but for those of us who haven't learned to use video editing software, those videos end up languishing, forgotten and neglected, in dark corners on our hard disks.

Lightroom 4 lets you import your videos, dust them off, catalog and organize them alongside your photos, make simple edits and grab still frames—even share them to Facebook or Flickr—and you can do it all without ever leaving the Library module.

You can import video in many common file formats used by digital still cameras, including AVI, MOV, MPG, MP4, and AVCHD, in exactly the same way that you import photos; in fact, you did just that at the beginning of this lesson.

1   Press the G key or click the Grid view button (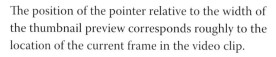) in the Toolbar. If you're working with very small thumbnails, use the Thumbnails slider in the Toolbar to make them a little larger.

2   Locate the video file TamilTemple.MPG; then, move the pointer slowly from left to right, and then back again over the thumbnail (or better still, just below it) to scrub forwards and backwards through the video.

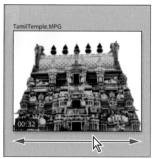

The position of the pointer relative to the width of the thumbnail preview corresponds roughly to the location of the current frame in the video clip.

3   Double-click the thumbnail to see the video in Loupe view; drag the circular current time indicator in the playback control bar to scrub through the video.

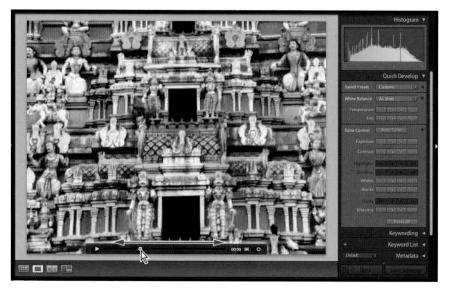

Trimming video clips

In the Loupe view, you can improve a video by snipping off a slow start or a shaky ending; the video file on your hard disk remains intact, but when you export the clip, or play it in Lightroom, it will be trimmed down to show only the real action.

1   Click the Trim Video button (⚙). The playback control bar expands to display a series of key frames from the video, representing a time-line or film-strip view of the clip. You can lengthen the expanded control bar by dragging either end.

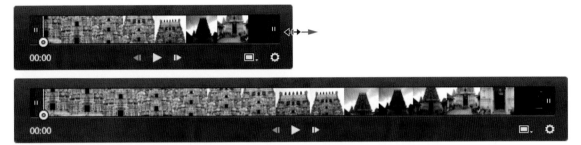

2   Watch the time count at the left end of the control bar as you drag the current time indicator to the last frame in the 19th second; then, drag the end marker in from the right end of the time-line to meet the current time indicator.

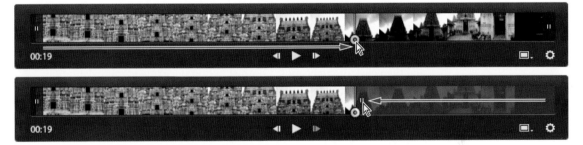

3   Click the Play button at the center of the control bar to view the trimmed clip.

Setting video thumbnails and grabbing still frames

Setting a distinctive poster frame (thumbnail image) for a video clip can make it easier to locate in the Grid view or the Filmstrip.

1   Make sure that you can see the video clip's thumbnail in the Filmstrip. In the Loupe view, move the current time indicator to the frame you want; then, click the Frame button (▣) at the right end of the control bar. Watch the video thumbnail in the Filmstrip as you choose Set Poster Frame.

2   Find a frame that you like somewhere in the range between 00:05 and 00:13; then, click the Frame button and choose Capture Frame to capture and save the current frame as a JPEG image that will be stacked with the clip. You'll use the captured frame later in this lesson.

Applying develop presets to videos

When you're working with a video in Loupe view, the Quick Develop controls for Highlights, Shadows, and Clarity are disabled. Although you can still access all the developing presets in the Saved Preset menu, only the supported settings within each preset will be applied. This means that for a particular clip, some presets not specifically intended for use with video may produce very little effect. Some other presets, including the Lightroom Effect category, will not work at all for video.

The colors in our lesson clip are cold and de-saturated, and the tone is flat and dull; the video was shot just a few seconds before the arrival of a tropical storm. In this exercise you'll try two very different developing presets to liven up the movie, and tweak the settings for each effect using the controls in the Quick Edit panel.

1   With the video still open at the same frame in the Loupe view, choose the Antique preset from the Lightroom B&W Toned Presets category.

Unless you've already disabled it, an alert appears warning that some settings are not supported for video and listing those that are. Check Don't Show Again to disable the alert if you wish, but it may be a good idea to make a note of the settings supported for video for future reference.

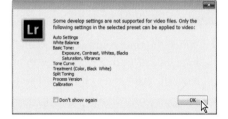

2   Click OK to dismiss the alert message. In the Quick Develop panel, click once on the third Exposure button to increase the exposure by one-third of a stop, and then click the right-most Contrast button once to add more definition. Drag the current time indicator to scrub through the clip, or click the Play button in the control bar, to see the effect in motion.

● **Note:** Resetting the Quick Develop controls will not affect the way you've trimmed your video clip; the start and end markers will stay in place unless you move them manually.

3   Click the Reset All button at the bottom of the Quick Develop panel, and then apply the Video Color Pop preset from the Lightroom Video Presets category. Choose Auto from the White Balance menu, and then click twice on both the right-most Contrast button and the left-most button for Whites. Scrub or play through the clip to assess the changes.

As imported

B&W Toned / Antique preset, plus Exposure and Contrast

Video Color Pop preset, plus White Balance, Contrast, and Whites

About process versions

Lightroom 4 uses updated Camera Raw technology to analyze, process, and render digital images, allowing finer control over color, tone, and detail adjustments than was possible in previous versions—so you'll get better results, with fewer artefacts. Taken as a whole, this technology constitutes the current *process version*, PV2012.

Lightroom 1 and 2 used the original process version, PV2003. Lightroom 3 applied the updated PV2010 by default, offering the option to either update images edited in Lightroom 1 or 2, or switch to the old process version to avoid modifying the existing adjustments. Process Version 2012 is applied by default to photos that are edited for the first time in Lightroom 4. For images edited in an earlier version of Lightroom, you can switch to either of the old process versions if you wish.

PV2012 incorporates improved sharpening and noise-reduction routines, as well as new adaptive tone-mapping algorithms that help to protect edge detail and minimize processing artefacts, enabling you to adjust exposure without clipping the whites in your image and to recover more detail from shadows and highlights.

Updating the process version

In this exercise, you'll update the process version for a raw image that was edited in Lightroom 3. Even if you're new to Lightroom and don't have photos that were edited in previous versions, this exercise will serve as an introduction to the new Develop controls in Lightroom 4.

1   In the Grid view or the Filmstrip, select the raw image DSC_7259.NEF, and then click Develop in the module picker at the top of the workspace.

In the Develop module, an exclamation point badge in, or near, the lower right corner of the image indicates it was edited with a process version earlier than PV2012.

> **Tip:** If you don't see the Filmstrip, press F6 or choose Window > Panels > Show Filmstrip.

2 Choose Settings > Process. The Process menu shows that this image was edited using the 2010 process version. For the moment, leave the setting unchanged.

3 To access update options, click the exclamation point badge, rather than using the Settings > Update To Current Process (2012) command, which updates the image using the default options, or those that were set for the last update.

4 In the Update Process Version dialog box, activate the option Review Changes Via Before/After; then, click Update.

▶ **Tip:** If you don't see the right panels, press F8 or choose Window > Panels > Show Right Module Panels.

5 If necessary, expand the Basic panel in the right panel group. Watch the Histogram and the Basic panel settings as you undo and redo the update by pressing Ctrl+Z / Command+Z, and then Shift+Ctrl+Z / Shift+Command+Z.

The histogram shows a significant improvement in the image's tonal spread. In the Basic panel, the old develop settings are mapped to a new set of slider controls.

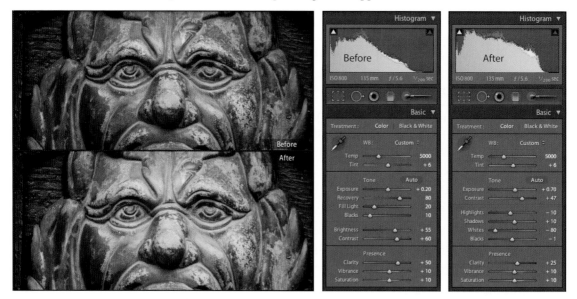

▶ **Tip:** Updating to Process Version 2012 may result in significant changes in the appearance of your photos; it's a good idea to update images one at a time until you're familiar with the new processes. Use one of the Before & After views while you tweak the PV2012 settings, to help you match the look of the photo before it was updated.

In PV2012, the Exposure setting combines elements of both the Exposure and Brightness settings from earlier process versions. The new Exposure control works more like camera exposure; shifting the midtones without clipping the highlights.

The Highlights and Shadows sliders replace Recovery and Fill Light, enabling you to bring out even more detail from the darkest and brightest parts of your photos. The improved processes in PV2012 target their respective tonal ranges more effectively, without affecting the rest of the image; your Highlights and Shadows adjustments won't overlap, so there's less chance of color shifts and other artefacts.

The Whites and Blacks controls correct clipping at the ends of the histogram; for PV2012, blacks are calculated automatically. The new Clarity process produces a different look, with less likelihood of halo effects; the upgraded setting is reduced.

About white balance

To be able to display the full range of color information contained in an image file correctly, it's critical to set the right white balance for the photo. For this reason, it's important to understand what the white balance is. An image's white point reflects the lighting conditions in which the photo was taken. The white point is defined by values on two scales: temperature and tint.

If the red, green, and blue components of a pixel on the screen all have exactly the same values, the pixel appears as a neutral gray—ranging from white to black. The higher the red component, the warmer the image appears. The higher the blue component, the cooler the image. The tint accounts for color shifts in the direction of green or magenta.

The sensors in a digital camera record the amount of red, green, and blue light that is reflected from an object. A neutral gray reflects all color components of the light source equally. If the light source is not pure white but has a predominant red component for example, a higher amount of red will be reflected to the sensors. Unless the composition of the light source is known—and the *white balance* or *white point* is corrected accordingly—the image will have a red color cast.

Different types of artificial lighting have different white points; they provide lighting that is dominated by one color or deficient in another. Weather conditions also have an effect on the white balance.

When shooting in auto white balance mode, your camera tries to estimate the composition of the light source from the color information measured by the sensors. Although modern cameras are doing better at automatically setting the white balance to meet conditions, it is never fail-proof. It is preferable—if your camera supports it—to have the camera measure the white point of the light source; this is usually done by taking a picture of a light gray object under the same lighting conditions as the subject.

As well as the color information recorded by the camera sensors, a Raw image also contains the "As Shot" white balance information. This enables Lightroom to correctly interpret the recorded color information for a given light source. The recorded white point information is used as a calibration point in reference to which the white balance can be corrected and the colors in the image will be shifted accordingly.

About white balance (continued)

If there is an area in your photo that you know should appear as a light neutral gray on screen you can use that area to set the point around which the image can be calibrated. Use the White Balance Selector tool, located in the top left corner of the Basic panel, to sample the color information in that area and Lightroom will set the image's white balance accordingly.

As you move the White Balance Selector tool across the image you will see a magnified view of the pixels under the eyedropper and RGB values for the central target pixel. To avoid too radical a color shift, try to click a pixel where the red, green, and blue values are as close as possible. Do not use white or a very light color as target neutral; for a very bright pixel a color component might already have been clipped.

Color temperature is defined with reference to a concept known as *black-body radiation* theory. When heated, a black-body will first start glowing red, then orange, yellow, white, and finally blue-white. A color's temperature is the temperature—in kelvin (K)—to which a black-body must be heated to emit that particular color. Zero K corresponds to −273.15 °C or −459.67 °F and an increment of one unit kelvin is equivalent to an increment of one degree Celsius.

What we generally refer to as a warm color (with a higher red component) actually has a lower color temperature (in kelvin) than what we would call a cool color (with a higher blue component). The color temperature of a visually warm scene lit by candlelight is about 1,500 K. In bright daylight you would measure around 5,500 K and light from an overcast sky results in a color temperature in the photo of about 6,000 to 7,000 K.

The Temp slider adjusts the color temperature (in kelvin) of the designated white point, from low at the left side of the range to high on the right side. Moving the Temp slider to the left reduces the color temperature of the white point. In consequence, the colors in the image are interpreted as having a higher color temperature relative to the adjusted white point and are shifted towards blue. The colors displayed inside the Temp slider control indicate the effect a change in that direction will have on the image. Moving the slider to the left will increase the blue in the image, moving the slider to the right will make the image look more yellow and red.

The Tint slider works in the same way. For example, to remove a green cast in an image you would move the Tint slider to the right, away from the green displayed inside the slider control. This increases the green component in the white point so the colors in the image are interpreted as less green relative to the adjusted white point.

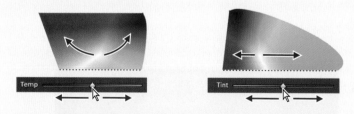

Adjusting the Temp and Tint sliders corresponds to shifting the white point in the color gamut.

The Develop module

Although the Quick Develop panel in the Library module offers access to many basic image editing options, you'll work in the Develop module to make more detailed adjustments and modifications to your photos. The Develop module is a comprehensive editing environment, presenting all the tools you'll need to correct and enhance your images in a single workspace. The controls are easy enough for a beginner to use, and yet have the depth and power required by the advanced user.

The Develop module offers two viewing modes: the Loupe view, where you can focus on a single image, and the Before/After view (with several layout options), which makes it easy to compare the original and edited versions of a photo. The Toolbar across the bottom of the work area presents buttons for switching between the views and a slightly different suite of controls for each viewing mode.

The tools and controls in the Develop module's right panel group are arranged from top to bottom in the order in which they would ordinarily be used: a layout that guides you intuitively through the editing workflow.

The left panel group contains the Navigator panel, which can be collapsed but not hidden, and any combination of the Presets, Snapshots, History, and Collections panels, which can be shown or hidden to suit the way you prefer to work.

At the top of the left panel group, the Navigator panel helps you find your way around a zoomed image, and lets you preview the effects of developing presets before you apply them. You can also use the Navigator to review past stages in an image's developing history. At the right of the Navigator's header is a zoom picker for setting the magnification levels in the working views.

The Navigator can be collapsed, but not hidden.

While the History panel keeps track of every modification made to the image, including Quick Edit adjustments made in the Library module, you can use the Snapshots panel to record important stages in a photo's development, so you can return to a key state quickly and easily, without searching through the history list.

At the top of the right panel group is the Histogram panel. Immediately below the Histogram is an array of tools for cropping, removing flaws and red eyes, applying graduated adjustments and painting develop settings directly onto an image selectively. Clicking any of these tools opens a drawer with controls and settings for that tool.

Below these editing tools is the Basic panel: your starting point for color correction and tonal adjustments. In many cases this may be the only panel you need to achieve the result you want. The remaining panels offer specialized tools for various image enhancement tasks.

For example, you can use the Tone Curve panel to fine-tune the distribution of the tonal range and increase mid-tone contrast. Use the controls in the Detail panel to sharpen an image and reduce noise.

It's not intended that you use every tool on every photo. In many circumstance you may make only a few slight adjustments to an image; however, when you wish to polish a special photo—or if you need to work with shots captured at less than ideal camera settings—the Develop module provides all the tools you need.

In the next exercise you'll crop and rotate an image, and then remove some spots.

Cropping and rotating images

The Crop Overlay tool makes it simple to improve your composition, crop away unwanted edge detail, and even straighten your image.

1   Click to select the raw image DSC_6058.NEF in the Filmstrip.

2   If you're not already in the Develop module, press the D key or choose View > Go To Develop. Hide the Filmstrip and the left panel group to expand the work area; you'll find keyboard shortcuts for showing and hiding any or all of the workspace panels listed beside the commands in the Window > Panels menu. If you're not already in the Loupe view, press the D key again, or click the Loupe view button (▣) in the Toolbar. If you don't see the Toolbar, press the T key.

3 Click the Crop Overlay tool ()button just below the Histogram panel, or press R. A crop overlay rectangle appears on the image in the Loupe view and a control pane for the Crop Overlay tool opens above the Basic panel.

4 From the Aspect menu, choose Original. If the lock button shows an open lock icon, click to close the lock. The closed lock will constrain the aspect ratio.

You can specify a custom crop ratio by choosing Enter Custom from the Aspect menu. Your new Aspect Ratio will be added to the Aspect menu for later use; it will also be listed as a sorting and filter criteria.

5 Drag the lower left handle of the crop overlay rectangle upwards and to the right. As you drag, the image moves so that the cropped portion is always centered in the Loupe view. Release the mouse button when the horizon is roughly aligned with the guideline one-third of the way up the image as shown below.

6 Click outside the crop overlay rectangle and drag to rotate the photo. As you drag, additional grid lines appear to help you straighten the image. Release the mouse button when the horizon is aligned with the grid.

7 Click inside the crop overlay rectangle and drag the image. You'll notice that you can't drag the photo downwards or to the left because the image will move only until its edge touches the border of the cropping rectangle. Position the photo so that the stone arch in the background is roughly centered in the frame.

8 To exit cropping mode, press R on your keyboard or click the Crop Overlay tool button again. The cropped image is displayed in the Loupe view.

▶ **Tip:** Thanks to non-destructive editing, you can return to adjust your crop at any time by simply reactivating the Crop Overlay tool. The crop becomes "live" again—the entire image becomes visible once more and you can resize the cropping rect-angle or reposition the image as you wish.

Removing spots

Unsightly spots or blurs caused by water droplets or dirt on the camera lens are not an uncommon problem, especially in photos captured outdoors or in harsh lighting conditions. The Spot Removal tool is ideal for fixing blemishes like these.

1 In Loupe view in the Develop module, click the Spot Removal tool just below the Histogram panel, or press Q on your keyboard. You'll notice that an extra pane opens below the tool buttons with controls and settings for the Spot Removal tool.

The Spot Removal tool works in either Clone mode or Heal mode. In Clone mode, the tool covers an imperfection in the photo (the target area) with an exact copy of another portion of the image (the sample area). Clone mode is ideal for repairing an area in the image that is patterned or where there are distinct repeated details such as bricks, stairs or even foliage. For areas with smooth color transitions, such as skin, or the sky—or fine, "noisy" textures, like the beach in our example—use the Heal mode. In Heal mode, the Spot Removal Tool blends the sampled area with the target area rather than replacing it.

2 In the Spot Removal Tool settings pane, choose Heal from the two brush options.

3 Choose Window > Panels > Show Left Module Panels or press F7. In the header of the Navigator panel, click 1:1 to zoom in to a pixel-for-pixel view. Drag the white rectangle in the Navigator preview to focus on the distant stretches of the beach, as shown in the illustration at the right.

OK, so they're tourists—not unsightly blemishes—but the principle is the same.

4 Use the sliders in the Spot Removal Tool settings pane to set the brush Size to 75 pixels and the brush Opacity to 100%.

5 Position the circular Spot Removal tool cursor over the nearest of the tourists; then, click—but don't drag. Release the mouse button and move the pointer away; Lightroom automatically finds an appropriate area to sample. On your screen you should see something similar to what you see in the illustration below: the lighter white circle with the cross-hairs is the target area centered on the tourists and the bolder white circle is the sample area.

▶ **Tip:** To cancel and remove an active spot correction, simply press Backspace / Delete.

6 If you see obvious repetition of nearby detail in the newly depopulated target area, as in the illustration above, click inside the circular sample area and drag it to a new position, watching the result in the target area.

7 If you wish, you can manually specify the area to be sampled by the Heal brush. Increase the brush size by clicking the Right Bracket (]) key until the Spot Removal tool cursor is large enough to cover the next group of tourists. Click to define the target area, but this time, don't release the mouse button immediately; instead, drag to find a sample that blends effectively. Watch the effect on the target area as you drag; then, release the pointer when you're satisfied with the result. A white arrow between the two circles indicates that data from the sample area has been applied to the target area.

8 Repeat the process, using either technique, to remove the rest of the unsightly tourists. Increase or decrease the brush size as necessary by pressing the Left and Right Bracket ([,]) keys. For the large group behind our targets, and the couple in the far distance, the shore-line runs through the target area; whichever technique you use, drag the sample area carefully to align the effect.
If you see blurred artefacts at the edges of the target area, use the slider in the tool settings pane to increase or decrease the brush size for the active spot edit.

9 When you're done, press Q to disable the Spot Removal tool. The circular tool overlays disappear from the image in the Loupe view.

10 Click the Spot Removal tool, or press Q, to activate the tool again. The circular tool overlays for your spot corrections reappear on the image in the Loupe view. These edits are all still "live"—you can adjust them at any time.

11 Click the Spot Removal tool, or press Q, to disable the Spot Removal tool. To return to the Fit zoom level click the image in the Loupe view, or choose from the zoom picker in the header of the Navigator panel.

12 If you're itching to get your hands on some authentic unsightly spots, show the Filmstrip and select the image DSC_6056.NEF—the other shot of the beach at Etretat, and then have some fun honing your new skills.

▶ **Tip:** The best way to evaluate the results of a spot removal operation—and many other image edits—is to inspect the photo at full size. Click 1:1 in the header of the Navigator panel to set a pixel-for-pixel zoom ratio for the Loupe view.

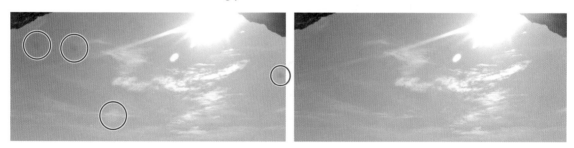

Adjusting a photo's tonal range

In the Develop module, the basic tone and color corrections your photos are likely to need are generally best made in the following order:

• Apply tonal corrections to set the correct white point and maximize the tonal range in the image using the Histogram and the controls in the Basic panel.

• Tweak the contrast using the Tone Curve panel.

• Adjust color problem selectively in the HSL / Color / B & W panel.

• Apply sharpening and noise reduction in the Detail panel.

• Add special effects such as duo-tone treatments, decorative lens vignetting, and simulated film grain, using the Split Toning, and Effects panels.

The order of these operations is reflected in the layout of the panels in the Develop module's right panel group; although you may often make only a handful of adjustments to any one image, you can work your way down the right panel group, using it as an image processing check-list.

In this exercise, you'll explore the Basic panel.

1 If necessary, press the D key to go to the Develop module. In the Filmstrip, select the image DSC_0357.NEF, a photo of an alpine vista shot in Germany.

2 Make sure that the Histogram and the Basic panel are expanded. Hide the Module picker (F5), the Toolbar (T), and the Filmstrip (F6); then, drag the left edge of the right panel group to make it as wide as possible—wider adjustment sliders give you finer control.

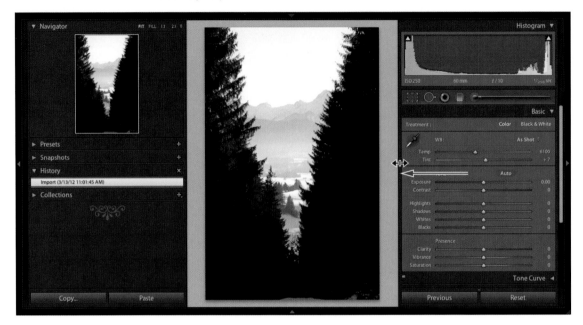

The controls in the Basic panel are also arranged from top to bottom in the order that's likely to produce the best results; if you're new to image correction, you can let the layout guide you through the workflow.

3 Starting at the top of the Basic panel, try a few of the White Balance (WB) presets; then set the white balance to the Cloudy preset for this exercise.

4 Moving down the Basic panel to the Tone controls, click Auto Tone. Undo and redo the Auto Tone adjustment, noting the effect it has on the Histogram and the tone settings in the Basic panel, as well the changes in the image itself.

Auto Tone improved the photo's tonal range markedly. The Histogram curve is still far from ideal, but the peaks in the Highlights and Whites have been shifted to fill out the mid-tones a little.

The adjustment to the photo's tonal distribution has unveiled the distant landscape that was hidden in the mist and glare, increased definition in mid-toned areas such as the sunlit branches of the trees on the left, and even retrieved some of the detail that was lost in the shadows. Overall, the image has far more color and depth.

The Auto Tone adjustment may be all you need for some photos, but for others, especially problem images, it may produce unexpected results. You can use it as a starting point for manual adjustment, or read the automatic settings as a diagnosis of your photo's deficiencies, and then undo and devise your own treatments.

Undoing, redoing, and remembering changes

Lightroom offers several options for undoing and redoing changes and recalling key stages in the develop process. The Edit > Undo command (Ctrl+Z / Command+Z) lets you undo the last command executed; pressing Ctrl+Y / Command+Shift+Z will redo the last command undone. To jump backward and forward in the editing history by more than one step at a time, you'll use the History panel.

The History panel

1   Press F7 or click the triangle at the left edge of the workspace to show the left panel group. If necessary, collapse any other panels that are open to see the History panel.

2   Expand the History panel; you'll see a list of every operation that has already been performed; with the most recent command at the top.

3   Watch the Navigator panel as you move the pointer slowly up the list of commands in the History panel. The Navigator preview shows how the image looked at each stage of its developing history.

4   Click the top entry—Auto Tone—to return the image to its most recent edited state.

Note: If you return an image to a previous state by clicking an entry in the History panel, and then make any new adjustment, all of the entries above your current position will be replaced by the new command.

Creating snapshots

The History list can quickly become long and unwieldy, so it's a good idea to save key steps in an image's developing history as Snapshots for quick and easy recovery. In this case, you'll use a snapshot as a reference to guide you as you work.

1   In the History panel, right-click / Control-click the Auto Tone entry and choose Create Snapshot from the context menu.

2   In the New Snapshot dialog box, type **Auto Tone** to name the snapshot; then, click Create. Your new Auto Tone snapshot appears in the Snapshots panel.

Changing the Before image

By default, the original, un-edited photo is displayed as the Before image in the Before / After view, but you can designate any other stage in the photo's developing history—or any saved snapshot—as the Before image.

Change the Before image when you're happy with your work so far, then work beside it so that you can see exactly what gains you're making.

1 Press T to show the Toolbar; then click the Before & After view button, repeatedly if necessary, until you see the two states of the photo side by side.

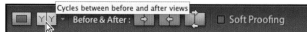

2 Right-click / Control-click your saved snapshot in the Snapshots panel and choose Copy Snapshot Settings To Before. Both sides of the view should now be showing the photo as it appears with the Auto Tone adjustment.

3 In the Basic panel, double-click the name of each of the top five controls in the Tone pane to zero the current settings.

▶ **Tip:** To quickly toggle between the last edited state of an image and the Before view state, press the Backslash key (\).

Each of these actions is listed as a new entry in the History panel. The Auto Tone adjustment was never actually undone—it merely became history. Once you've zeroed all six controls, the After view is identical to the history state just before you applied the Auto Tone adjustment.

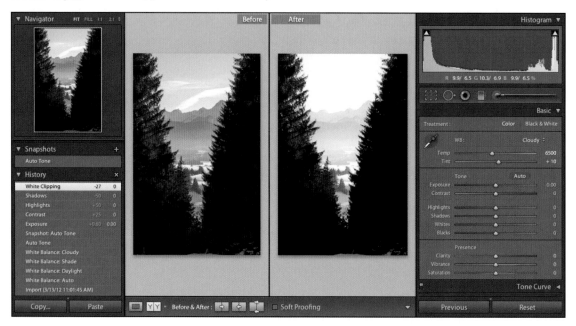

Now you can go back to your exploration of the Basic panel, with a visual benchmark to which you can compare your efforts.

Working with the Tone controls

As with the panels in the right panel group, you'll start at the top.

The first step is to use the Exposure control to set the overall image brightness by correcting the midtones range; then, you can retrieve detail from the lightest and darkest areas with the Highlights and Shadows controls and correct clipping at the ends of the curve by tweaking the Whites and Blacks settings.

1   Hide the left panel group to make more room for your working view.

2   In the Basic panel, drag the Exposure slider all the way to the left, and then back up through its range. Watch the effect on the curve in the Histogram as well as in the After image. Set the Exposure value to **-0.2**.

3   Experiment with the Contrast slider, and then set the contrast to **+10** (%)

4   Watch the Histogram, as well as the After image, as you drag the Highlights slider slowly, all the way to the left. Notice the dramatic effect on the lighter parts of the image, while very little changes elsewhere, even in the adjacent mid-tones. The peak in the Whites zone of the Histogram curve disappears, and the right end of the curve moves towards the center. Set the Highlights to **-80**.

5   Drag the Shadows slider slowly, all the way to the right. Watch how little effect this has on the mid-tones and highlights in the image, relative to the gain in the darkest areas. When you're done, leave the Shadows set to **+80**.

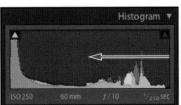
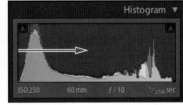

After WB, Exposure and Contrast   Highlights -80   Shadows +80

These Highlights and Shadows settings are somewhat extreme; at these levels you'll notice a glowing halo effect where light and dark areas meet, giving the scene an unreal look—and there is also the risk of introducing noticeable noise.

As a general rule, set values between -50 and +50 for image correction, and use higher settings sparingly to rescue problem photos or to achieve creative effects.

Note: The Exposure value is expressed in terms of camera f-stops: a setting of +1 is the equivalent of opening the aperture one stop.

Tip: To modify any of the settings, you can either drag the slider, scrub horizontally over the numerical value, or click the setting's name to activate it, and then use the Plus (+) and Minus (-) keys.

Note: Clarity adjusts local contrast between small adjacent areas of light and dark. Vibrance boosts saturation selectively, without affecting skin tones or colors that are already saturated.

6 Set the Whites control to **+10**, and the Blacks to **-10**: settings not far short of levels that would result in clipping at the ends of the Histogram curve.

7 Set both the Clarity and Vibrance controls in the Presence pane to **+20**. Both of these controls are useful for enhancing image definition.

The photo now has very nearly as much detail in the brightest areas as the auto-toned Before image, and a lot more detail in the mid-tones and shadows.

8 Show the left panels. Right-click / Control-click the Import entry in the History panel and choose Copy History Step Settings To Before; then, hide the left panels.

Creating your own developing presets

When you've spent time setting up an effect that you'd like to use again, you can save all your current settings as a developing preset that will be listed in both the Develop module's Presets panel and the Library module's Quick Develop panel.

In this exercise, you'll create a custom preset tailored to very specific purpose. Earlier in this lesson you edited a video clip in the Library module, where your options were limited to those offered in the Quick Develop panel. You can't bring video into the Develop module, but by working on a captured frame, and then saving your settings as a custom preset, you can effectively bring the power and subtlety of Develop module editing back to your video in the Library module.

▶ **Tip:** You can set up a preset to achieve a consistent look for every image in a photo book or web gallery, to add a romantic glow to wedding shots, or even to correct the color in your underwater photos. Whatever the purpose, develop presets streamline your workflow by letting you apply your favorite develop settings with a single click.

1   Staying in the Develop module, click the Loupe view button (![icon]) in the Toolbar. Show the Filmstrip, if it's hidden, and then select the still image that you captured from the TamilTemple video earlier in the lesson.

2   Starting at the top of the Basic panel, set the Temperature and Tint to **+15** and **+30**, respectively. Set a Contrast value of **55**, reduce the Whites setting to **-100**, and increase the Blacks to **+100**.

3   Choose Develop > New Preset. Name your custom preset **IceCreamCake** and accept the User Presets folder as the destination to which it will be saved.

Note: This preset is intended for use with our lesson video, so no values are specified for Highlights, Shadows, or Clarity settings; those adjustments are amongst those not supported for video.

4 Inspect the Settings pane in the lower half of the New Develop Preset dialog box. You won't need to change the defaults for this preset, but the Settings options will give you an overview of just how many developing adjustments you can include in a single preset. When you're done, click Create.

Settings

☑ White Balance	☑ Treatment (Color)	☐ Lens Corrections
		☐ Lens Profile Corrections
☑ Basic Tone	☑ Color	☐ Transform
☑ Exposure	☑ Saturation	☐ Lens Vignetting
☑ Contrast	☑ Vibrance	☐ Chromatic Aberration
☑ Highlights	☑ Color Adjustments	
☑ Shadows		☐ Effects
☑ White Clipping	☐ Split Toning	☐ Post-Crop Vignetting
☑ Black Clipping		☐ Grain
	☐ Graduated Filters	
☐ Tone Curve		☑ Process Version
	☐ Noise Reduction	☑ Calibration
☐ Clarity	☐ Luminance	
	☐ Color	
☐ Sharpening		

(Check All)   (Check None)   (Cancel)   (Create)

If you apply your custom preset to the lesson video now, you'll lose the work you did earlier. In the next exercise, you'll create a *virtual copy* of the video file, so that you can keep and compare the two edited versions.

Working with virtual copies

Note: In fact, *every* photo or video in your catalog is a virtual copy of the master file.

When you wish to explore different treatments for a photo or video, without losing the work you've already done, you can create *virtual* copies of your image or clip, and edit each one independently, just as if they were separate master files.

If a particular photo is included in more than one collection, any changes you make to that image while you're working in one collection will be visible in all the others. If you wish to modify an image for a specific collection without affecting the way the photo appears elsewhere in your catalog, you should use a virtual copy.

You might include a full-frame, full-color version of your photo in a collection that you've assembled for a slideshow—and a tightly cropped, sepia-toned virtual copy in another collection intended for a print layout. You can apply a unifying special effect to an entire collection of virtual copies for a photo book without affecting the way the same images appear in any of your other projects and presentations.

Another important advantage of working with virtual copies is that you save a great deal of disk space by keeping only one master file for each photo. A virtual copy is actually just an additional catalog entry for that master file. This new entry will be updated to record every change you make to the virtual copy, while your developing settings for other virtual copies—and the master file—remain unchanged.

1   If you're still in the Develop module, switch to the Grid view in the Library. In the Grid view or the Filmstrip, right-click / control click the video file TamilTemple.MPG and choose Create Virtual Copy from the context menu.

2   If necessary, press F6 to show the Filmstrip. You can see that there are now two copies of the video side by side in the Filmstrip.

In both the Grid view and the Filmstrip, virtual copies are identified by a page peel icon in the lower left corner of the thumbnail, though this is difficult to see on video thumbnails, as it appears behind of the duration indicator.

By default, Lightroom will automatically stack the virtual copy with the original video. In this case, the original video was already stacked with the still frame you captured, so Lightroom has added the virtual copy to the existing stack. The video at the top of the stack is marked with a stack badge.

3   Move the pointer over either of the stacked videos to see a file count indicating the position of that copy in the stack.

> **Tip:** To unstack photos or videos, select one of the thumbnails in the stack in the Grid view; then, right-click / Control-click the stack icon on the selected thumbnail and choose Unstack from the menu.

You can use the Kind filter—one of the Attribute filters in the Filter bar—to filter your library by file kind, isolating master images, virtual copies, or video files.

4   If you don't see the Filter bar above the Grid view, choose View > Show Filter Bar, or press Backslash (\) on your keyboard. Click Attribute in the filter picker; then click the third of the Kind filters—the button with a film-strip icon—at the right end of the Filter bar. The Grid view displays both videos. Click the next Kind filter to the left—the button with a turned-up corner—to isolate the virtual copy.

5 Click None in the filter picker; then, press Backslash (\) to hide the Filter bar.

6 Double-click the virtual copy, TamilTemple.MPG / Copy 1, in the Grid view or the Filmstrip, to open the clip in the Loupe view. Expand the Quick Develop panel, if necessary, and click the Reset All button at the bottom of the panel to clear all of the current settings and set the copy to the video's un-edited state.

7 Click the Saved Preset menu (currently set to the Default Settings preset) and choose your custom IceCreamCake preset from the User Presets category. Scrub or play through the clip to see the effect.

Your custom preset has improved the video significantly, correcting the cold, blue-green color cast, boosting the flat tonal range to add contrast and definition, and replacing the dull, de-saturated hues with the cheerful colors of the candy counter.

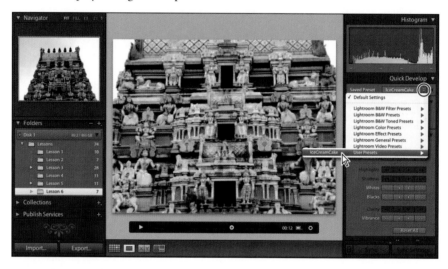

8 Choose Edit > Select None. In the Filmstrip, select the original video; then, hold down the Ctrl / Command key and click the virtual copy. Press the C key to switch to Compare view where you can see the two treatments side by side.

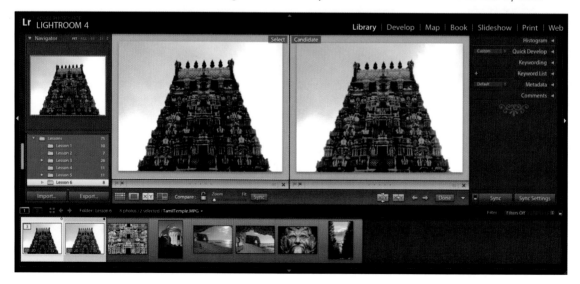

Beyond the Basic panel

Once you've adjusted the white balance and the tonal distribution in the Basic panel, you can move on to the rest of the panels in the right panel group.

1   In the Filmstrip, select the photo of the church: DSC_0299.NEF; then, press D on your keyboard to switch to the Develop module.

2   You can make more space in the Loupe view for this portrait-format photo by hiding the top panel (F5) and the Filmstrip (F6). Press T to hide the Toolbar. In the right panel group, expand the Histogram and Tone Curve panels. For a clear view, collapse any other panels that are currently open.

3   Inspect the settings in the Basic panel; you can see that the developing settings for this image have already been modified to adjust the tonal range.

Adjusting contrast using the tone curve

Working with the Tone Curve enables you to adjust contrast in different parts of the tonal range selectively. Tone curve corrections should not be applied until after the imaged has been processed as necessary with the controls in the Basic panel.

The tone curve maps the distribution of tonal values in the input image along the x-axis to a new distribution of tonal values in the output image along the y-axis. The dark end of the range is at the lower left and the light at the upper right.

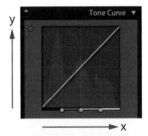

A linear tone curve at a 45° incline from the lower left corner to the upper right corner has no effect on the image; each tone value in the input image is mapped to the identical tone value in the output image. Raising the tone curve above this line maps tone values to a lighter value; lowering it darkens the tonal values.

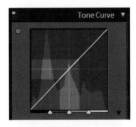

A tone curve section that is flatter than 45° compresses a range of tone values from the input image (x axis) to a narrower range in the output image (y axis). Some tone values which were distinguishable in the input image become indistinguishable in the output image, resulting in a loss of image detail.

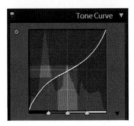

A tone curve section that is steeper than 45° expands tone values; the differences between tone values becomes more noticeable and the image contrast is increased.

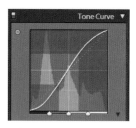

In Lightroom, the tone curve is constrained so that the curve is always ascending. This means that if you increase the incline of one section of the curve you'll end up with a decreased incline somewhere else; you'll have to make a compromise. When using the tone curve, the trick is to increase the contrast in the range where you have the most tonal information; recognizable by a peak in the histogram. At the same time, try to place the flatter parts of the tone curve in ranges where there is less information in the image (troughs in the histogram) or where a lack of contrast is not as disturbing or noticeable.

A typical tone curve intended to increase mid-range contrast starts flat in the lower left corner (less contrast in the shadows), is steep in the center (more contrast in the mid-tones), and ends flat in the upper right corner (less contrast in the highlights).

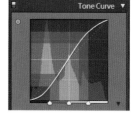

For the image at hand we'll customize the tone curve to selectively increase the contrast in the well-lit wall area of the church, which is the focus of attention in the photo. For this substantial enhancement it will be worthwhile sacrificing a little of the contrast in the shadowed area at the lower left and in the sky.

1 In the Navigator, set the Loupe view zoom level to Fit.

● **Note:** The choice of point curve preset also constrains the amount of play in the adjustment controls.

2 From the Point Curve menu at the bottom of the Tone Curve panel, choose Linear, Medium Contrast, and Strong Contrast in turn and notice the effect each setting has on the image. You can use a tone curve preset as a starting point for your adjustments; for this image, set a Medium Contrast curve.

Note the silhouette of the histogram plotted in the background in the tone curve display. This gives you an indication of the tonal ranges where an increase in contrast might be most effective.

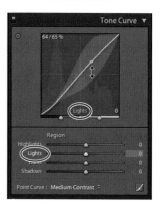

▶ **Tip:** By default, the four tonal ranges are of equal width. You can change their width by dragging the controls below the tone curve to reposition the dividing lines between adjacent tonal ranges.

3 Position the pointer over the tone curve. As you move from left to right you'll notice the names of the ranges you're moving over displayed at the bottom of the tone curve grid, while the corresponding slider is highlighted in the Region controls below.

Whether you use the sliders, enter numeric values, or drag directly in the tone curve grid, the tone curve controls raise or lower the curve by moving the center points of these four ranges: Shadows, Darks, Lights, and Highlights. The overall shape of the tone curve changes to accommodate your adjustments, becoming flatter in one place and steeper in another.

The extent to which you can adjust each section of the tone curve is indicated by the gray area that appears when you position the pointer over that section.

4 To see which areas in the image correspond to the different tonal ranges, click the Target button (◉) in the top left corner of the Tone Curve panel and move the pointer over the image in the Loupe view. As you move the pointer over the shadowed area in the lower left of the image you can see that these tones account for much of the first peak in the histogram around the 25% mark. Most of the tonal values in the blue sky are represented in the second peak in the histogram close to the 50% input level. The tones in the well-lit parts of the church wall are mostly spread between input levels of 60% to 90%.

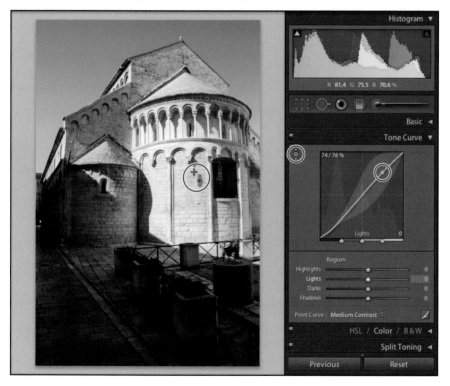

Lowering the Lights value in the tone curve should produce the effect we're after: increasing the contrast in the well-lit church wall by steepening the curve for the input values above 60%. The compromise is a flattening of the curve for lower input values; reducing contrast in the sky and shadow areas where a loss of detail is less noticeable.

5 Watch the tone curve as you move the target cursor over the church wall. When you see the Lights adjustment control selected on the Tone Curve, click and drag downwards in the image. Release the mouse button when the Lights value is adjusted to –45. Remember: you can only adjust the tone curve by dragging directly in the image when you are using the Tone Curve Target mode.

6 Click the Target button again to turn off target mode.

7 To compare your image with and without the tone curve adjustment, switch the tone curve controls off and on by clicking the On/Off switch at the left side of the Tone Curve panel's header. Review the effect in the image at 100% zoom level. Note how much your adjustment enhanced the detail in the stone wall.

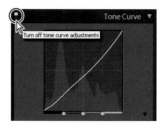

The image was also darkened as a whole because the tone curve was pushed below the diagonal. This works quite well for the image at hand. In another case, you could lessen the effect, if you wished, by raising the Shadows value in the Tone Curve or by readjusting the levels using the controls in the Basic panel.

8 When you're done, set the zoom level to Fit and make sure the tone curve adjustment is turned on.

The image now looks quite acceptable. To improve it even further you can apply additional sharpening and reduce some of the noise that's visible in the sky area.

Sharpening detail and reducing noise

The Detail panel contains controls for sharpening image detail and reducing noise. Sharpening helps make edges more pronounced and gives the image a crisper look.

Lightroom applies a slight amount of sharpening to your Raw images by default, so you should apply additional sharpening with caution.

The Detail panel offers separate controls for reducing luminance noise and color noise. The image for this exercise was shot at an ISO setting of 800 and contains a slight amount of noise, mostly noticeable the sky area.

Note: Noise is most noticeable in images that were captured under low lighting conditions or at a high ISO setting. The image for this exercise was shot at an ISO setting of 800.

1   In the Navigator panel, set the zoom level for the Loupe view to 1:1 (100%). Image sharpening and noise reduction are always best executed at 100%; the pixel-for-pixel zoom level view gives you the clearest view of the results.

2   Scroll down in the right panel group, or collapse other panels if necessary, and then expand the Detail panel.

3   For this image, the sharpening amount is already set to 25%. To compare the image with and without this default sharpening, switch the Detail controls off and on by clicking the On/Off switch at the left of the panel header. Review the effect in several areas of the image at 100% magnification.
When you're done, make sure that the Detail settings are switched on.

Though the default sharpening has done a good job of emphasizing the edges in this image, you can still make it crisper. Before you apply extra sharpening, however, it's best to set up a mask that will restrict your adjustment to areas with edge detail. For our lesson image, this will let you to sharpen architectural detail while you avoid accentuating the noise in the sky area where it will be easily noticeable.

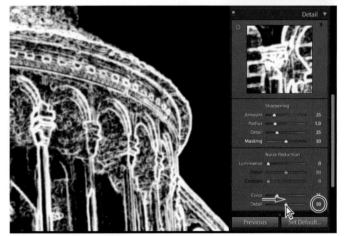

4   Position the photo in the Loupe view so that you can see some of the sky and part of the church at the same time. Hold down the Alt / Option key and drag the Masking slider to the right. The mask is displayed in the Detail panel preview and in the Loupe view when the zoom level is set to 1:1 or higher. Release the pointer when most of the sky area is masked (black) but the edge detail on the church is still unmasked (white). We used a value of 50.

5   To sharpen the image further, drag the Amount slider to the right. With the extensive mask in place, you can afford to increase the value by a relatively large amount. We raised the setting to 100.

6 Compare the image with and without sharpening once again by clicking the On/Off switch icon at the left side of the header of the Detail panel.

▶ **Tip:** If you can't see the effect clearly, click a higher zoom ratio in the header bar of the Navigator panel.

7 To assess the effect of the sharpening mask, make sure the detail controls are turned on and drag the Masking slider all the way back to its default setting of 0. Undo and Redo to see the effect of applying sharpening with and without the mask. Pay particular attention to the sky area where unmasked sharpening accentuates noise. When you're done, return the Masking setting to 50.

Most of the noise apparent in this image is *luminance noise*—variations in the brightness of pixels which should be equally bright. Luminance noise looks a little like film grain and is in general less of a problem than color noise, or *chrominance noise*—bright blue, red and purple spots in an area that should be a uniform hue. In the Noise Reduction pane at the bottom of the detail panel, you can see that a small amount of Color noise reduction has been applied to this image by default.

8 To assess the effect of the default reduction in color noise, focus on an area of sky in the image and drag the Color slider all the way to the left. Undo and Redo to see the image with and without the color noise reduction. When you're done, return the zoom to 1:1 and the Color noise reduction value to 25.

▶ **Tip:** You should use Noise Reduction with caution; both forms can blur image detail. You can use the Detail sliders for the Noise Reduction controls to help maintain the sharpness of the image, despite this effect.

9 Position the photo in the Loupe view so that you can some of the sky and part of the church wall at the same time, as shown in the illustration below. Drag the Luminance slider all the way to the right to a value of 100. The luminance noise in the sky has now disappeared—however, there is marked blurring of the detail in the church wall. You'll need to find a compromise between reducing noise and maintaining the sharpness. Drag the Luminance slider back to 0, and then slowly to the right until you notice that the sky area is improved with only slight blurring of the details on the church wall. We used a value of 40.

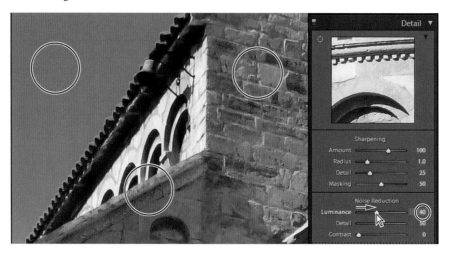

10 Use the Detail and Contrast controls below the Luminance slider to reduce the blurring effect. Try Detail and Contrast values of 70 and 25 respectively.

Correcting lens effects

As well as the Transform sliders you used in Lesson 1, the Lens Corrections panel in manual mode presents controls for correcting Lens Vignetting and Chromatic Aberration—unwanted effects that can be caused by your camera lens.

Lens vignetting is a phenomenon that results in reduced brightness or saturation of color towards the edges of an image—usually an accidental effect caused by a combination of the focal length, type of lens, and filters used.

Chromatic Aberration is most noticeable near the edges of an image shot with a wide-angle lens, resulting in color fringes where the lens has been unable to focus the different wavelengths of incoming light correctly on the sensor. There is only a very slight chromatic aberration in the image used for this exercise.

Tip: For information on using the Profile mode to make lens corrections tailored to your camera, please refer to Lightroom Help.

The slight amount of color aberration in this photo is apparent as a blue fringe around the top of the sunlit arches. The Remove Chromatic Aberration control is in the Lens Corrections panel's Profile mode.

Adding effects

In the Lens Corrections panel, you can remove accidental lens vignetting; in the Effects panel you can deliberately put it back. A post-crop vignette can be used creatively to frame a photo, to draw the viewer's attention to the center of an image, or even to simulate an accidental vignette for an atmospheric or "antique" effect.

The Effects panel also offers a Grain effect that simulates the distinctive look of a film photograph by adding grain.

This illustration shows a fairly extreme application of Post-Crop Vignetting that suggests the look of a film transparency. You can control the softness and shape of the vignette, and specify how you want it to interact with colors and highlights.

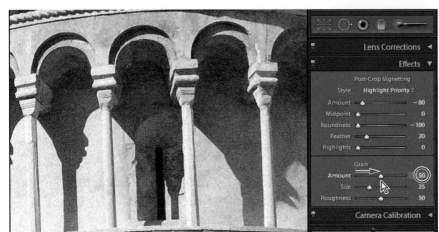

Making discrete color adjustments

You can use the controls in the HSL / Color / B & W panel to adjust discrete shades of color in your image, changing the hue, saturation, or luminance values for specific color ranges independently.

When converting an image to black and white, you can fine-tune the way that each color in the image will contribute to the grayscale mix. Use the Split Toning panel to apply creative duotone effects to a black and white image.

Understanding hue, saturation, and luminance

The color of each pixel in your image can be expressed either as a set of RGB values or as a combination of hue, saturation, and luminance values. Hue, saturation, and luminance values can be calculated from from RGB values, and vice versa.

Once you understand hue, saturation, and luminance, defining color in these terms seems far more natural than using RGB values, especially when it comes to describing changes made to color.

For example, darkening the blue colors in your image can be done by reducing the luminance value for the blue color component. Expressed in RGB values, a light blue might be composed of R: 42, G: 45, and B: 63, while a darker blue uses R: 35, G: 38, and B: 56—certainly not a very intuitive model for describing color adjustments.

When you describe a color by name—red, yellow, green, blue—you're referring to its hue. The full range of hues can be displayed as a color wheel. Adjusting the hue moves a given color around the wheel in one direction or the other.

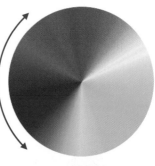

Saturation is the boldness or intensity of a hue, ranging from neutral and grayed to vivid and un-muted. Saturation can be visualized on a color wheel with fully saturated colors around the edge of the circle and less saturated colors closer to the center. As the saturation of a color is increased it moves from a neutral gray in the center of the wheel to a pure, vivid hue on the rim.

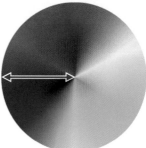

Luminance is the measure of brightness of a color, ranging from the minimum value for black to the maximum value for white. On the color wheel model, luminance can be represented by adding a third dimension, with a completely underexposed—or black—wheel below the color wheel and a completely overexposed—or white—wheel above it.

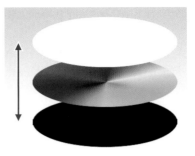

The terms tint, shade, and tone can all be expressed with reference to hue, saturation, and luminance.

A *tint* is a pure hue mixed with white; a hue with increased luminance and a reduced saturation. In our three-dimensional color wheel model the tints of a hue are found along the line from the pure hue on the rim of the wheel in the middle to the center point of the white wheel at the top.

A *shade* is a pure hue mixed with black; a hue with decreased luminance and saturation, located along a line from the pure hue on the rim of the wheel in the middle to the center point of the black wheel at the bottom.

A *tone* is a pure hue mixed with a neutral gray, located along a line from the pure hue on the rim of the wheel in the middle to the respective gray on the central axis.

Adjusting colors selectively

Understanding color in an image in terms of hue, saturation and luminance can help you both in identifying the changes you need to make to achieve the effect you want and in choosing the most effective way to make those changes.

In this exercise you'll darken the blue of the sky in the photo of the stone church. You can do this by reducing the luminance of the blue color range while leaving the hue and saturation unchanged.

1   You should still be in the Develop module, with the image of the stone church, DSC_0299.NEF, open in the Loupe view.

2   In the Navigator panel, set the zoom level to Fit.

3   In the right panel group, scroll up or collapse other panels, if necessary, and then expand the HSL / Color / B & W panel. If not already selected, click HSL (Hue, Saturation, Luminance) in the panel header, and then click the Luminance tab.

4 Click the Target tool button () in the upper left corner of the Luminance pane.

5 In the Loupe view, click in the sky area and drag the pointer downwards to reduce the luminance of the color range under the pointer. Release the mouse button when the Luminance value for Blue reaches −20. Depending on where you click, you may see a small shift in the Aqua or Purple values.

6 Click the Target button again to disable target mode.

Note: The luminance adjustment is not restricted to one discrete color but is applied across a range of colors to either side of the target hue.

7 To compare the image with and without the luminance adjustment applied, switch the HSL / Color / B & W adjustment off and on by clicking the On/Off switch icon at the left side of the panel header. Note that the adjustment has not affected the gradient from lighter blue near the horizon to darker blue at the top. When you're done, make sure the HSL / Color / B & W adjustment is turned on.

You can adjust the hue or saturation in the same way. Select the Hue or Saturation tab, then use the Target tool to adjust the color in a specific area in the image. You could also use the respective slider controls. Click the All tab for access to all the sliders for Hue, Saturation, and Luminance at the same time. In the Color tab the sliders are grouped by color rather than by hue, saturation, and luminance. The All tab displays the sliders for all of the colors at the same time.

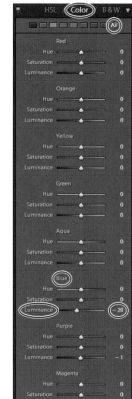

Converting an image to black and white

Lightroom converts a photo to black and white by mapping each color in the image to a different tone of gray according to a default routine. You can create very different grayscale looks by adjusting the relative predominance of each color in the mix.

1 Click B & W in the header of the HSL / Color / B & W panel. You can see the result of the default black and white mix in the Loupe view.

If you wish, you can even adjust the black and white mix selectively for different areas of the same image.

2 Click the Target button (⊚) in the upper left of the Black And White Mix pane. In the Loupe view, click the sky and drag upwards to set the Blue value to +30; then, click the church wall and drag down to reduce the value for Orange to –20.

3 Click the Black And White Mix Target button (⊚) again to turn target mode off.

4 To compare the image before and after your adjustments to the grayscale mix, switch the Black And White Mix adjustments off and on by clicking the On/Off switch icon at the left side of the HSL / Color / B & W panel header. When you're done, make sure the Black And White Mix control is turned on.

Split toning

A split toning effect replaces the dark tones (shadows) in a black and white image with shades of one color and the lighter tones (highlights) with tints of another. The effect can be quite subtle and restrained or very striking and unusual depending on your choice of colors and your intention.

1   In the right panel group, expand the Split Toning panel. If possible, keep the HSL / Color / B & W panel open so you can see the settings for the grayscale mix at the same time.

2   Right-click / Control-click the image in the Loupe view and choose Settings > Lightroom BW Toned Presets > Antique from the menu. Note the changes in the Split Toning panel. The Antique effect uses a sepia tone for the highlights and a less saturated and slightly warmer color for the shadows.

3   In the right panel group, expand the Basic, Tone Curve, Detail, and Lens Corrections panels in turn, using Undo and Redo to see how the Antique preset changes the settings. Collapse each panel when you're done with it.

If you wish, you can copy only a subset of the settings from a preset or another image. In this case, you'll copy just the color settings from the Split Toning panel.

4   Right-click / Control-click the antique grayscale image in the Loupe view, and then choose Settings > Copy Settings from the context menu. In the Copy Settings dialog box, first click the Check None button, and then activate only the Split Toning option. Click Copy.

5 Choose Edit > Undo Antique to return to the black and white image with all your customized settings. Right-click / Control-click the image in the Loupe view and choose Settings > Paste Settings from the context menu. By checking the panels in the right panel group, you can see that this time only the settings in the Split Toning panel have been altered.

Antique preset applied

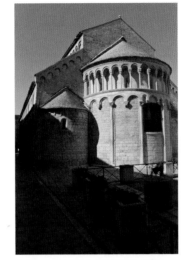

Antique preset's Split Toning only

Synchronizing settings

You can copy, or *synchronize*, settings from one photo to a multiple selection of images by using the Synchronize Settings command.

1 Select all five of the raw images in the Filmstrip, avoiding the two video files and the associated JPEG image. Click the image of the church to make sure it's the active (the most selected) image.

2 Click the Sync button below the right panel group. In the Synchronize Settings dialog box, click the Check None button, and then activate both the Treatment (Black & White) and Split Toning options. Click Synchronize.

All five images have been converted to black and white and have had the duo-tone effect that you copied from the Antique Grayscale preset applied.

▶ **Tip:** The Synchronize Settings command in the Develop module copies absolute values from one image to the others. To apply relative changes to a selection of images—such as increasing exposure by 1/3 step independent of the current exposure settings in each of the destination images— you can use the Quick Development panel in the Library module.

Local corrections

All the adjustments you've made in this lesson so far have been applied globally—across the entire image. For example, increasing the Shadows setting affects all the darker areas in a photo; you can't lighten one area selectively or some areas more than others. With the local correction tools—the Graduated Filter tool and the Adjustment Brush tool—you can do both.

Using the Graduated Filter tool

With the Graduated Filter tool you can created a gradient mask through which you can apply an adjustment so that the effect is stronger in one area and fades off across the rest of the image.

1   In the Filmstrip, select just the image of the stone church. Click the Graduated Filter button below the Histogram panel, or press M. Controls for the tool appear below the tool buttons.

2   Make sure New is selected as the Mask setting; then, choose Exposure from the Effect menu above the Temperature and Tint sliders. Use the slider or type a new value in the text box at the right to set the Exposure setting to **0.36**.

3   With the Graduated Filter tool, drag from a point near the lower left corner of the image upwards and to the right, and then release the pointer.

You have just created a basic gradient mask, through which your adjustment has been applied. Next you'll fine-tune both the mask and the adjustment.

You can see the effect on the image at a glance; the exposure is gradually increased towards the lower left corner. In the Graduated Filter controls, the Mask setting has changed to Edit. You can still change the settings for the adjustment and reposition, rotate, resize, and fine-tune the gradient mask.

4   Increase the Exposure setting to **1.00**. Then adjust the gradient mask as shown in the illustration below. Drag the pin to reposition the center of the gradient beside the kerb-stone. Drag the center line to rotate the mask so that its orientation is parallel to the kerb, and then drag either of the outer lines to make the band of the gradient narrower or broader.

▶ **Tip:** You can use more than one graduated filter in a single image, each with its own position, direction, size, and adjustment settings.

The broader the band, the "softer" the gradient—the narrower the band, the more abruptly the adjustment is faded into the image. While you're dragging the outer lines, you can keep the center line fixed at its current position by holding down the Alt / Option key. The outer lines represent the boundaries beyond which the adjustment is applied at 100% of the specified value on one side and 0% on the other. Press the H key to hide or show the adjustment pin.

5   To evaluate the image with and without the graduated filter adjustment, click the On/Off switch icon in the lower left corner of the Graduated Filter controls pane. When you're done, make sure the graduated filter adjustment is activated.

6   Click the Graduated Filter button again to disable the Graduated Filter tool.

Using the Adjustment Brush tool

You can use the Adjustment Brush tool to paint adjustments directly onto different areas of the image selectively.

1 Click the Adjustment Brush button below the Histogram panel (circled at right), or press K. The Adjustment Brush tool settings appear below the tool buttons. Make sure that Mask is set to New in the Adjustment Brush tool controls pane.

In addition to the Effect pane, the Adjustment Brush tool settings also present controls for setting up brushes. You can set a different size, softness, flow, and density for two brushes that will apply the adjustment or effect and one that will erase it.

2 Reset the Exposure value to **0**. Click the color box to choose a color for a tint effect. We chose a strong, saturated red.

3 Click brush A and activate the Auto Mask option. With the Auto Mask option activated, the brush will detect the edges of the area you're painting, and will mask those parts of the image outside those edges.

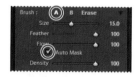

4 Paint over the entire sky area. Avoid moving the center of the brush outside the area. Hold down the Alt key / Option key and drag to erase any mistakes.

▶ **Tip:** You can use the Adjustment Brush to create more than one local adjustment in a single image, each with its own settings. To delete a local adjustment, select its pin, and then press delete.

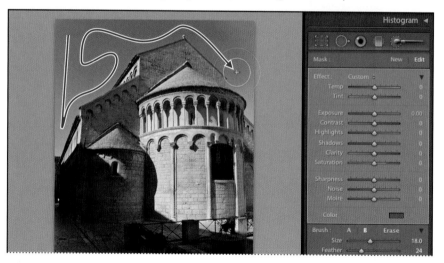

5 Click the Adjustment Brush tool again to disable it.

This exercise completes the lesson. You are now familiar with a wide variety of basic skills as well as some specialized techniques for more sophisticated image editing tasks. Experiment with the tools, settings, and options on your own photos to discover more of the depth and power of the Develop module. Take a moment to refresh what you've learned by reading through the review on the facing page.

Review questions

1 How do you undo changes or return quickly to a previous develop state?

2 How can you edit a video with the Develop module's tools, even though video is not supported in the Develop module?

3 What is white balance?

4 What does a tone curve represent and what is it used for?

5 What are the two kinds of noise you might encounter in a digital image and what can you do about them?

6 Which tools are used to perform local corrections?

Review answers

1 You can undo one modification at a time using the Undo command. You can jump back multiple steps at once in the History panel. You can create snapshots of important develop states so that you can return to them quickly.

2 Capture a still frame from the video; then, open the captured frame in the Develop module, make your adjustments, and save the results as a custom developing preset. Your saved preset is listed in the Library module's Quick Develop panel, where you can apply it to your video clip.

3 An image's white balance reflects the composition of the red, green, and blue components in the light source when the picture was taken. It is used as a calibration benchmark to correctly render the color information recorded by the camera's sensors.

4 A tone curve adjusts the distribution of the tonal ranges in an image. The curve shows the way tonal information from the original image will be mapped to the adjusted image. It can be used to increase or decrease the contrast in specific tonal ranges.

5 Digital images may contain two kinds of noise: luminance noise, which is a result of variation in the brightness of pixels which should be of the same luminance, and color (chrominance) noise: bright blue, red and purple spots in an area that should be a uniform hue. Each kind of noise can be reduced using the appropriate noise reduction slider in the Detail panel.

6 You can restrict adjustments to selected areas of your image with the Graduated Filter tool and the Adjustment Brush tool.

7 CREATING A PHOTO BOOK

Lesson overview

Whether it's produced for a client or as a professional portfolio, designed as a gift or simply to preserve precious memories, a photo book makes a great way to share and showcase your images.

The Book module makes it easy to design beautiful, sophisticated book layouts, and then publish them without leaving Lightroom.

In this lesson, you'll learn the skills you need to create your own high-quality photo book:

- Grouping the images for your photo book as a collection

- Setting up a photo book

- Modifying page layouts

- Setting a page background

- Placing and arranging images in a layout

- Adding text to a book design

- Working with text cells and photo cells

- Using the Text Adjustment Tool

- Saving a photo book

- Exporting your creation

 You'll probably need between one and two hours to complete this lesson.

The Book module, new in Lightroom 4, delivers everything you need to create stylish book designs that can be uploaded directly from Lightroom for printing through the on-demand book vendor Blurb, or exported to PDF and printed on your own printer. Template-based layout, an intuitive editing environment, and state-of-the-art text tools make it easy to present your photographs in their best light.

Getting started

This lesson assumes that you are already familiar with the Lightroom workspace and with moving between the different modules. If you find that you need more background information, refer to Lightroom Help, or review the previous lessons.

Before you begin, make sure that you have correctly copied the Lessons folder from the CD in the back of this book onto your computer's hard disk as detailed in "Copying the Classroom in a Book files" on page 2, and created the LR4CIB Library Catalog file to manage the lesson files as described in "Creating a catalog file for working with this book" on page 3.

1 Start Lightroom.

2 In the Adobe Photoshop Lightroom - Select Catalog dialog box, make sure the file LR4CIB Library Catalog.lrcat is selected under Select A Recent Catalog To Open, and then click Open.

Tip: The first time you enter any of the Lightroom modules, you'll see module tips that will help you get started by identifying the components of the Lightroom workspace and stepping you through the workflow. Dismiss the tips by clicking the Close button. To reactivate the tips for any module, choose [*Module name*] Tips from the Help menu.

3 Lightroom will open in the screen mode and workspace module that were active when you last quit. If necessary, switch to the Library module by clicking Library in the Module Picker at the top of the workspace.

Importing images into the library

The first step is to import the images for this lesson into the Lightroom library.

1 In the Library module, click the Import button below the left panel group.

2   If the Import dialog box appears in compact mode, click the Show More Options button at the lower left of the dialog box to see all the options in the expanded Import dialog box.

3   In the Source panel at the left of the Import dialog box, navigate to and select the LR4CIB > Lessons > Lesson 7 folder. Ensure that all nineteen images are checked for import.

4   In the import options above the thumbnail previews, select Add so that the imported photos will be added to your catalog without being moved or copied. Under File Handling at the right of the expanded Import dialog box, choose Minimal from the Render Previews menu and ensure that the Don't Import Suspected Duplicates option is activated. Under Apply During Import, choose None from both the Develop Settings menu and the Metadata menu and type **Lesson 7, Architecture** in the Keywords text box. Make sure that the Import dialog box is set up as shown in the illustration below, and then click Import.

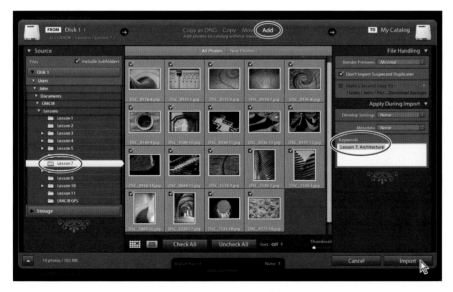

The nineteen images are imported from the Lesson 7 folder and now appear in the Grid view of the Library module and also in the Filmstrip across the bottom of the Lightroom workspace.

Assembling photos for a book

The first step in creating a book is to assemble the photos you wish to include.
Having just been imported, the images for this
lesson are already isolated from the rest of your
catalog. In the Catalog panel, the Previous Import
folder is selected as the active image source.

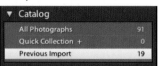

The Previous Import folder is merely a temporary grouping and, as an image
source, it is not flexible—you can't rearrange the images inside it, or exclude a
photo from your project without removing it from the catalog entirely.

You should always use either a collection or a single folder without subfolders as
the source for the images in your book; both will let you reorder photos in the Grid
view or the Filmstrip. For this exercise, you'll create a collection—a virtual grouping
from which you can also exclude an image without deleting it from your catalog.

1 Make sure that either the Previous Import folder in the Catalog panel, or the
   Lesson 7 folder in the Folders panel, is selected as the image source; then,
   press Ctrl+A / Command+A or choose Edit > Select All.

2 Click the New Collection button (➕) in the header of the Collections panel and
   choose Create Collection from the menu. In the Create Collection dialog box,
   type **Details** as the name for the new collection, and make sure that Top Level
   is selected in the Placement options. Under Collection Options, activate Include
   Selected Photos and disable Make New Virtual Copies; then, click Create.

Your new collection appears in the Collections
panel, where it is automatically selected as the
active image source. The image count indicates
that the Details collection contains 19 photos.

3 Choose Edit > Select None; then, click Book in
   the Module Picker to switch to the Book module.

Working in the Book module

Whether you want to commemorate a family milestone, frame your memories from
a special trip, or put together a photographic package for a client, a photo book is
an attractive and sophisticated way to showcase your work. The Book module, new
in Lightroom 4, delivers everything you need to create stylish book designs that can
be uploaded directly from Lightroom for printing through the on-demand book
vendor Blurb, or exported to PDF and printed on your own printer.

Setting up a photo book

In the work area, you may or may not see photos already placed in page layouts, depending on whether you've already experimented with the Book module's tools and controls. You can start this project by clearing the layout and setting up the workspace so that we're all on the same page.

1 Click the Clear Book button in the header bar across the top of the work area. If you don't see the header bar, choose View > Show Header Bar.

2 In the Book Settings panel at the top of the right panel group, choose Blurb from the Book menu and make sure that the Size, Cover, Paper Type, and Logo Page are set to Standard Landscape, Hardcover Image Wrap, Premium Lustre, and On, respectively. The estimated price of printing the book at the current settings is displayed at the bottom of the Book Settings panel.

3 If it's not already selected, click the Multi-Page View button at the far left of the Toolbar at the bottom of the work area. In the View menu, disable Show Info Overlay.

4 Choose Book > Book Preferences. Examine the options; you can choose whether photos are zoomed to fit their image cells or cropped to fit them, toggle the Autofill feature for new books, and set your preferences for text behaviors. Leave the settings at the defaults and close the Book Preferences dialog box.

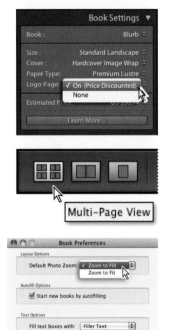

The Autofill feature is activated by default; if you just entered the Book module for the first time, you would have seen the images from the Details collection already placed in the default book layout. An automatically generated layout can be a great starting point for a new book design, especially if you're beginning without a clear idea of exactly what you want.

5 Expand the Auto Layout panel, if necessary. From the Auto Layout Preset menu, choose Left Blank, Right One Photo, Caption; then, click the Auto Layout button. Scroll down in the work area, if necessary, to see all the page thumbnails. Click the Clear Layout button and repeat the procedure for the auto-layout preset One Photo Per Page.

● **Note:** If you're publishing to Blurb.com, auto-layout is limited to books of 240 pages. There is no auto-layout page limit for books published to PDF.

6 Examine the result in the work area; scroll down, if necessary, to see all the page thumbnails arranged as two-page spreads in the Multi-Page view. Hide the module picker and the left panel group by pressing F5, and then F7, or by clicking the triangles at the top and left edges of the Lightroom workspace. Drag the Thumbnails slider in the Toolbar to reduce or enlarge the thumbnails.

Tip: Blurb offers a discounted price for photo books that incorporate the Blurb logo on the last page.

Lightroom generates a book with a cover, a separate page for each of the nineteen lesson photos—placed in the order in which they appear in the Filmstrip—and a twentieth page reserved for the Blurb logo. You can't place a photo on the Blurb logo page, but you can disable it in the Book Settings panel, if you wish.

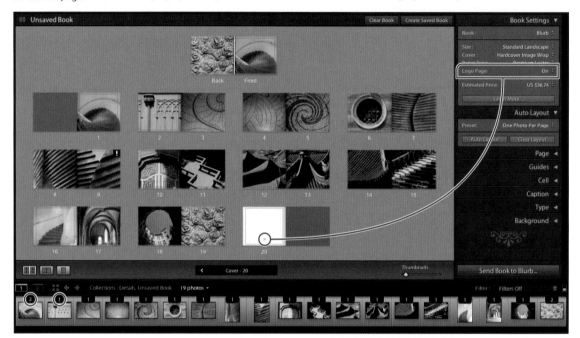

Note: If you want to rearrange the order of images in the Filmstrip before you click Auto Layout, you'll first need to save your book.

The first photo in the Filmstrip becomes the front cover image; the last image in the series is placed on the back cover. The number above each photo in the Filmstrip indicates how many times it has been used in the book; the first and last images have each been used twice—on the cover and also on pages 1 and 19.

Changing page layouts

Using an auto-layout preset can help you get started on your book; you can then focus on individual spreads and pages to introduce subtlety and variety to the design. For this project, however, you'll build your book layout from scratch.

1 In the Auto Layout panel, click the Clear Layout button.

2 Right-click / Control-click the header of the Page panel and choose Solo Mode from the context menu.

3 In the Multi-Page view, double-click the front cover.

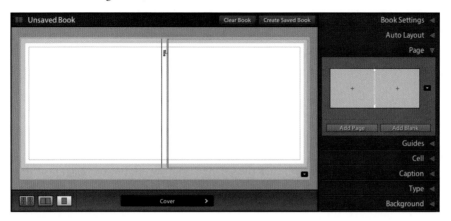

The cover layout fills the work area, with the front cover selected, as indicated by the yellow border. The Page panel displays a diagrammatic preview of the default cover template: two image cells (identifiable by central cross-hairs) and a narrow text cell positioned along the book's spine.

4 Click the Change Page Layout button ( ) to the right of the layout preview thumbnail in the Page panel, or in the lower right corner of the cover spread displayed in the work area.

5 Scroll down in the page template picker to see all of the available cover layout templates. Grey areas with central cross-hairs indicate image cells; rectangles filled with horizontal lines represent text cells. Click to select the third template in the list. The single cross-hairs at the center of the spread shows that this template has a single image cell that extends across both covers, and three text cells: one on the back cover, one on the spine, and one on the front cover.

6 Expand the Guides panel. Make sure that the Show Guides option is activated; then, watch the layout in the work area as you toggle each of the four guides in turn. When you're done disable Photo Cells, leaving the other guides visible. Move the pointer over the layout to see the borders of the text cells.

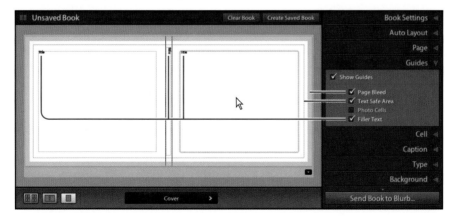

The Page Bleed guide's wide gray border shows the area to be cut off after the page is printed. A thin gray line borders the Text Safe Area, where your text will be well clear of accidental trimming. The Filler Text guide shows filler text (here, the word "Title") to indicate the position of text cells. The filler text will disappear when you click a text cell.

7 Click the Multi-Page View button (⊞) in the Toolbar.

The first page in a photo book is always on the right side of the first spread; the grayed-out left side represents the inside of the front cover, which is not printed. Likewise, the last page in a photo book to be published to Blurb must always occupy the left side of the final spread. At this stage, your book consists of a cover and a single, double-sided page, the back of which is the Blurb logo page.

8 Right-click / Control-click page 1 and choose Add Page from the context menu. Lightroom adds a second double-sided page to the book, which appears as an additional two-page spread in the Multi-Page view.

9 Click to select page 2; then, click the Change Page Layout button (🔽) near the lower right corner of the page.

For an inside page, the page template picker offers a choice of layout categories to help you search the layout templates by style, or by the number of photos per page.

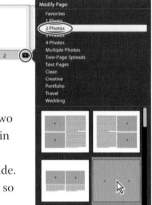

10 Click 2 Photos to see all the layout templates with two image cells; then click to select the fourth template in the list: a layout without text cells that fills the page with two portrait-format images arranged side by side. Activate the Photo Cells option in the Guides panel so that you can see the changed page layout.

Adding photos to a book layout

You can add photos to a page layout in any of the three Book Editor views.

1 Drag the image DSC_1534.jpg—the seventh photo in the Filmstrip—to the cover spread in the Multi-Page view.

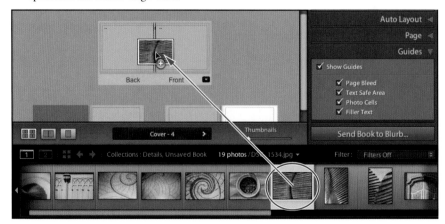

2   Drag the image DSC_6230.jpg from the Filmstrip to page 1 in the Multi-Page view. Place the photos DSC_0180.jpg and DSC_5865.jpg in the left and right image cells on page 2, respectively, and the sixth image DSC_0149.jpg on page 3.

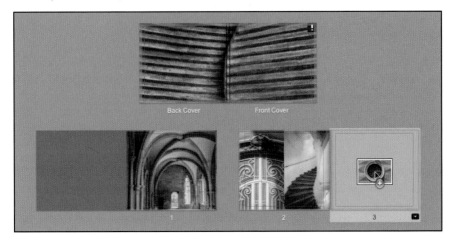

● **Note:** An exclamation mark badge in the upper right corner of an image cell indicates that the image may not be of a high enough resolution to print well at the current size. You can either reduce the size of the image in your layout, or ignore the alert if you are prepared to accept a lower print resolution.

Changing the images in a photo book

You can remove a photo from a page layout by right-clicking / Control-clicking the image in the Book Editor and choosing Remove Photo from the context menu. If you simply want to replace a photo, you needn't remove it first.

1   Drag the photo DSC_0131.jpg—the second image in the Filmstrip—onto the right-hand image on page 2. DSC_0131.jpg replaces the original image.

2   In the Multi-Page view, drag the image on page 1—DSC_0131.jpg—onto the photo on page 3; the photos on pages 1 and 3 swap places.

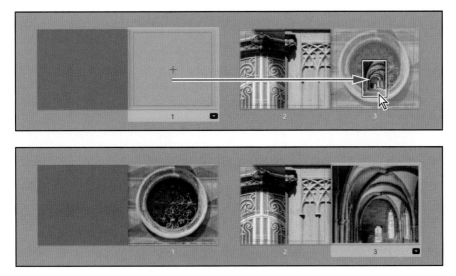

▶ **Tip:** You should see the thumbnail as you drag, leaving page 1 in place. If you see the page move instead, drag it back into place and try again, making sure to drag from well inside the photo cell.

▶ **Tip:** You can easily rearrange the order of the pages in your photo book—or even shuffle entire spreads—in the same way; simply drag them to new positions in the Multi-Page view.

Working with photo cells

The photo cells in a page layout template are fixed in place; you can't delete them, resize them, or move them on the page. Instead, you can use the *cell padding*—the adjustable space around a photo within its cell—to position the images in your page layout exactly as you want them.

1 Double-click page 3. The Book Editor switches from Multi-Page view to Single Page view; in the Toolbar, the Single Page View button is highlighted.

2 Click the photo to select it, and then experiment with the Zoom slider. When you enlarge the image too much (for this photo, above 43%), an exclamation-point badge appears in the upper right corner to alert you that the photo may not print well. Right-click / Control-click the photo and choose Zoom Photo To Fill Cell; the image is scaled so that its shortest edge fills the cell (at a zoom value of 29%, for this photo). Drag the photo to position it vertically within the cell. Drag the slider all the way to the left; the minimum setting reduces the image so that its longest edge fits within the image cell. Click well within the borders of the photo and drag it to the right side of the cell.

3 Leave the photo at the 0% zoom setting. Expand the Cell panel and increase the padding by dragging the Padding Amount slider or typing a new value of **150 pt**.

4 In the Cell panel, click the black triangle above the Padding value to expand the padding controls. By default, the four controls are linked; the adjustment you made in the previous step changed all four values. Disable Link All, and then set the Right and Top padding to **0** pt and the Bottom value to **300** pt.

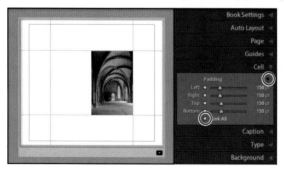
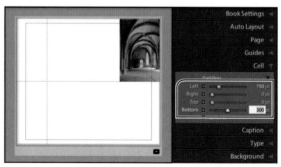

5 Set the Left and Right padding to **250** pt, and the Top and Bottom padding to **205** pt. Click the photo in the Single Page view to select it; then, use the slider to set the zoom level to 22% and drag the image to position it within its cell padding as shown in the illustration at the right.

By starting with the right template, and then setting the photo cell padding, you can position an image anywhere on the page, cropped however you wish.

6 In the Cell panel, activate Link All, and then drag any of the sliders to set all of the padding settings to zero. Right-click / Control-click the photo in the Single Image view and choose Zoom Photo To Fill Cell from the context menu. Drag the image vertically inside its cell to find a pleasing crop.

7 Click the Spread View button in the Toolbar to see pages 2 and 3 as a spread.

8 Select the image on the left of page 2. Set the linked padding controls to **50** pt, then unlink them and reduce the Right padding to **15** pt. Repeat the process for the photo on the right side of page 2, but this time, reduce the Left padding to 15, rather than the Right.

9 Double-click the yellow frame below page 2 to see it enlarged in the Single Image view. Zoom the photo on the left to 70%; then, drag the image inside its cell padding to position it as shown in the illustration at the right. Reposition the photo on the right without changing the zoom level. For a clearer view, click the gray space outside the page to deselect it.

10 In the Toolbar below the Single Image view, click the left navigation arrow to jump to page 1. The circular grille is slightly off-center; zoom the photo to 21% and drag in the photo cell to center the image on the page.

11 Click away from the page to deselect it, and then click the Multi-Page View button (⊞⊞) in the Toolbar for an overview of the changes you've made.

Setting a page background

By default, all the pages in a new book share a plain white background. You can change the background color, set up a partially transparent backdrop image, or choose from a library of graphic motifs, applying your background design to the entire book, or just a selected page.

You can start by adding two more spreads to your book layout.

1   Right-click / Control-click the Blurb logo page and choose Add Page from the context menu. To add another double-sided page, right-click / Control-click page 5 and choose Add Page.

2   Select any of the four new pages in the Multi-Page view, and then click the Spread View button (▮▮) in the Toolbar.

▶ **Tip:** You can also apply a background image to a selected page (or pages) by dragging a photo directly onto the page background area from the Filmstrip, making sure not to drop the image into a photo cell.

3   Expand the Background panel. Disable the option Apply Background Globally; then, drag the last photo in the Filmstrip, DSC_9777.jpg, to the preview pane in the Background panel. Drag the slider to set the opacity of the image to 50%.

4   Activate the Background Color option, and then click the associated color swatch to open the color picker. Drag the saturation slider at the right of the color picker about a third way up its range; then, drag the eyedropper cursor in the color field to find a muted tone; we chose a color with R, G, and B values of 70, 55, and 90, respectively. Click away from the color picker to dismiss it.

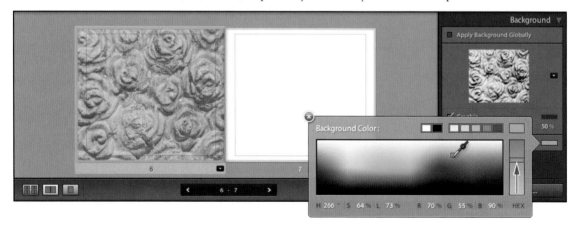

5   In the Background panel, activate the Apply Background Globally option, and then click the Multi-Page View button (▦) in the Toolbar.

Your composite background is applied to every page (except the Blurb logo page, where only the color is applied); it can be seen behind the images on page 2.

6   Disable the Background Color option; then, right-click / Control-click the image in the background preview pane and choose Remove Image. Disable Apply Background Globally.

7   Select page 2 in the Multi-Page view, and then reactivate the Background Color option. Click the color swatch to open the color picker, and then click the black swatch at the top of the picker. Click away from the color picker to dismiss it.

8   Refresh the skills you've learned in this lesson by replicating the pages in the illustration below. You'll need to adjust photo cell padding on pages 5, 6, and 7.

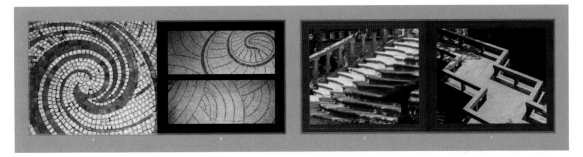

Adding text to a photo book

There are several ways to add text to your pages in the Book module, each useful in different situations:

- Text cells that are built into page layout templates are fixed in position; they can't be deleted, moved, or resized, but you can use the adjustable cell padding to position text anywhere on a page.

- Photo captions are associated with a single image in the layout; a photo caption can be positioned above or below an image, or overlaid on the photo, and can be moved vertically on the page.

- Page captions span the full width of the page and are not attached to any particular image, but to the page as a whole. Page captions let you place custom text anywhere on a page; you can move them vertically, and then use the cell padding for horizontal positioning.

Depending on the layout template, a single book page might include more than one fixed text cell, a page caption, and a separate photo caption for each image.

Fixed text cells and photo captions can be configured for custom text, or set to display captions or titles extracted automatically from your photos' metadata. The Book module incorporates state-of-the-art text tools that give you total control over every aspect of the text styling. Type attributes can be adjusted using sliders or numerical input, or tweaked visually with the Text Adjustment Tool.

Working with text cells

Text cells incorporated in a page layout template are fixed in place; you can't delete them, resize them, or move them on the page. Instead, you can use the adjustable cell padding—the space surrounding text within its cell—to position text in your page layout exactly as you want it.

▶ **Tip:** To select a page or a spread, rather than the text and image cells in the layout, click near the edge of the thumb-nail, or just below it.

1 Click the Multi-Page View button (▦) in the Toolbar to see your entire book layout; then, double-click the cover spread to zoom in on the layout. Select the text cell on the front cover.

2 Expand the Type panel. Make sure that the Text Style Preset is set to Custom, to accommodate manually entered text, rather than metadata from the image.

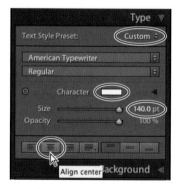

3 Choose a font and type style from the menus below the preset setting. We chose American Typewriter, Regular. Click the Character color swatch to open the color picker; click the white swatch at the left of the row at the top of the picker; then, click away from the color picker to dismiss it. Set the type size to 70 pt, and leave the opacity set to 100%. Click the Align Center button at the lower left of the Type panel.

4 Type the words **in the**; then, press Enter / Return and type **detail**. Swipe to select the word detail, and then type in the Size text box to increase the size of the selected text to **140** pt.

5 Keeping the text selected, click the black triangle to the right of the Character color swatch to see the type attribute controls. Reduce the Leading—the spacing between the selected text and the line above it—to **100** pt.

▶ **Tip:** Once you've changed the Leading value, the Auto Leading button becomes available below the text adjustment controls, making it easy for you to quickly reinstate the default setting. The Auto Kerning button works the same way.

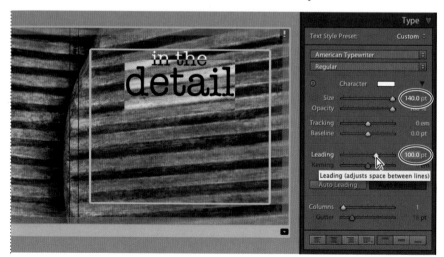

6 Click inside the text cell, but away from the text, to keep the cell selected while deselecting the text; then, expand the Cell panel. Disable the Link All option, and then increase the Top padding to **320** pt.

Fine-tuning type

In The Type panel, Lightroom incorporates a suite of sophisticated yet easy-to-use type tools that allow you detailed control over the text styling. You can use the adjustment sliders and numerical input to set type attributes in the Type panel, or tweak your text visually in any view using the intuitive Text Adjustment Tool.

1 Expand the Type panel and examine the four controls below the Size and Opacity sliders: Be sure to undo any changes you make at this stage.

- **Tracking** adjusts the letter spacing throughout a text selection. You can use tracking to change the overall appearance and readability of your text, making it look either more open or more dense.

- **Baseline** adjusts the vertical position of selected text relative to the baseline—the imaginary line on which the text sits.

- **Leading** adjusts the space between selected text and the line above it.

- **Kerning** adjusts the letter spacing between specific pairs of letters. Some pairings produce optical effects that cause letter spacing to appear uneven; place the text insertion cursor between two letters to adjust the kerning.

2 Swipe across all of the text in the front cover text cell to select it, and then click to activate the Text Adjustment Tool, to the left of the Character color setting in the Type panel.

3 Drag horizontally across the selection to adjust the text size. The adjustment is applied relatively; the different sizes of text are changed by relative amounts. Choose Edit > Undo or press Ctrl+Z / Command+Z to undo the change.

4 Drag vertically over the selection to adjust the leading; then, choose Edit > Undo or press Ctrl+Z / Command+Z to reverse the change.

5 Hold down the Alt / Option key—to temporarily disable the Text Adjustment Tool—and drag to select the words **in the**, leaving the word **detail** deselected; then, release the Alt / Option key and hold down the Ctrl / Command key as you drag horizontally over the selected text to increase the tracking slightly. Watch the Tracking control in the Type panel as you drag to set a value of **5** em.

6 Hold down the Alt / Option key and drag to select the word **the**, leaving the rest of the text deselected. Release the Alt / Option key, and then hold down the Ctrl / Command key and drag vertically over the selected text to shift it in relation to its baseline. Undo the change and click away from the text to deselect it.

7 If necessary, press F7, or choose Window > Panels > Show Left Module Panels. In the zoom ratio picker in the header of the Preview panel, click 1:1. Drag the white rectangle in the preview to focus on the front cover text. Make sure that the Text Adjustment Tool is still active; then, click once to position the text insertion cursor to the left of the word **in**. Drag to the right over the insertion point. Watch the Type panel as you drag to set a value of **135** em.

At this large point size, the first three letters of the word **detail** appear to be more loosely spaced than the last four.

8 Click once to place the insertion point between the letters **e** and **t**, and then drag to the left over the insertion point to set the Kerning value to -**30**. Set the Kerning value to -**40** for the **d-e** pair.

9 Click the Text Adjustment Tool in the Type panel to disable it; then, click the Multi-Page View button (▦) in the Toolbar to see your entire book layout. Double-click page 1 to zoom to the Single Page view.

Working with captions

Text cells incorporated in a page layout template are fixed in place; you can't delete them, resize them, or move them on the page. Instead, you can use the adjustable cell padding—the space surrounding text within its cell—to position text in your page layout exactly as you want it.

1 Click the black triangle to the right of the Character color swatch in the Type panel to hide the text adjustment controls; then, right-click / Control-click the header of the panel and disable Solo Mode. Expand the Caption and Cell panels. In the Caption panel, activate the Page Caption option.

2 In the Caption panel, activate the Page Caption option. Drag the Offset slider to set a value of **110** pt. If your page caption appeared towards the bottom of the page, click the Top button below the Offset slider.

3 With the page caption selected in the Single Page view, set up the Type panel just as you did for steps 2 and 3 of the exercise "Working with text cells" on page 236, other than the text size. Set the size to **40** pt.

4 Type whatever you like in the page caption, using the Enter/Return key to break the lines so that the text is shaped to fit the photo, as in the illustration below.

● **Note:** Unlike fixed template text cells and photo captions, page captions can't be set to display information drawn from a photo's metadata; they can only be used for custom text.

5 Click the Multi-Page View button (▦) in the Toolbar.

Creating a custom text preset

You can save your text settings as a custom text preset, so you can add text in the same style elsewhere in your book, or re-use the same style in a different project.

1 In the Type panel, expand the text adjustment controls and examine the current combination of settings.

2 At the top of the Type panel, click Custom: the current Text Style Preset setting. Choose Save Current Settings As New Preset. Type **Details caption 40 pt** as the name for the new preset and click Create.

Your custom text style preset is added to the Text Style Preset menu.

Re-using custom book page layouts

You can save time and effort by copying a customized page layout—or even a full spread—and then pasting it to a page or spread elsewhere in your book. You can use a copied layout as is, or as a starting point for a new design.

1   In any of the three Book Editor views, select the page or spread you wish to copy. Take care to select the page (or pages) and not the component text or image cells. Right-click / Control-click the yellow selection border and choose Copy Layout from the context menu.

2   Select the destination page or spread; then right-click / Control-click the yellow selection border and choose Paste Layout from the context menu.

Creating a saved book

Since you entered the Book module, you've been working with an *unsaved book*, as is indicated in the bar across the top of the Book Editor work area.

| Unsaved Book | Clear Book | Create Saved Book |

Until you save your book layout, the Book module works like a scratch pad. You can move to another module, or even close Lightroom, and find your settings unchanged when you return, but if you need to clear the layout to begin another project, all your work will be lost.

Converting your project to a Saved Book not only preserves your work, but also links your book layout to the particular set of images for which it was designed.

Your photo book is saved as a special kind of collection—an *output collection*—with its own listing in the Collections panel. Clicking this listing will instantly retrieve the images you were working with, and reinstate all of your settings, no matter how many times the book layout scratch pad has been cleared.

1   Click the Create Saved Book button in the bar at the top of the preview pane, or click the New Collection button (⊕) in the header of the Collections panel and choose Create Book.

2   In the Create Book dialog box, type **Details Book** as the name for your saved layout. In the Placement options, activate Inside and choose the collection Details from the menu; then, click Create.

Your saved book appears in the Collections panel, marked with a Saved Book icon (), and nested inside the original source collection, Details. The image count shows that the new output collection includes only ten of the nineteen photos in the source collection. The bar above the work area shows the name of the saved book.

Tip: Adding more images to your saved photo book is easy: simply drag photos to the book's listing in the Collections panel. To jump directly from the Library to your layout in the Book module, move the pointer over your saved book in the Collections panel and click the white arrow that appears to the right of the image count.

Depending on the way you like to work, you can save your book layout at any point in the process; you could create a Saved Book as soon as you enter the Book module with a selection of images or wait until your layout is polished. Once you've saved your book project, any changes you make to the design are auto-saved as you work.

Copying a saved book

Your saved photo book design represents a lot of effort; if you want to go ahead and try something different, or add pages and photos without a clear idea of what you'd like to achieve, you can duplicate your output collection and make changes to the copy without the risk of losing your work thus far.

1 Right-click / Control-click your saved book in the Collections panel and choose Duplicate Book from the context menu.

If you're happy with your extended design, you can delete the original saved book, and then rename the duplicate.

2 Right-click / Control-click the original saved book in the Collections panel and choose Delete from the context menu.

3 Right-click / Control-click the duplicated book in the Collections panel and choose Rename from the context menu. In the Rename Book dialog box, delete the word Copy from the end of the book's name, and then click Rename.

Exporting a photo book

You can upload your book to Blurb.com, or export it to PDF and print it at home.

1 To publish your photo book to Blurb.com, click the Send Book To Blurb button below the right panel group.

2 In the Purchase Book dialog box, either sign in to Blurb.com with your email address and password, or click "Not A Member?" in the lower left corner and register to get started.

3 Enter a book title, subtitle, and author name. You'll see an alert at this stage warning that your book must contain at least twenty pages; the Upload button is disabled. Click Cancel, or sign out of Blurb.com first, and then cancel.

Books published to Blurb must have between 20 and 240 pages, not including the front and back covers. Blurb.com prints at 300 dpi; if a photo's resolution is less than 300 dpi, an exclamation point badge (!) appears in the upper-right corner of the image cell in the work area. Click the exclamation point to find out what print resolution can be achieved for that photo. Blurb.com recommends a minimum of 200 dpi for optimum quality.

For help with printing, pricing, ordering, and other Blurb.com issues, visit the-Blurb.com Customer Support page.

4   To export your photo book as a PDF file, first choose PDF from the Book menu at the top of the Book Settings panel. Examine the controls that appear in the lower half of the Book Settings panel. You can leave the JPEG Quality, Color Profile, File Resolution, Sharpening, and Media Type settings unchanged for now. Click the Export Book To PDF button below the right panel group

5   In the Save dialog box, type InTheDetail as the name for the exported book. Navigate to your LR4CIB > Lessons > Lesson 7 folder, and then click Save.

6   To export your Blurb photo book as a PDF file for proofing purposes, without changing the book settings, click the Export Book To PDF button below the left panel group.

Well done! You've successfully completed another Lightroom lesson. In this lesson you learned how to put together an attractive photo book to showcase your images.

In the process, you've explored the Book module and used the control panels to customize page templates, refine the layout, set a backdrop, and add text.

In the next chapter you'll find out how to present your work in a dynamic slide-show, but before you move on, take a few moments to reinforce what you've learned by reading through the review questions and answers on the next page.

Review questions

1 How do you modify a photo book page layout?

2 What is cell padding and how is it used?

3 What text attributes are affected by the Tracking, Baseline, Leading, and Kerning controls in the Type panel?

4 How can you use the Text Adjustment Tool to fine-tune text?

Review answers

1 Click the Change Page Layout button () to the right of the layout preview thumbnail in the Page panel, or in the lower right corner of a selected page or spread displayed in the work area. Choose a layout category, and then click a layout thumbnail to apply that template. Use cell padding to tweak the layout.

2 Cell padding is the adjustable space around an image or text within its cell; it can be used to position text or a photo anywhere on the page. In combination with the Zoom slider, photo cell padding can be used to crop an image any way you wish.

3 Tracking adjusts the letter spacing throughout a text selection. You can use tracking to change the overall appearance and readability of your text, making it look either more open or more dense. The Baseline setting shifts selected text vertically in relation to the baseline. The Leading control affects the space between selected text and the line above it. Kerning adjusts the letter spacing between specific pairs of letters.

4 Drag horizontally across selected text to adjust the text size. Drag vertically over the selection to increase or decrease the leading (line spacing). Hold down the Ctrl / Command key as you drag horizontally over selected text to adjust the tracking. Hold down the Ctrl / Command key and drag vertically over a text selection to shift it in relation to its baseline. Hold down the Alt / Option key to temporarily disable the Text Adjustment Tool when you wish to change the text selection. Click between a pair of letters to place the text insertion cursor, and then drag horizontally across the text insertion point to adjust kerning.

8 CREATING A SLIDESHOW

Lesson overview

Once you've spent time in Lightroom getting the best out of your photos, showing them off on-screen in a slideshow is one of the easiest and most effective ways to share them with friends and family or present them to a client. Choose a template as a starting point; then customize the layout, color scheme, and timing. Add backdrops, borders, text—even music—to create a dynamic, stylish presentation that will complement your work and captivate your audience.

In this lesson, you'll create your own slideshow by following these easy steps:

- Grouping the images for your slideshow as a collection
- Choosing a slideshow template
- Adjusting the slide layout and setting a backdrop image
- Adding a text overlay
- Adding music and adjusting the playback settings
- Previewing and playing your slideshow
- Saving your slideshow and your customized template
- Exporting your presentation
- Viewing an impromptu slideshow

 You'll probably need between one and two hours to complete this lesson.

In the Slideshow module you can quickly put together an impressive on-screen presentation complete with stylish graphic effects, transitions, text overlays, and even music. Lightroom 3 makes it easier than ever to share your images with family and friends, clients, or the world at large by giving you the option of exporting your slideshow as a video.

Getting started

This lesson assumes that you are already familiar with the Lightroom workspace and with moving between the different modules. If you find that you need more background information as you go, refer to Lightroom Help, or review the previous lessons in this book.

Before you start on the exercises in this section, make sure that you have correctly copied the Lessons folder from the CD in the back of this book onto your computer's hard disk as detailed in "Copying the Classroom in a Book files" on page 2, and created the LR4CIB Library Catalog file to manage the lesson files as described in "Creating a catalog file for working with this book" on page 3.

1 Start Lightroom.

2 In the Adobe Photoshop Lightroom - Select Catalog dialog box, make sure that the file LR4CIB Library Catalog.lrcat is selected under Select A Recent Catalog To Open, and then click Open.

3 Lightroom will open in the screen mode and workspace module that were active when you last quit. If necessary, switch to the Library module by clicking Library in the Module Picker at the top of the workspace.

Importing images into the library

The first step is to import the images for this lesson into the Lightroom library.

1 In the Library module, click the Import button below the left panel group.

2   If the Import dialog box appears in compact mode, click the Show More
    Options button at the lower left of the dialog box to see all the options in the
    expanded Import dialog box.

3   At the top of the Source panel, just below the Select A Source menu, activate the
    option Include Subfolders; then, navigate to and select the LR4CIB > Lessons >
    Lesson 8 folder. Ensure that all twelve images are checked for import.

4   In the import options above the thumbnail previews, select Add so that the
    imported photos will be added to your catalog without being moved or copied.
    Under File Handling at the right of the expanded Import dialog box, choose
    Minimal from the Render Previews menu and ensure that the Don't Import
    Suspected Duplicates option is activated. Under Apply During Import, choose
    None from both the Develop Settings menu and the Metadata menu and type
    Lesson 8, Egypt, Art in the Keywords text box. Make sure that your import
    is set up as shown in the illustration below, and then click Import.

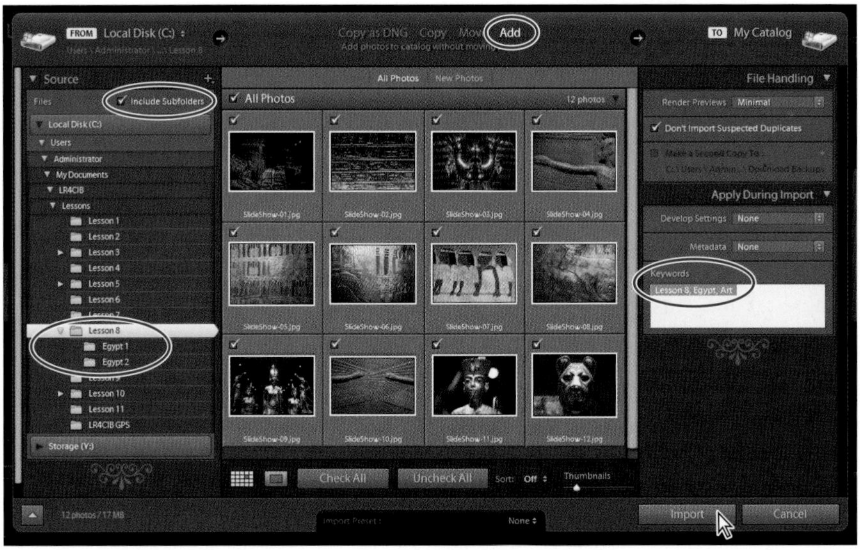

The twelve images are imported from the Egypt 1 and Egypt 2 subfolders inside the
Lesson 8 folder and now appear in the Grid view of the Library module and also
in the Filmstrip across the bottom of the Lightroom workspace.

Assembling photos for a slideshow

The first step in creating a slideshow is to assemble the images you wish to include.

Having just been imported, the images for this lesson are already isolated from the rest of your catalog. In the Catalog panel, the Previous Import folder is selected as the active image source.

▼ Catalog	
All Photographs	101
Quick Collection +	0
Previous Import	12

Although you could move to the Slideshow module now, the result would be less than ideal. The Previous Import folder is merely a temporary grouping and, as an image source, it is not flexible—you can't rearrange the images inside it, or exclude a photo from your slideshow without removing it from the catalog entirely.

1   In the Folders panel, click to select the Lesson 8 folder. If you don't see the twelve lesson images in the Grid view and the Filmstrip, activate the option Show Photos In Subfolders in the Library menu.

2   In the Grid view or the Filmstrip, drag any of the lesson images to a new position in the group. An alert message appears to let you know that you can't reorder the images in a folder that contains subfolders; click OK to dismiss it.

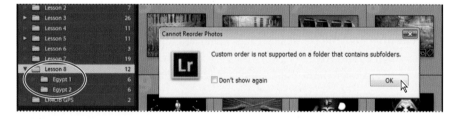

If the selected image source for your slideshow was a folder without subfolders, you *would* be able to rearrange photos in the Grid view or the Filmstrip to create a custom order for your slideshow, but you would still not be able to exclude an image without removing it from the catalog.

▶ **Tip:** You can reorder photos in a collection by simply dragging the thumbnails in the Grid view or the Filmstrip. Your custom display order will be saved with the collection.

The solution is to create a collection to group the photos for your project, where you can rearrange the image order—just as you can with a single folder—and also remove an image from the virtual grouping, without deleting it from your catalog. A collection has a permanent listing in the Collections panel, making it easy to retrieve the set of images you've assembled at any time, even if they're stored across multiple folders, as is often the case for the results of a complex search.

3   Check that the Lesson 8 folder is still selected in the Folders panel; then, press Ctrl+A / Command+A or choose Edit > Select All.

4   Click the New Collection button (➕) in the header of the Collections panel and choose Create Collection from the menu. In the Create Collection dialog box, type **Egypt** as the name for the new collection, and make sure that Top Level is selected in the Placement options. Under Collection Options, activate Include Selected Photos and disable Make New Virtual Copies; then, click Create.

Your new collection appears in the Collections panel, where it is automatically selected as the active image source. The image count indicates that the Egypt collection contains twelve photos.

5 Choose Edit > Select None; then, press Ctrl+Alt+5 / Option+Command+5, or click Slideshow in the Module Picker to switch to the Slideshow module.

Working in the Slideshow module

At center stage in the Slideshow module is the Slide Editor view where you can work on your slide layouts and preview your slideshow in operation.

In the left panel group, the Preview panel displays a thumbnail preview of the layout template that is currently selected (or under the pointer) in the Template Browser panel, while the Collections panel offers easy access to your photos.

The Toolbar below the Slide Editor view presents controls for navigating the images in your collection, previewing your slideshow, and adding text to your slides.

The settings and controls in the right panel group enable you to customize the selected template by tweaking the layout, adding borders, shadows, and overlays, changing the backdrop, adding title screens, and adjusting the playback settings.

Choosing a slideshow template

Each of the preset Lightroom slideshow templates incorporates a different combination of layout settings, such as image size, borders, backgrounds, shadows, and text overlays, and can be customized to create your own slide designs.

▶ **Tip:** The Plus sign (+) after the name of the Default template is not part of its name but denotes that this template will be used when you launch the Impromptu Slideshow from another module. To specify a different template for this purpose, right-click / Control-click the name in the Template Browser and choose Use For Impromptu Slideshow.

1 In the Template Browser panel, expand the Lightroom Templates folder, if necessary; then, move the pointer over the list of Lightroom templates. The Preview panel shows you how the selected image looks in each template layout. Select a different image in the Filmstrip, and then preview the templates again.

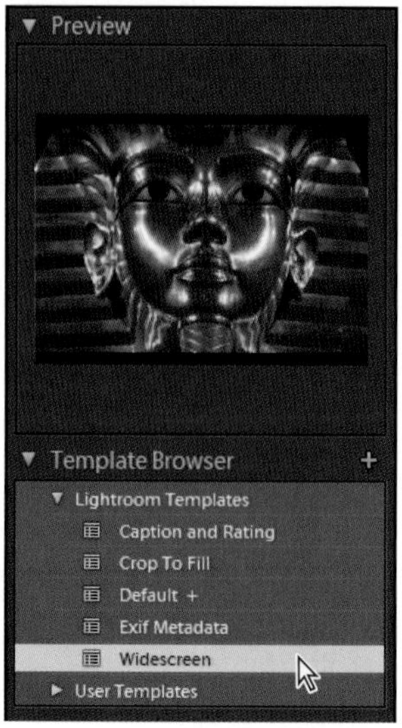

2 When you're done previewing the options in the Template Browser, click to select the Widescreen template.

3 In the Filmstrip, select the first image, Slideshow-01.jpg. From the Use menu in the Toolbar, choose All Filmstrip Photos.

4 Click the Preview button at the bottom of the right panel group to preview your presentation in the Slide Editor view. When you're done, press the Esc key on your keyboard, or click in the Slide Editor view to stop the preview.

Template options for slideshows

As a convenient starting-point for creating your own slide layouts, you can choose from these customizable Lightroom templates:

Caption And Rating   This template centers the images on a grey background and displays the star rating and caption metadata for each photo.

Crop To Fill   Your photos fill the screen and may be cropped to fit the screen's aspect ratio, so this is probably not a good option for images in portrait format.

Default   This template centers your photographs on a black background and incorporates your custom identity plate.

EXIF Metadata   The slides are centered on a black background and include star-ratings, EXIF (Exchangeable Image Format) information, and your identity plate.

Widescreen   Your images are centered and sized to fit the screen without being cropped: any empty space outside the image is filled with black.

Customizing your slideshow template

For the purposes of this lesson, you won't be adding an identity plate or metadata information to your slides, so the Widescreen template will serve as a good basis. You'll customize the template by tweaking the layout, creating a background, and overlaying text, and then liven up the show by adding a soundtrack.

Adjusting the slide layout

Once you've chosen a slide template, you can use the controls in the right panel group to customize it. For this project you'll start by modifying the layout, and then change the background to set up the overall look of the design before you make decisions about the style and color of borders and overlaid text. The Layout panel enables you to change the size and position of the photo in the slide layout by setting the margins that define the image cell.

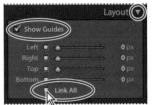

1   If the Layout panel in the right panel group is currently collapsed, expand it by clicking the triangle beside its name. Make sure that the Show Guides and Link All options are activated.

2   Move the pointer over the lower edge of the image in the Slide Editor view. When the pointer changes to a double-arrow cursor, drag the edge of the image upwards. As you drag, grey layout guide lines appear against the black background around the scaled-down image. All four guides move at the same time because the Link All option is activated in the Layout panel. As you drag upwards, watch the linked sliders and numerical values change in the Layout panel and release the mouse button when the values reach 75 px (pixels).

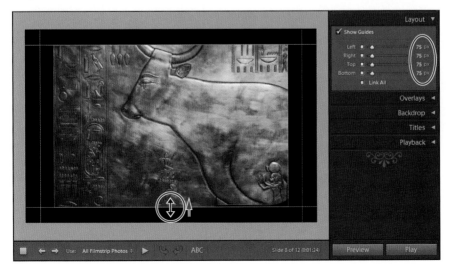

▶ **Tip:** You could also drag the sliders in the Layout panel—or click the pixel values at the right and type new numbers—to adjust the size of the image in the slide layout. In this case you would only need to drag one slider or enter one value because the settings are linked.

Now you can increase the width of the slide's top margin to create a space where you can add text later in the lesson.

3 In the Layout panel, disable the Link All option, and then either drag the Top slider to the right, type over the adjacent pixel value, or drag the top guide in the Slide Editor, to set a value of 150 px (pixels). Disable the Show Guides option, and then collapse the Layout panel.

Setting up the slide background

● **Note:** When all three of the backdrop options are disabled, the slide background is black.

▶ **Tip:** You can also drag an image from the Filmstrip directly onto the slide background in the Slide Editor view.

In the Backdrop panel you can set a flat background color for your slides, apply a graduated color wash, or place a background image—you can even mix all three elements to create an atmospheric frame for your photos.

1 In the Filmstrip, select any photo other than the second in the series.

2 If necessary, expand the Backdrop panel in the right panel group. Activate the Background Image option, and then drag the second image, Slideshow-02.jpg, from the Filmstrip into the Background Image pane. Drag the Opacity slider to the left to reduce the value to 75%, or click the Opacity value and type **75**.

The background image is still competing too much with the featured photos. You can use the Color Wash to darken the backdrop a little more and to create an angled lighting effect. The Color Wash option applies an angled graduated wash over the background. The overlaid gradient fades from whatever color is set in the Color Wash swatch to the background color or, as in our example, to the background image that you set for the slide.

3 Activate the Color Wash option. Click the Color Wash swatch, and then click the black swatch in the row at the upper right of the Color Picker.

4 Click the Close button at the upper left of the Color Picker, and then use the Opacity slider to set the color wash opacity to **75%**. Set the Angle of the wash to **135°**. When you're done, collapse the Backdrop panel.

With the background photo set to partial transparency, your backdrop design is now a composite of all three optional elements: a graduated color wash, an image, and the default background color.

▶ **Tip:** A sophisticated backdrop design that includes a related background image can be a stylish and effective way to create an overall theme or atmosphere for your slideshow.

Adjusting stroke borders and shadows

Now that you've established the overall layout and feel for your slides, you can "lift" the images to make them stand out more against the background by adding a thin stroke border and a drop shadow. We'll stay within our established color scheme, so that the design doesn't become too busy.

1 In the right panel group, expand the Options panel. Activate the Stroke Border option, and then click the color swatch beside it to open the Color Picker.

2 To set a dull gold color for the stroke border, click to select the R, G, and B percentages at the lower right of the Color Picker in turn and type values of **55**, **45**, and **20** respectively. Click outside the Color Picker to close it.

3 Use the Width slider to set a width of 2 pixels or type **2** in the text box.

4 Activate the Cast Shadow option in the Options panel and experiment with the controls. You can adjust the opacity of the shadow, the distance the shadow is offset from the image, the angle at which it is cast, and the Radius setting, which affects the softness of the shadow's edge. When you're done experimenting, set the controls as in the illustration at the right and collapse the Options panel.

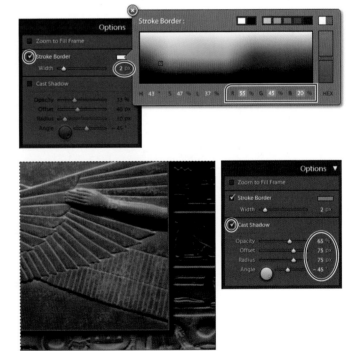

Adding a text overlay

● **Note:** For this exercise, you won't incorporate an identity plate in your slideshow. For more information on identity plates, refer to Lesson 2, Lesson 10, or the Lightroom Help topic "Add your identity plate to a slideshow."

In the Overlays panel you can add text, an identity plate, or a watermark to your slides and have Lightroom display the rating stars you've assigned to your images or the captions that you've added to their metadata. In this exercise, you'll add a simple headline that will be overlaid on the background of every slide.

1 In the Filmstrip, select the last image, Slideshow-12.jpg; this is one of the narrower photos in the series, so we'll use it as reference when placing text. Expand the Overlays panel and activate the Text Overlays option.

2 If the Toolbar is not visible just below the Slide Editor view, press the T key. In the Toolbar, click the Add Text To Slide button (ABC).

3 Type **TREASURES FROM THE TOMB** in the Custom Text box.

4 Press Enter / Return. The text appears in the lower left corner of the Slide Editor view, surrounded by a bounding box. The Text Overlays settings are updated to show the font details (Myriad Web Pro is selected in the illustration below).

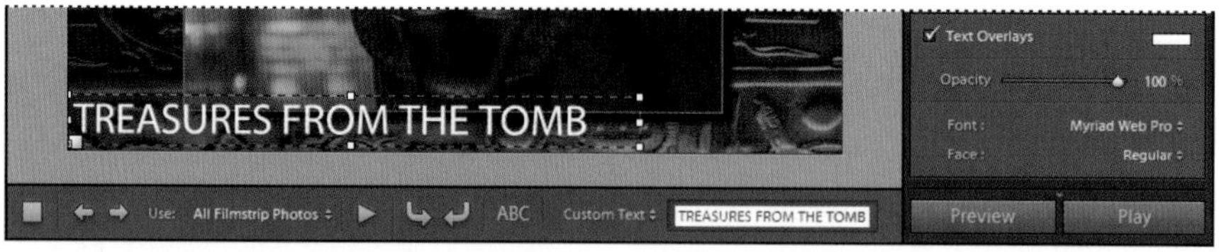

5 Click the double triangle beside the font name and choose a different font. We chose Papyrus, but Optima or even Lithos Pro would suit our design. From the Face menu, we chose Bold on Windows, and Black on Mac OS.

6 Drag the text upwards and allow it to attach itself to the anchor at the center of the upper edge of the slide. Drag the handle at the bottom of the text bounding box upwards to scale the text to the width of the photo; then, use the up and down arrow keys to center the text vertically in the space above the image.

As you drag text on a slide, Lightroom tethers the bounding box either to the nearest of various reference points around the edge of the slide, or to a point on the border of the image itself.

7 To see this in operation, drag the text around the slide, both inside and outside of the image, and watch the white tether-line jump from point to point. When you're done, return the text to its original position.

Throughout a slideshow, the tethered text will maintain the same position either relative to the slide as a whole or to the border of each image, whatever its shape.

You can use this feature to ensure that a caption, for instance, will always appear just below the left corner of each image no matter what its size or orientation, while a title that applies to the presentation as a whole—as does the text in our example—will remain in a constant position on the screen.

The color and opacity controls in the Text Overlays operate just as they do for the Color Wash and Stroke Border. On Mac OS, you can also set up a drop shadow for your text. For this exercise, we'll use the default white at 100% opacity.

8 Collapse the Overlays panel and deselect the text box in the Slideshow Editor.

9 Select the first slide in the Filmstrip and click the Preview button at the bottom of the right panel group to preview your slideshow in the Slideshow Editor view. When you're done, press Esc to stop playback.

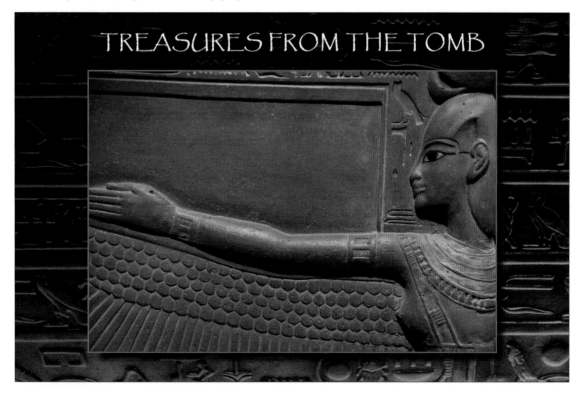

Using the Text Template Editor

In the Slideshow module, you can use the Text Template Editor to access and edit the information that is stored as metadata in your images and to specify which elements of that information you would like to display as text overlays on each slide.

You can add titles that differ from the original file names, or display captions, capture dates, image sizes, or any of numerous other options. You can save your choices as a text template preset and create presets with different sets of information for different types of presentation.

In the Slideshow module, click the Add Text To Slide button (ABC) in the Toolbar. Type anything at all in the Custom Text box and press Enter / Return. The text appears as an overlay in the Slide Editor. Make sure the text overlay is selected; then click the double triangle beside the Custom Text box in the Toolbar and choose Edit from the menu.

The Text Template Editor appears. In the Example text box, you will see a Custom Text *token*.

A token is a placeholder for whatever custom text you wish to specify. If you did not specify any other content for the token in the Text Template Editor the token would represent whatever custom text you already entered in the Toolbar.

Click the token to select it and type anything at all in the example box. Click Done and the new custom text replaces the original in the Slide Editor view.

Open the Text Template Editor again by clicking the double triangle beside the Custom Text box in the Toolbar and choosing Edit from the menu. This time you will replace the custom text with another token chosen from the options in the Text Template Editor. Select the custom text in the Example box and delete it. In the Image Name options, click the top Insert button. A Filename token appears in the Example box. Click Done and the file name appears in the Slide Editor view.

Drag the file name overlay to the upper left corner of the slide and click outside the bounding box to deselect it. Click the Add Text To Slide button (ABC) in the Toolbar; then click the double triangle beside the Custom Text box and choose Edit from the menu. The text "untitled" appears on the slide as a new text overlay. In the Text Template Editor, select the new Custom Text token in the Example box and choose Image # (01) from the upper menu in the Numbering options. Click Done and the image number (in two-digit format) replaces the text "untitled" on the slide in the Slide Editor view.

(continues on next page)

Using the Text Template Editor (continued)

In this way you can create as many text overlays as you wish and each text overlay can contain more than one token. Change the font, color and other options for your overlays using the Text Overlays controls in the Overlays panel. Resize the text by dragging the handles of the bounding box.

Explore the options in the Text Template Editor:

Preset menu   Apply, save, delete, or rename presets, which are saved sets of information tokens customized for different presentation purposes.

Image Name   Specify a text string containing the filename, folder name, or a custom name.

Numbering   Number the slideshow images and display image capture dates in various formats.

EXIF Data   Choose from Exchangeable Image Format data including image dimensions, exposure, flash settings and numerous other options.

IPTC Data   Choose from International Press Telecommunications Council data including copyright and creator details and numerous other options.

Custom   Add a custom text string.

For more details on using the Text Template Editor please refer to Lightroom Help.

Creating a Saved Slideshow

Since you entered the Slideshow module, you've been working with an *unsaved slideshow*, as is indicated in the bar across the top of the Slideshow Editor view.

Unsaved Slideshow	Create Saved Slideshow

Until you save your slideshow, the Slideshow module works like a scratch pad. You can move to another module, or even close Lightroom, and find your settings unchanged when you return, but if you click a new slideshow template—or even the one you started with—in the Template Browser, the "scratch pad" will be cleared and all your work will be lost.

Converting your project to a Saved Slideshow not only preserves your layout and playback settings, but also links your design to the particular set of images for which it was designed. Your slideshow is saved as a special kind of collection—an *output collection*—with its own listing in the Collections panel. Clicking this listing will instantly retrieve the images you were working with, and reinstate all of your settings, no matter how many times the slideshow scratch pad has been cleared.

▶ **Tip:** Once you've saved your slideshow, any changes you make to the layout or playback settings are auto-saved as you work.

1   Click the Create Saved Slideshow button in the bar at the top of the Slideshow Editor view, or click the New Collection button (➕) in the header of the Collections panel and choose Create Slideshow.

▶ Tip: The Make New Virtual Copies option is useful if you wish to apply a particular treatment, such as an antique monochrome developing preset, to all the pictures in your slideshow, without affecting the photos in the source collection.

2   In the Create Slideshow dialog box, type Egypt Slideshow as the name for your saved presentation. In the Placement options, activate Inside and choose the collection Egypt from the associated menu; then, click Create.

▶ Tip: Adding more photos to your saved slideshow is easy: simply drag images to the slideshow's listing in the Collections panel. Click the white arrow that appears to the right of the image count when you move the pointer over your saved slideshow in the Collections panel to jump from the Library to your presentation in the Slideshow module.

Your saved slideshow appears in the Collections panel, marked with a Saved Slideshow icon (▶), and nested inside the original source collection, Egypt. The image count shows that the new output collection, like the source, contains twelve photos.

The title bar above the Slide Editor now displays the name of your saved slideshow, and no longer presents the Create Saved Slideshow button.

Depending on the way you like to work, you can save your slideshow at any point in the process; you could create a Saved Slideshow as soon as you enter the Slideshow module with a selection of images or wait until your presentation is polished.

For the purposes of this lesson, saving the project at this stage enables you to go ahead and delete or rearrange slides to refine your presentation, without affecting the original source collection—any image you exclude from the slideshow now will be removed from the Egypt Slideshow output collection, but will remain a part of your Egypt collection. This could be useful if you also intended to use the photos in the Egypt collection to produce a print layout and a web gallery, for instance— your original collection will remain intact, while the output collection for each project might contain a different subset of images, arranged in a different order.

Refining your slideshow

It's a good idea to finalize the photo set for your slideshow at this point, before you go on to specify playback settings—if you remove an image later, you might need to readjust the time allocated for each slide and transition, especially if your slideshow is timed to match the duration of a sound file.

1   In the Filmstrip, right-click / Control-click the image Slideshow-02.jpg—the photo you used as a background image—and choose Remove From Collection.

Note that although the photo disappears from the Filmstrip, and will not feature on any slide in the presentation it is not removed from the slide background in the Slide Editor view. The background image has become part of the slide layout, rather than merely one of the selection photos to be displayed. Even if you "re-fill" your slideshow with a different set of photos entirely, the background image will remain in place. Your saved slideshow includes a link to the photo that is independent of the output collection or its parent collection.

In the Collections panel, the nested Egypt Slideshow output collection now shows an image count of eleven photos, while its parent collection still contains the original count of twelve.

2   In the Filmstrip, drag the photo Slideshow-07 to a new position between the images Slideshow-05 and Slideshow-06, releasing the mouse button when the black insertion bar appears.

Adjusting the playback settings

Now that you've finalized the photo set for the slideshow, you can go ahead and fine-tune your presentation by specifying the playback settings.

In the Playback panel you can add a soundtrack to your presentation, set the duration for slides and transitions, or set the slideshow to display your images in random order. Adding a soundtrack can make your slideshow much more dynamic and compelling, so let's start with that.

Adding music to your slideshow

You'll find a sound file named Iteru.m4a in your Lesson 8 folder. This piece of music will underline the middle-eastern feel of the slideshow. However, feel free to choose any other file from your music library that you'd like to audition.

1   Expand the Playback panel in the right panel group, and then activate the Soundtrack option.

2   Click the Select Music button; then, navigate to your LR4CIB > Lessons > Lesson 8 folder, select the file Iteru.m4a, and click Open / Choose.

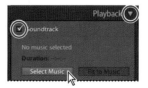

> **Tip:** If you have more than one screen attached to your computer you'll see the Playback Screen pane in the Playback panel. You can choose which screen will be used when your slideshow is played at full-screen and whether to blank the other screens during playback.

The name of the sound file and its duration are now displayed in the Soundtrack pane of the Playback panel.

3   Click the Preview button at the bottom of the right panel group to preview the slideshow in the Slideshow Editor view. The new soundtrack adds atmosphere to the slideshow. When you're done, press Esc to stop playback.

The next step is to fine-tune the timing of the slideshow by setting the duration of slides and fades to match the length of the music file.

4   In the Soundtrack pane, click the Fit To Music button, keeping an eye on the default Slides and Fades values in the Slide Duration settings towards the bottom of the Playback panel as you do so.

▶ **Tip:** The Playback Settings panel's Slide Duration pane also includes a color control for setting the color to which images will fade during slide transitions.

Lightroom adjusts the Slides and Fades values to fit the duration of the music file.

5   Drag the Fades slider to the right to increase the duration of the fade transitions by two seconds, and then click the Fit To Music button once more, keeping an eye on the Slides value in the Slide Duration settings as you do so.

Lightroom automatically re-calculates the duration for which each slide will be shown so that the slideshow still fits to the music file despite the lengthened fades.

6   At the bottom of the Playback panel, disable Random Order and Repeat.

7   Select the first photo in the Filmstrip, and then click the Play button at the bottom of the right panel group to see the slideshow in full-screen mode.

8   Play the slideshow once more; this time, press the spacebar to pause and resume playback, the Right Arrow key to advance to the next slide, the Left Arrow key to return to the previous slide, and the Esc key to end the slideshow.

Saving a customized slideshow template

Having spent so much time customizing your slideshow template, you should now save it so that it becomes available as a new choice in the Template Browser menu.

This is different from saving your slideshow, as you did earlier.

A saved slideshow is actually an output collection—an arranged grouping of images, saved together with a slide layout, text overlays, and playback settings. In contrast, a saved custom template records only your slide layout and playback settings—it is an empty container that is not linked to any particular set of images.

Saving your customized slideshow template will save you a lot of time later should you wish to put together a related presentation, or simply use the template as a starting-point for creating a new design.

Modifying and organizing user templates

The Template Browser offers numerous options for organizing your templates and template folders:

Renaming a template or template folder
You cannot rename the Lightroom Templates folder, any of the Lightroom templates, or the default User Templates folder. To rename any of the templates or template folders that you have created, right-click / Control-click the template or folder in the Template Browser and choose Rename from the context menu.

Moving a template
If you wish to move a template into another folder in the Template Browser, simply drag the template to that folder. If you wish to move a template into a new folder, right-click / Control-click the template and choose New Folder from the context menu. The selected template will be moved into the new folder as it is created. If you try to move one of the Lightroom templates, the template will be copied to the new folder but will still remain in the Lightroom Templates folder.

Updating a custom template's settings
If you wish to modify one of your own custom templates select it in the Template Browser and make your changes using any of the controls in the right panel group. To save your changes, right-click / Control-click the template in the Template Browser and choose Update with Current Settings.

Creating a copy of a template
You may wish to create a copy of a template so that you can safely make modifications without affecting the original. If you wish to create a copy of the currently selected template in an existing template folder, click the Create New Preset button (+) in the Template Browser panel header. In the New Template dialog box, type a name for the copy, choose the destination folder from the Folder menu, and click Create. If you wish to create a copy of the currently selected template in a new folder, click the Create New Preset button (+) in the Template Browser panel header. In the New Template dialog box, type a name for the copy and choose New Folder from the Folder menu. In the New Folder dialog box, type a name for the new folder and click Create. The new folder appears in the Template Browser. Click Create in the New Template dialog box to dismiss it. The copied template will be created in the new folder.

Exporting a custom template
To export your custom slideshow template so that you can use it in Lightroom on another computer, right-click / Control-click the template name in the Template Browser menu and choose Export from the context menu.

Importing a custom template
To import a custom template that has been created in Lightroom on another computer, right-click / Control-click the User Templates header or any of the templates in the User Templates menu and choose Import from the context menu. In the Import Template dialog box, locate the template file and click Import.

(continues on next page)

Modifying and organizing
user templates (continued)

Deleting a template

To delete a custom template, right-click / Control-click the template name in the Template Browser and choose Delete from the context menu. You can also select the template and click the Delete Selected Preset button in the header of the Template Browser. You cannot delete the templates in the Lightroom Templates folder.

Creating a new templates folder

To create a new empty folder in the Templates Browser, right-click / Control-click the header of any other folder and choose New Folder from the context menu. You can drag templates into the new folder.

Deleting a templates folder

To delete a template folder, you'll first need to delete all the templates within that folder—or drag them to another folder. Right-click / Control-click the empty folder, and choose Delete Folder from the context menu or simply select the empty folder and click the Remove button at the bottom of the right panel group.

By default, your customized template will be listed with the User Templates in the Template Browser panel.

1 With your slideshow still open, click the Create New Preset button (➕) in the header of the Template Browser panel, or choose Slideshow > New Template.

▶ **Tip:** When saving a customized template it's a good idea to give it a descriptive name. This will make it easier to find as you add more choices to the Template Browser menu.

2 In the New Template dialog box, type **Titled Exhibition** as the new template name. Leaving the default User Templates folder selected as the destination folder in the Folder menu, click Create.

Your new customized template is now listed under User Templates in the Template Browser panel.

Exporting a slideshow

To send your slideshow to a friend or client, play it on another computer, or share it on the Web, you can export it as a PDF file or as a high-quality video file.

1 In the Slideshow module, click the Export PDF button at the bottom of the left panel group.

2 Review the options available in the Export Slideshow To PDF dialog box, noting the settings for size and quality, and then click Cancel.

Note: PDF slide-show transitions work when viewed using the free Adobe Reader® or Adobe Acrobat®. However, slideshows exported to PDF will not include music, random-ized playback order, or your customized slide duration settings.

3 Repeat the process for the Export Video button. Review the Export Slideshow To Video dialog box, noting the range of options available in the Video Preset menu. Select each export option in turn to see a brief description below the Video Preset menu.

Lightroom exports slideshows in the mp4 movie format so that you can share your slideshow movies on popular video sharing sites or optimize them for playback on mobile media. Preset size and quality settings range from 320 x 240, optimized for personal media players and email, to 1080p, optimized for high quality HD video.

4 In the Export Slideshow To Video dialog box, type a name for your exported video and specify a destination folder. Choose an option from the Video Preset menu, and then click Export.

A progress bar in the upper left corner of the workspace shows the status of the export process.

Playing an impromptu slideshow

Even outside the Slideshow module you can play an impromptu slideshow. In the Library module, for instance, this makes a convenient way to see a full-screen preview of the photos you've just imported.

The Impromptu Slideshow can be launched from any of the Lightroom modules. The slide layout, timing, and transitions for the Impromptu Slideshow will depend on the template currently set in the Slideshow module for use with the Impromptu Slideshow.

Tip: To change the slideshow template used for the impromptu slideshow, right-click / Control-click a template in the Slideshow module Template Browser and choose Use For Impromptu Slideshow.

1 Switch to the Library module.

2 Use the Sort menu in the Grid view Toolbar to set the sorting order to either Capture Time or File Name. Choose View > Sort > Ascending, or click the Sort Direction button (🔀) beside the Sort menu, if necessary, to set an ascending sort direction (the Sort Direction button should show an "a" above a "z").

3 Press Ctrl+A / Command+A or choose Edit > Select All to select all of the images that you've just imported.

4 Choose Window > Impromptu Slideshow or press Ctrl+Enter / Command+Return to start the impromptu slideshow.

5 Press the Right Arrow key to advance to the next slide or the Left Arrow key to return to the previous slide. Use the spacebar to pause and resume playback. The slideshow will repeat, cycling through the selected images until you either press the Esc key on your keyboard or click the screen to stop playback.

Tip: In the Library and Develop modules, you can also use the Impromptu Slideshow button in the Toolbar. If you don't see the Impromptu Slideshow button in the Toolbar, choose Slideshow from the content menu at the right end of the Toolbar.

Well done! You have successfully completed another Lightroom lesson. In this lesson you learned how to create your own stylish slideshow presentation.

In the process, you've explored the Slideshow module and used the control panels to customize a slideshow template—refining the layout and playback settings and adding a backdrop, text, borders, and a soundtrack.

In the next chapter you'll find out how to present your work in printed format, but before you move on, take a few moments to reinforce what you've learned by reading through the review questions and answers on the next page.

Review questions

1 How can you change which template is used for an Impromptu Slideshow?

2 Which Lightroom slideshow template would you pick if you wished to display metadata for your images?

3 What options do you have when customizing a slideshow template?

4 What are the four Cast Shadow controls and what are their effects?

5 What is the difference between saving your customized slideshow template and saving the slideshow you've created?

Review answers

1 In the Slideshow module, right-click / Control-click the name of a slideshow template in the Template Browser and choose Use For Impromptu Slideshow.

2 The EXIF Metadata template, which centers photos on a black background and displays star ratings and EXIF information for the images, as well as an identity plate.

3 In the right panel group you can modify the slide layout, add borders and text overlays, create shadow effects for images or text, change the background color or add a backdrop image, adjust the durations of slides and fades, and add a soundtrack.

4 The four Cast Shadow controls have the following effects:

- Opacity: Controls the opacity of the shadow ranging from 0% (invisible) to 100% (fully opaque).

- Offset: Affects the distance that the shadow is offset from the slide. As the offset is increased, more shadow becomes visible.

- Radius: Controls how sharp (lower settings) or soft (higher settings) the edges of the shadow appear.

- Angle: Sets the direction of the light source, which affects the angle at which the shadow is cast.

5 A saved custom template records only your layout and playback settings—it is like an empty container that is not linked to any particular set of images, whereas a saved slideshow is actually an output collection—an arranged grouping of images, saved together with a slide layout, text overlays, and playback settings.

9 PRINTING IMAGES

Lesson overview

The Lightroom Print module offers all the tools you'll need to quickly prepare any selection of images from your library for printing.

You can print a single photo, repeat one image at different sizes on the same sheet, or create an attractive layout for multiple images. Add borders, text, and graphics, and then adjust print resolution, sharpening, paper type, and color management with just a few clicks.

In this lesson, you'll explore the Print module as you become familiar with the steps in the printing workflow:

- Choosing a print template

- Customizing the layout and output settings

- Creating a Custom Package print layout

- Adding an identity plate, borders and a background color

- Captioning photos with information from their metadata

- Saving a custom print template

- Specifying print settings and printer driver options

- Choosing appropriate color management options

- Saving a print job as an output collection

 You'll probably need between one and two hours to complete this lesson.

Whether you need to print a contact sheet or a fine art mat, Lightroom makes it easy to achieve professional results with a choice of highly customizable layout templates.

Getting started

This lesson assumes that you are already familiar with the Lightroom workspace and with moving between the different modules. If you find that you need more background information, refer to Lightroom Help, or review the previous lessons.

Before you begin, make sure that you have correctly copied the Lessons folder from the CD in the back of this book onto your computer's hard disk as detailed in "Copying the Classroom in a Book files" on page 2, and created the LR4CIB Library Catalog file to manage the lesson files as described in "Creating a catalog file for working with this book" on page 3.

1 Start Lightroom.

2 In the Adobe Photoshop Lightroom - Select Catalog dialog box, make sure the file LR4CIB Library Catalog.lrcat is selected under Select A Recent Catalog To Open, and then click Open.

▶ Tip: The first time you enter any of the Lightroom modules, you'll see module tips that will help you get started by identifying the components of the Lightroom workspace and stepping you through the workflow. Dismiss the tips by clicking the Close button. To reactivate the tips for any module, choose [*Module name*] Tips from the Help menu.

3 Lightroom will open in the screen mode and workspace module that were active when you last quit. If necessary, switch to the Library module by clicking Library in the Module Picker at the top of the workspace.

Importing images into the library

The first step is to import the images for this lesson into the Lightroom library.

1 In the Library module, click the Import button below the left panel group.

2 If the Import dialog box appears in compact mode, click the Show More Options button at the lower left to expand it.

3 Under Source at the left of the Import dialog box, navigate to and select the Lesson 9 folder (inside the LR4CIB > Lessons folder). Make sure that all six images in the Lesson 9 folder are checked for import.

4 In the import options picker above the thumbnail previews, select Add so that the imported photos will be added to your catalog without being moved or copied. Under File Handling at the right of the Import dialog box, choose Minimal from the Render Previews menu and ensure that the Don't Import Suspected Duplicates option is activated. Under Apply During Import, choose None from both the Develop Settings menu and the Metadata menu, and type **Lesson 9, Portraits** in the Keywords text box. Make sure that your import is set up as shown in the illustration below, and then click Import.

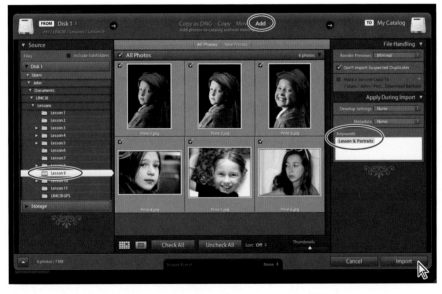

The six images from the Lesson 9 folder appear in both the Library module Grid view and the Filmstrip across the bottom of the Lightroom workspace.

5 You won't be able to rearrange the images for your print job as long as Previous Import is selected as the image source in the Catalog panel. In the Folders panel, click the Lesson 9 folder to change the image source. In the Toolbar, set the Sort order to File Name; then, click Print in the Module Picker at the top of the workspace to switch to the Print Module.

Library | Develop | Map | Book | Slideshow | Print | Web

About the Lightroom Print module

In the Print module you'll find tools and controls for each step in the printing workflow. Change the order of your photos, choose a print template and refine the layout, add borders, text, and graphics, and then adjust the output settings; everything you need to produce professional-looking prints is at your fingertips.

The left panel group contains the Preview, Template Browser, and Collections panels. Move the pointer over the list in the Template Browser to see a thumbnail preview of each layout template displayed in the Preview panel. When you choose a new template from the list, the Print Editor view—at center-stage in the workspace—is updated to show how the selected photos look in the new layout.

You can quickly select and rearrange the photos for your print job in the Filmstrip, where the source menu provides easy access to the images in your library, listing your favorites and recently used source folders and collections.

You'll use the controls in the right panel group to customize your layout template and to specify output settings.

The Template Browser contains templates of three distinct types: Single Image / Contact Sheet layouts, Picture Package layouts, and Custom Package layouts.

Four of the first fifteen preset Lightroom templates in the menu are Picture Package layouts, which repeat a single image at a variety of sizes on the same page. The other eleven are Single Image / Contact Sheet layouts, which can be used to print multiple photos at the same size on a single sheet. Single Image / Contact Sheet layouts are based on an adjustable grid of image cells. They range from contact sheets with many cells to single-cell layouts such as the Fine Art Mat and Maximize Size templates. The Custom layout templates further down the menu enable you to print multiple images at any size on the same page. All of the templates can be customized; you can save your modified layouts as user-defined templates, which will be listed in the Template Browser.

Once you've chosen a layout from the Template Browser, the Layout Style panel at the top of the right panel group indicates which type of template you're working with. The suite of panels you see below the Layout Style panel will vary slightly, depending on which type of template you have chosen.

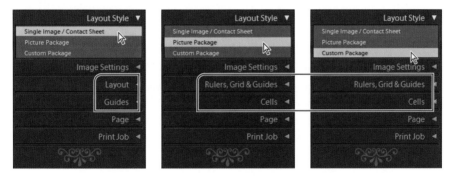

The controls in the Image Settings panel enable you to add photo borders and to specify the way your pictures are fitted to their image cells.

For a Single Image / Contact Sheet template, you can use the Layout panel to adjust margins, cell size and spacing, and to change the number of rows and columns that make up the grid. For a Picture Package or Custom package template, you'll modify your layout with the Rulers, Grid & Guides panel and the Cells panel. Use the Guides panel to show or hide a selection of layout guides. The Page panel has controls for watermarking your images and adding text, graphics, or a background color to your print layout. In the Print Job panel you can set the print resolution, print sharpening, paper type, and color management options.

About layout styles and print templates

The Template Browser offers a wide choice of preset Lightroom print templates that differ not only in basic layout but may also include a variety of design features such as borders and overlaid text or graphics.

Templates may also differ in their output settings: the print resolution setting for a contact sheet will be lower than the resolution set for a template designed for producing finished prints.

You can save time and effort setting up your print job by selecting the print template that most closely suits your purpose. In this exercise you'll be introduced to the different types of templates and use the panels in the right panel group to examine the characteristics of each layout.

1   In the left panel group, make sure that the Preview and Template Browser panels are expanded. If necessary, drag the top border of the Filmstrip down so that you can see as many of the templates in the Template Browser as possible. In the right panel group, expand the Layout Style panel and collapse the others.

2   Choose Edit > Select None, and then select just one of the images in the Filmstrip. The Print Editor view at the center of the workspace is updated to display the selected photo in the current layout.

3   If necessary, expand the Lightroom Templates folder inside the Template Browser panel. Move the pointer slowly over the list of preset templates to see a preview of each layout in the Preview panel.

4   Click the second template in the Template Browser: "(1) 4 × 6, (6) 2 × 3." The new template is applied to the image in the Print Editor view. Scroll up in the right panel group, if necessary, and inspect the Layout Style panel. You'll see that the Layout Style panel indicates that this template is a Picture Package layout. In the Template Browser, click the sixth Lightroom template "(2) 7 × 5." The Layout Style panel indicates that this is also a Picture Package layout.

5   Now choose the ninth preset template in the Template Browser: "2-Up Greeting Card." The Layout Style panel indicates that the template "2-Up Greeting Card" is a Single Image / Contact Sheet layout, and the Print Editor view at the center of the workspace displays the new template.

6   In the Layout Style panel, click Picture Package. The Print Editor is updated to display the last selected Picture Package layout: "(2) 7 × 5." Click Single Image / Contact Sheet in the Layout Style panel and the Print Editor view returns to the last selected Single Image / Contact Sheet layout: "2-Up Greeting Card."

You'll notice that different control panels become available in the right panel group as you move between the Single Image / Contact Sheet and Picture Package layout styles. Panels common to both layout styles may differ in content.

7 In the right panel group, expand the Image Settings panel. In the Layout Style panel, click Picture Package and expand the Image Settings panel again. Toggle between the Picture Package and Single Image / Contact Sheet layouts and notice how the options available in the Image Settings panel change.

You can see that the selected photo fits to the image cell differently for each of these templates. In the Picture Package layout "(2) 7 × 5," the Zoom To Fill option is activated in the Image Settings panel so that the photo is zoomed and cropped to fill the image cell. In the Single Image / Contact Sheet "2-Up Greeting Card," the Zoom to Fill option is disabled and the photo is not cropped. Take a moment to examine the other differences in the Image Settings panel.

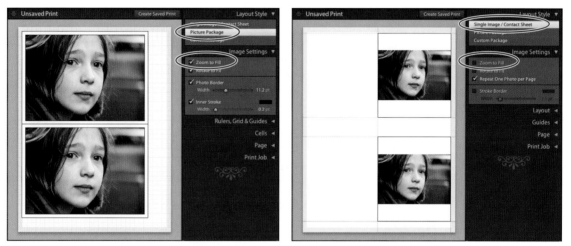

(2) 7 × 5 template   2-Up Greeting Card template

8 Select the Single Image / Contact Sheet layout style. Look at the page count at the right of the Toolbar below the Print Editor view: it reads "Page 1 of 1." Press Ctrl+A / Command+A or choose Edit > Select All to select all six images in the Filmstrip. The page count in the Toolbar now reads "Page x of 6." The template "2-Up Greeting Card" is now applied to all six photos, resulting in a print job of six pages. Use the navigation buttons at the left the Toolbar to move between the pages and see the layout applied to each image in turn.

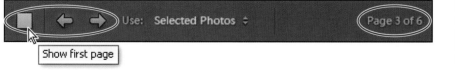

> **Tip:** You can also navigate your multi-page print document by using the Home, End, Page Up, Page Down, and left and right arrow keys on your keyboard, or choosing from the navigation commands in the Print menu.

9 For the last step in this exercise, collapse the Image Settings panel and expand the Print Job panel. You'll notice that in the Print Job panel, the Print Resolution for the "2-Up Greeting Card" template is set to 240 ppi. Select the template "4×5 Contact Sheet" in the Template Browser. The Print Resolution option in the Print Job panel is disabled and the Draft Mode Printing option is activated.

Selecting a print template

Now that you've explored the Template Browser, it's time to choose the template that you'll customize in the next exercise.

1 In the Template Browser, click the template "4 Wide." Later in this lesson you'll customize your identity plate, but for now, uncheck the Identity Plate option in the Page panel to hide the default design.

2 Choose Edit > Select None. In the Filmstrip, select the images Print-4.jpg, Print-5.jpg, and Print-6.jpg. The images will be arranged in the template in the same order in which they appear in the Filmstrip. Drag the images inside their grid cells to reposition them as shown in the illustration below.

▶ **Tip:** By default, each photo will be centered in its own image cell. To expose a different portion of an image that is cropped by the boundaries of its cell, simply drag the photo to reposition it within its image cell.

▶ **Tip:** Lightroom automatically scales your photos in the print layout template to fit the paper size you have specified. In the Print Setup / Page Setup dialog box, leave the scale setting at the default 100% and let Lightroom fit the template to the page—that way, what you see in the Print Editor view will be what you'll get from your printer.

Specifying the printer and paper size

Before you customize the template, you'll need to specify the paper size and page orientation for your print job. Doing this now may save you the time and effort of readjusting the layout later.

1 Choose File > Page Setup.

2 In the Print Setup / Page Setup dialog box, choose the desired printer from the Name / Format For menu. From the Paper Size menu, choose Letter (Windows) / US Letter > US Letter (Mac OS). Under Orientation, choose portrait format (vertical), and then click OK.

Customizing print templates

Having established the overall layout of your print job, you can use the controls in the Layout panel to fine-tune the template so that the images fit better to the page.

Changing the number of cells

For the purposes of this exercise, we need only three of the four preset image cells.

1   If necessary, expand the Layout panel in the right panel group. Under Page Grid, drag the Rows slider to the left or type **3** in the text box to the right of the slider.

2   Experiment with the Margins, Cell Spacing, and Cell Size sliders—making sure to undo (Ctrl+Z / Command+Z) after each change. Activate the Keep Square option below the Cell Size sliders. The Cell Width and Cell Height sliders are locked together at the same value. Disable the Keep Square option.

3   The black lines you might see around the photos are merely guides indicating the image cell boundaries; they will not appear on your printed page. These guides are helpful while you're adjusting the cell size and spacing but they'll be distracting when you add printable borders to your layout in the next exercise.

If necessary, expand the Guides panel below the Layout panel and disable the Image Cells option; then collapse the Layout and Guides panels.

Modifying the page layout of a print template

Layout controls for Single Image / Contact Sheet and Picture Package templates

Depending on which type of print template you are working with, you'll find a slightly different suite of panels in the right panel group. The Image Settings, Page, and Print Job panels are available for all template types but the controls for modifying the page layout differ. If you've chosen a Single Image / Contact Sheet template, you'll customize your layout using the Layout and Guides panels. For a Picture Package template, you'll use the Rulers, Grids & Guides panel and the Cells panel. For Custom Package layouts you'll also use the Rulers, Grids & Guides panel and the Cells panel—where you'll find a few minor differences from the options offered in the same panels for a Picture Package.

Picture Package templates and Custom Package layouts and are not grid-based so they are very flexible to work with; you can arrange the image cells on the page either by simply dragging them in the Print Editor view or by using the controls in the Cells panel. You can resize a cell using the width and height sliders or simply drag the handles of its bounding box. Add more photos to your layout with the Cells panel controls or Alt-drag / Option-drag a cell to duplicate it and resize it as you wish.

Lightroom provides a variety of guides to help you adjust your layout. Guides are not printed: they appear only in the Print Editor view. To show or hide the guides, activate Show Guides in the Guides panel, or choose View > Show Guides (Ctrl+Shift+H / Command+Shift+H). In the Guides panel you can specify which types of guides will be displayed in the Print Editor view.

Note: The Margins and Gutters guides and Image Cells guides—available only for Single Image / Contact Sheet layouts—are interactive; you can adjust your layout directly by dragging the guides themselves in the Print Editor view. When you move these guides, the Margins, Cell Spacing and Cell Size sliders in the Layout panel will move with them.

Using the Layout panel to modify a Contact Sheet / Grid layout

Ruler Units sets the units of measurement for most of the other controls in the Layouts panel and for the Rulers guide in the Guides panel. Click the Ruler Units setting and choose Inches, Centimeters, Millimeters, Points or Picas from the menu. The default setting is Inches.

Margins sets the boundaries for the grid of image cells in your layout. Most printers don't support borderless printing, so the minimum value for the margins is dependent on the capabilities of your printer. Even if your printer does support borderless printing, you may first need to activate this feature in the printer settings before you can set the margins to zero.

Page Grid specifies the number of rows and columns of image cells in the layout. The grid can contain anything from one image cell (Rows: 1, Columns: 1) to 225 image cells (Rows: 15, Columns: 15).

Cell Spacing and Cell Size settings are linked so that changes you make to one will affect the other. The Cell Spacing sliders set the vertical and horizontal spaces between the image cells in the grid; the Cell Size controls change the height and width of the cells. The Keep Square option links the height and width settings so that the image cells remain square.

Modifying the page layout of a print template (continued)

Using the Guides panel to modify a Contact Sheet / Grid layout

Rulers are displayed across the top and at the left of the Print Editor view. If Show Guides is activated, you can also show the rulers by choosing View > Show Rulers (Ctrl+R / Command+R). To change the ruler units, click the setting in the Layout panel.

Page Bleed shades the non-printable edges of the page, as defined by your printer settings.

Margins and Gutters guides reflect the Margins settings in the Layout panel; in fact, dragging these guides in the Print Editor view will move the respective sliders in the Layout panel.

Image Cells shows a black border around each image cell. When the Margins and Gutters guides are not visible, dragging the Image Cells guides in the Print Editor view will change the Margins, Cell Spacing, and Cell Size settings in the Layout panel.

Dimensions displays the measurements of each image cell in its top left corner, expressed in whatever units of measurement you have chosen for the Ruler Units.

Using the Rulers, Grids & Guides panel to modify a Picture Package layout

Rulers shows the rulers and lets you set the units of measurement just as you would in the Layout panel when you're working with a Contact Sheet / Grid template.

Grid displays a grid guide behind the image cells in the Print Editor view. As you drag the cells, you can have them snap to each other or to the grid (or turn the snap behavior off) by choosing Cells, Grid, or Off from the Snap menu options. The grid divisions are affected by your choice of ruler units.

Note: The snap behavior helps you to position the image cells accurately on the page. If you accidentally overlap your photos, Lightroom will let you know by showing a triangular yellow warning icon (!) in the top right corner of the page.

Bleeds and **Dimensions** are the Picture Package equivalents of the Page Bleed and Dimensions guides.

Using the Cells panel to modify a Picture Package layout

Add To Package offers six preset image cell sizes that can be placed in your layout at the click of a button. You can change which of the presets is assigned to each button by clicking its menu triangle. The default presets are standard photo sizes but you can edit them if you wish.

New Page adds a page to your layout, though Lightroom automatically adds pages if you use the Add to Package buttons to add more photos than fit on a page. To delete a page from your layout, click the red X in its upper left corner of the page in the Print Editor view.

Auto Layout optimizes the arrangement of the photos on the page for the fewest cuts.

Clear Layout removes all the image cells from the layout.

Adjust Selected Cell lets you change the height and width of an image cell using sliders or numerical input.

Rearranging the photos in a print layout

Lightroom places your photos in the cells of a multiple-image print layout in the order in which they appear in the Filmstrip (and the Library module Grid view).

If your image source is a Collection, or a folder without subfolders nested inside it, you can change the placement of your images in the print job by simply dragging their thumbnails to new positions in the Filmstrip. Rearranging photos in this way is not possible if either the All Photographs folder or Previous Import folder is the selected image source.

1   In the header bar of the Filmstrip, the Lesson 9 folder is listed as the source of the images displayed. Click the white triangle to the right of the image source information in the header bar of the Filmstrip to see the options available in the source menu.

If you enter the Print module with the Previous Import folder selected as the image source, making it impossible to reorder the photos for your print job, you can choose from recently opened folders and collections in the Filmstrip source menu.

2   Choose Edit > Select None, or press Ctrl+D / Command+D on your keyboard; then, drag the thumbnails in the Filmstrip to reverse the order of the last three photos, Print-4, Print-5, and Print-6.

3   Ctrl-click / Command-click to group-select the three reordered photos in the Filmstrip.

The three photos are rearranged in your modified layout template to reflect the new sorting order in the Filmstrip.

For a Picture Package layout, which repeats a single photo at various sizes on the same page, a new page is added to the print job for each selected photo; reordering the photos in the Filmstrip will affect only the page order.

Creating stroke and photo borders

For our Single Image / Contact Sheet layout, the Image Settings panel offers options that affect the way your photos are placed in the image cells, and a control for adding borders. In this exercise you'll add a stroke border around each of the three images and adjust the width of the stroke.

1 Expand the Image Settings panel. For the 4 Wide template, the Zoom To Fill option is activated. This means that our photos are cropped in height to fit the proportions of the image cells.

Tip: You can change the color of the border by clicking the Stroke Border color swatch and choosing a color from the Color Picker.

2 Click the checkbox to activate the Stroke Border option, and then drag the Width slider to the right or type **2.0** in the text box to the right of the slider. For your reference, 72 points (pt) are one inch.

3 In the Layout Type panel, click Picture Package. In the Rulers, Grid & Guides panel, activate the Image cells option to see the borders of the cells. For a Picture Package template, the Image Settings panel offers two controls for borders. An Inner Stroke border is the Picture Package equivalent of a Stroke Border. The Photo Border control lets you set the width of a blank frame between the edge of each photo and the boundary of its image cell.

4 Experiment with the Inner Stroke and Photo Border settings.

5 Disable the Image Cell guides. In the Layout Type panel, click Single Image / Contact Sheet to return to your modified 4 Wide template.

Using the Rotate To Fit option

By default, Lightroom will place photos so that they are upright within their image cells. The Rotate To Fit option in the Image Settings panel will override this behavior so that your photos are rotated to match the orientation of the image cells. For presentation layouts you would not wish to have images displayed in different orientations on the same page but in some situations this feature can be very helpful and save on expensive photo paper too! The Rotate To Fit option is particularly useful when you wish to print photos in both portrait and landscape formats on the same sheet, as large as possible and without wasting paper, as shown in the illustration on the right.

Another situation where you might choose to use the Rotate To Fit setting is when you are printing contact sheets. As you can see in the next illustration, Rotate To Fit enables you to see all the photos at the same size regardless of the image orientation.

Customizing your identity plate

In the Page panel you'll find controls for adding an identity plate, crop marks, page numbers, and text information from your photos' metadata to your layout. To begin with, you'll edit the identity plate to suit your layout.

1 Expand the Page panel; then click the checkbox to activate the Identity Plate option. The illustration at the right shows a preview of the default Identity Plate on Windows; on Mac OS, the default design will feature your user name. Click the triangle in the lower right corner of the identity plate preview pane and choose Edit from the menu.

2 In the Identity Plate Editor dialog box, activate the Use A Styled Text Identity Plate option. Choose Arial, Regular, and 36 point from the font menus. To change the text color, swipe over the text in the text box to select it, and then click the color swatch to the right of the font size menu; we chose a slightly darker gray than the default. Swipe to select the text again, if necessary, and type **Manneken Photography** (or a name of your own choice); then click OK.

▶ **Tip:** If your text is too long to be fully visible in the text box, either resize the dialog box or reduce the font size until you've finished editing.

3 In the Page panel, drag the Scale slider to the right so that the identity plate text is the same width as the image. You can also scale the identity plate by clicking it in the Print Editor view and dragging the handles of its bounding box.

▶ **Tip:** By default the identity plate will be oriented horizontally. This setting (0°) is indicated at the top right of the Identity Plate pane in the Page panel. To re-orient your identity plate on the page, click on the 0° indicator and choose 90°, 180°, or −90° from the menu. To move your identity plate, simply drag it in the Print Editor view.

4 Now you'll change the color of the identity plate. Click the Override Color checkbox to set the color of the identity plate for this layout only—without affecting the defined color settings for the identity plate.

5 Click the Override Color swatch to open the Color Picker. Set the RGB values: R: **45%**, G: **25%**, B: **20%**, and then close the Color Picker. The color of the text identity plate now reflects the tones of the photo at the top of the page.

Tip: If you see a hexadecimal value displayed in the lower right corner of the Color Picker rather than RGB values, click RGB below the color slider.

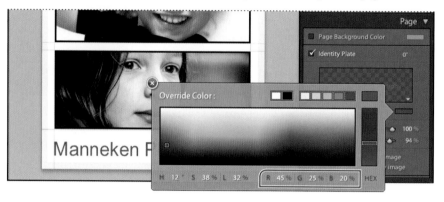

6 In the Identity Plate pane, use the Opacity slider or type **75** in the text box beside it to set an opacity value of 75% for the identity plate. This feature can be particularly effective if you wish to position your identity plate over an image.

Printing captions and metadata information

In this exercise, you will add a caption and metadata information—in this case, titles for the images—to your print layout using the Page panel and the Text Template Editor.

1 At the bottom of the the Page panel, click the checkbox to activate the Photo Info overlay option; then choose Edit from the menu to the right. Most of the other options in the Photo Info menu are drawn from the images' existing metadata.

The Text Template Editor enables you to combine custom text with the metadata embedded in your image files, and then save your edited template as a new preset, making it easy to add the same items of text information to future print jobs.

The names of the subjects of our lesson photos have been entered in the Title field of the images' metadata; you'll base your text captions on these photo titles.

▶ **Tip:** You'll find more detailed information on the Text Template Editor in the section "Using the Text Template Editor" in Lesson 8.

2 Choose Title from the Preset menu at the top of the Text Template Editor dialog box.

3 Click to place the insertion cursor just before the Title token in the Example text box. Type **Portraits:**, making sure to add the colon; then, type a space between your text and the token.

4 Click to place the cursor after the Title token in the Example box. Type a comma and a space; then choose Date (Month) from the second Numbering menu. If the Date (Month) token does not appear in the Example box, click the Insert button to the right of the Date menu.

5 Add a space after the Date (Month) token; then, choose Date (YYYY) from the second Numbering menu and click the Insert button if necessary.

6 Click Done to close the Text Template Editor dialog box. The images in the Print Editor view are now titled and dated.

Portraits: Lilly, February 2012

7 Click the triangle beside the Font Size menu at the bottom of the Page panel and choose 12 pt; then collapse the Page panel.

Saving your customized print template

Having started with a preset print template, you've created your own page design by modifying the layout and adding borders, an identity plate, and caption text to the images. You can now save your customized layout for future use.

1 Click the Create New Preset button (+) in the header of the Template Browser panel header, or choose Print > New Template.

2 In the New Template dialog box, type **My Wide Triptych** in the Template Name text box. By default, new templates are saved to the User Templates folder. For this exercise, accept the default User Templates as the destination folder and click Create.

3 Your saved template appears in the User Templates folder in the Template Browser panel where you can access it quickly for use with a new set of images. With your new template selected in the Template Browser, select the first three images in the Filmstrip, Print-1.jpg, Print-2.jpg, and Print-3.jpg.

Creating a Custom Package print layout

Every Single Image / Contact Sheet template is based on a grid of image cells that are all the same size. If you want a more free-form layout, or you prefer to create your own page layout from scratch, without using any of the preset templates as a starting point, you can use the Custom Package option in the Layout Style panel.

► **Tip:** If you'd prefer to work without using a template, start by clicking Custom Package in the Layout Style panel; then, click Clear Layout in the Cells panel and drag photos from the Filmstrip directly onto the page preview.

1　Choose Edit > Select None, or press Ctrl+D / Command+D on your keyboard. In the Template Browser, scroll down the list of Lightroom templates, if necessary, and select the Custom Overlap × 3 layout. Click the Page Setup button below the left panels and make sure that the paper size is set to A4.

2　In The Rulers, Grid & Guides panel, click the double triangle beside the Grid Snap setting and choose Grid from the menu. This will make it easier to arrange the images in your print layout. Activate the Show Guides option, if necessary, and then click the checkboxes to show only the Page Bleed and Page Grid guides.

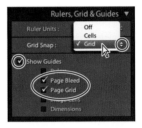

3　Click to select the central image cell in the Print Editor view, and then right-click / Control-click inside the selected cell. Note the options available in the context menu.

In a Custom Package images can be arranged so that they overlap. The first four commands in the context menu for a Custom Package image cell enable you to move an image backwards or forwards in the stacking order.

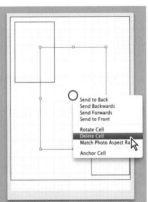

4　For now, choose Delete Cell from the context menu; then, delete either of the small cells.

5　Activate the Lock To Photo Aspect Ratio option in the Cells panel. Drag the image Print-1.jpg from the Filmstrip into the smaller image cell; then, drag the photo Print_3.jpg into the larger cell.

6 Select the smaller cell and use the Width slider in the Cells panel, or type in the text box, to set the width of the cell to **3** inches, and then press Enter / Return. Set the width of the larger image cell to **6.25** inches. Keep the large cell selected.

▶ **Tip:** To reposition a photo inside its image cell, hold down the Ctrl / Command key as you drag the image.

7 Disable the Lock To Photo Aspect Ratio option, and then drag the handle at the top of the large cell's bounding box downwards, or use the controls in the Cells panel to set the Height to **5.05** inches. With the Lock To Photo Aspect Ratio option disabled, the image is cropped to fill the resized cell.

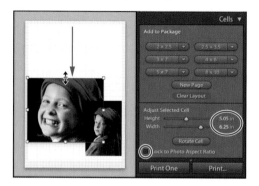

8 Hold down the Alt / Option key and drag the smaller image in the Print Editor view to produce a copy. Replace the photo in the copied cell by dragging the image Print-2.jpg from the Filmstrip.

9 Drag the three images in the Print Editor view to position them on the page as shown in the illustration below.

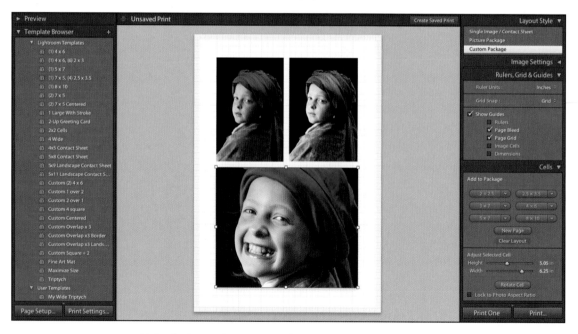

10 In the Image Settings panel, activate the Inner Stroke option. Move the Width slider to the left to set the width of the stroke to 0.5 pt. Leave the stroke color set to the default white; the white stroke borders will become visible when you set a background color in the next exercise.

Changing the page background color

To save on printer ink, you may prefer not to print a page with large areas of bold color or black in the background on your home printer, but when you're ordering professional prints this can be a striking choice. For this exercise, you'll set the background to reflect the blue in the girl's headdress.

1 In the Rulers, Grid & Guides panel, disable Show Guides.

2 In the Page panel, click the checkbox to activate the Page Background Color option. Click the Page Background Color color swatch to open the Color Picker.

3 In the Color Picker, Click the R, G, and B percentages in turn and type values of **5%**, **20%**, and **35%** respectively, and then click the Close button (x) or click outside the Color Picker to close it.

The new color appears in the Page Background Color color swatch and in the page preview in the Print Editor view.

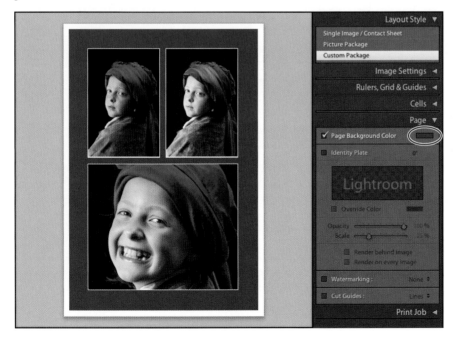

Soft proofing photos before printing

Each type of monitor and printer operates within its own *color gamut* or *color space*, which defines the range of colors that can be reproduced accurately by that device. By default, Lightroom uses your monitor's *color profile*—a mathematical description of its color space—to make your photos look as good as possible on screen. When you print an image, the image data must be reinterpreted for the printer's color space, which can sometimes result in unexpected shifts in color and tone.

You can avoid such unpleasant surprises by soft proofing your photos in the Develop module before you bring them into the Print module. Soft proofing lets you preview how your photos will look when they're printed; you can have Lightroom simulate the color space of your printer, and even the inks and paper you're using, giving you the opportunity to optimize your photos before printing them.

To activate soft proofing, open a photo in the Develop module and click the Soft Proofing checkbox in the Toolbar, or press the S key on your keyboard. The background surrounding the image changes to white "paper" and a Proof Preview label appears in the corner of the work area. Use the view button in the Toolbar to switch between the Loupe view and a choice of before and after views.

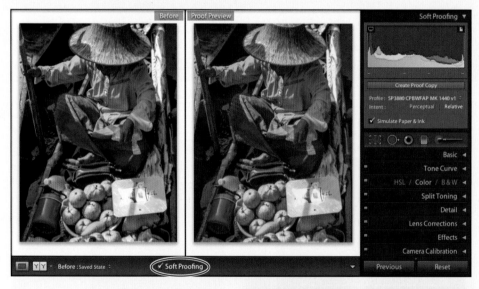

When you activate soft proofing, the Histogram panel changes to the Soft Proofing panel, which provides access to proofing options. The tonal distribution graph is updated according to the currently selected color profile. In the illustration at the right, the graph in the Histogram panel corresponds to the Before image in the illustration above. The graph in the Soft Proofing panel reflects the comparative flatness of the Proof Preview.

To soft proof your photo for a different printer, choose another color profile from the Profile menu in the Soft Proofing panel. If you don't see the profile you want in the menu, choose Other, and then select from the list of installed color profiles in the Choose Profiles dialog box.

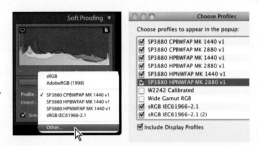

The Intent setting determines the rendering intent, which affects how colors are converted from one color space to another. The Perceptual rendering intent aims to preserve the visual relationship between colors so they look natural, though the color values may change. Relative rendering prints the in-gamut colors as they are and shifts out-of-gamut colors to the closest printable colors, retaining more of the original colors, though the relationships between some of them may be altered.

Once you've chosen a printer profile, you can activate the Simulate Paper & Ink option to simulate the off-white of real paper and the dark gray of real black ink. This option is not available for all profiles.

To check if your colors are in-gamut for the selected profile and rendering intent, use the buttons in the upper corners of the histogram in the Soft Proofing panel. Move the pointer over the Show /Hide Monitor Gamut Warning button on the left; colors that are outside your display's capabilities turn blue in the Proof Preview. Move the pointer over the Show/Hide Destination Gamut Warning button on the right; colors that cannot be rendered by your printer turn red in the preview. Colors that are out-of-gamut for both the monitor and the printer turn pink. Click the buttons to show the gamut warning colors permanently; click again to hide them.

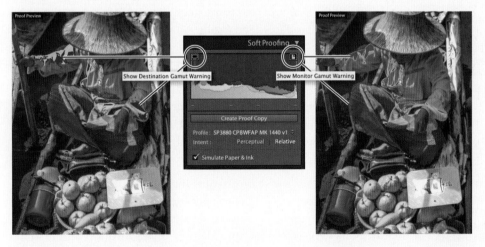

Click Create Proof Copy to generate a virtual copy that you can adjust without affecting your master settings. If you start adjusting a photo while soft proofing is on without first creating a proof copy, Lightroom asks if you want to create a virtual copy for soft proofing or make the master image a proof.

Configuring the output settings

The final step before you're ready to print your layout is to adjust the output settings in the Print Job panel.

1 Expand the Print Job panel in the right panel group.

From the Print To menu at the top of the Print Job panel you can choose to send the job directly to your printer or generate a JPEG file, which you can print later or send out for professional printing. The controls in the Print Job panel vary slightly depending on which option is selected in the Print To menu.

2 Choose Printer from the Print To menu at the top of the Print Job panel.

Note: The terms "print resolution" and "printer resolution" have different meanings. "Print resolution" refers to the number of printed pixels per inch (ppi); "printer resolution" refers to the capability of the printer, called dots per inch (dpi). A printed pixel of a particular color is created by patterns of tiny dots of the few ink colors available.

Activating the Draft Mode Printing option will disable the other options in the Print Job panel. Draft Mode Printing results in high speed output at a relatively low quality, which is an efficient option for printing contact sheets or for assessing your layout before you commit it to high quality photo paper. The 4 × 5 Contact Sheet and the 5 × 8 Contact Sheet templates are preset for Draft Mode Printing.

The Print Resolution setting that is appropriate for your print job depends on the intended print size, the resolution of your image files, the capabilities of your printer, and the quality of your paper stock. The default print resolution is 240 ppi, which generally produces good results. As a rule of thumb, use a higher resolution for smaller, high quality prints (around 360 ppi for letter size). You can use a lower resolution setting for larger prints (around 180 ppi for 16″ × 20″) without compromising too much on quality.

3 The Print Resolution control has a range of 72 ppi to 1440 ppi. For this exercise, type **200** in the Print Resolution text box.

Note: The purpose of the Sharpening feature in the Develop module is to compensate for blurriness in the original photo, while Print Sharpening improves the crispness of printed output on a particular paper type.

Images tend to look less sharp on paper than they do on screen. The Print Sharpening options can help to compensate for this by increasing the crispness of your printed output. You can choose between Low, Standard, and High Print Sharpening settings, and specify a Matte or Glossy Media Type. You won't notice the effects of these settings on screen so it's useful to experiment by printing at different settings to familiarize yourself with the results.

4 If it's not already selected, choose Low from the Print Sharpening menu.

Working with 16 Bit Output on Mac OS

If you are running Mac OS and are using a 16-bit printer, you can activate the 16 Bit Output setting in the Print Job panel. This will result in less image degradation and color artifacts in files that have been extensively edited.

Note: If you select 16 Bit Output and print to a printer that does not support it, print performance is slowed, but quality is not affected.

For detailed information on working with 16-bit output, consult the documentation for your printer or check with your output center.

Using color management

Printing your digital images can be challenging: what you see on screen is not always what you get on paper. Lightroom is able to handle a very large color space but your printer may operate within a much more limited gamut.

In the Print Job panel, you can choose whether to have Lightroom handle color management or leave it up to your printer.

Color managed by your printer

The default Color Management setting in the Print Job panel is Managed By Printer. This can be the easiest option and, given the continuing improvement of printing technology, will generally produce satisfactory results. In the Print Setup / Print dialog box (File > Print Settings), you can specify the paper type, color handling, and other print settings. On Windows, click Properties in the Print Setup dialog box to access additional printer specific settings.

● **Note:** For Draft Mode Printing, color management is automatically assigned to the printer.

● **Note:** The options available in the Print Setup / Print dialog box may vary depending on your printer.

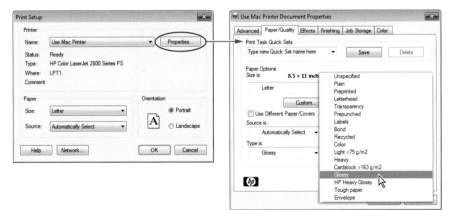

If you choose Managed By Printer, enable the ICM Method for Image Color Management (Windows) or activate the ColorSync option in the Color Management settings for the printer driver software (Mac OS) so that the correct profile is applied before printing. Depending on the printer driver software, you can usually find the color settings in the Print Document dialog box under Setup / Properties / Advanced (Windows), or in the menu below the Presets in the Print dialog box (Mac OS).

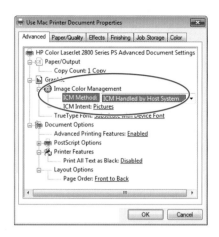

Color management controlled by Lightroom

Letting your printer manage color may be acceptable for general printing purposes but to achieve really high quality results it's best to have Lightroom do it. If you choose this option you can specify a printing profile tailored to a particular type of paper or custom inks.

1   In the Print Job panel, choose Other from the Color Management Profile menu.

You can choose this option when the profile you want isn't listed in the Profile menu. Lightroom searches your computer for custom printer profiles, which are usually installed by the software that came with your printer. If Lightroom is unable to locate any profiles, choose Managed By Printer and let the printer driver handle the color management.

2   Depending on your printer and paper stock, choose one or more printer profiles. In this illustration a profile for the Epson Stylus Pro R800 using glossy photo paper has been selected. Each profile you choose will be added to the Profile menu under Color Management in the Print Job panel for easy access next time you print.

Once you've chosen a printer profile from the Profile menu, the Rendering Intent options become available in the Print Job panel. The color space of an image is usually much larger than that within which most printers operate, which means that your printer may not be able to accurately reproduce the colors you see on screen. This may result in printing artifacts such as posterization or banding in color gradients as the printer attempts to deal with out-of-gamut colors. The Rendering Intent options help to minimize these problems. You can choose between two settings:

- **Perceptual** rendering aims at preserving the visual relationship between colors. The entire range of colors in the image will be re-mapped to fit within the color gamut your printer is able to reproduce. In this way, the relationships between all the colors are preserved but in the process even colors that were already in-gamut may be shifted as the out-of-gamut colors are moved into the printable range. This may mean that your printed image will be less vivid than it appeared on screen.

- **Relative** rendering prints all the in-gamut colors as they are and shifts out-of-gamut colors to the closest printable colors. Using this option means that more of the original color of the image is retained but some of the relationships between colors may be altered.

In most cases the differences between the two rendering methods are quite subtle. As a general rule, perceptual rendering is the best option for an image with many out-of-gamut colors and relative rendering works better for an image with only a few. However, unless you are very experienced it may be hard to tell which is which. The best policy is to do some testing with your printer. Print a very colorful, vivid photo at both settings and then do the same with a more muted image.

3 For the purposes of this exercise, choose Relative rendering.

Tweaking printed color manually

Printed results don't always match the bright and saturated look of the colors you see on-screen in Lightroom—even when you've spent time setting up the color management for your print job.

The problem may be related to your printer, the inks or paper stock you're using, or an incorrectly calibrated monitor; whatever the cause, you can make quick and easy adjustments with the Brightness and Contrast sliders in the Color Management pane of the Print Job panel.

> **Tip:** The tone curve adjustments produced by the Print Adjustment sliders do not appear in the on-screen. preview. You may need to experiment a little to find the settings that work best for your printer.

Your Print Adjustment settings are specific to the combination of printer, paper, and ink that you're using—they'll stay in place as long as you're working with the same output settings, and will be saved in the Lightroom catalog file with your custom template or saved print job.

Saving print settings as an output collection

Since you entered the Print module, you've been working with an *unsaved print*, as is indicated in the bar across the top of the Print Editor view.

Unsaved Print   Create Saved Print

Until you save your print job, the Print module works like a scratch pad. You can move to another module, or even close Lightroom, and find your settings unchanged when you return, but if you click a new layout template—or even the one you started with—in the Template Browser, the "scratch pad" will be cleared and all your work will be lost.

▶ **Tip:** Once you've saved your print job, any changes you make to the layout or output settings are auto-saved as you work.

Converting your print job to a Saved Print not only preserves your layout and output settings, but also links your layout to the particular set of images for which it was designed. Your print job is saved as a special kind of collection—an *output collection*—with its own listing in the Collections panel. Clicking this listing will instantly retrieve the images you were working with, and reinstate all of your settings, no matter how many times the print layout scratch pad has been cleared.

Depending on the way you like to work, you can save your print job at any point in the process; you could create a Saved Print as soon as you enter the Print module with a selection of images or wait until your layout is polished.

A print output collection is different from a normal photo collection. A photo collection is merely a grouping of images to which you can apply any template or output settings you wish. An output collection links a photo collection (or a selection of images from that collection) to a particular template and specific output settings.

For the sake of clarity: an output collection also differs from a custom template. A template includes all your settings but no images; you can apply the template to any selection of images. An output collection links the template and all its settings to a particular selection of images.

1 Click the Create Saved Print button in the bar at the top of the Slideshow Editor view, or click the New Collection button (➕) in the header of the Collections panel and choose Create Print

▶ **Tip:** The Make New Virtual Copies option (Windows only) is useful if you wish to apply a particular treatment, such as a developing preset, to all the pictures in your print job, without affecting the photos in the source folder or collection.

2 In the Create Print dialog box, type **Portrait Prints** as the name for your saved print job. In the Placement options, activate Top Level, and then click Create.

Your saved print appears in the Collections panel, marked with a Saved Print icon (🖶) to differentiate it from an image collection, which has a stacked photos icon. The image count shows that the new output collection contains three photos.

Tip: Adding more photos to a saved print job is easy: simply drag images to the gallery's listing in the Collections panel. To open your layout in the Print module from the Library, click the white arrow that appears to the right of the image count when you move the pointer over your saved layout in the Collections panel.

The title bar above the Print Editor now displays the name of your saved print job, and no longer presents the Create Saved Print button.

Printing your job

1 Click the Print button at the bottom of the right panel group or choose File > Print.

2 Verify the settings in the Print dialog box and click OK / Print to print your page, or click Cancel to close the Print dialog box without printing.

Clicking the Print One button will send your print job to the printer queue without opening the Print dialog box. This is useful if you print repeatedly using the same settings and don't need to confirm or change any settings in the Print dialog.

To achieve the best results when you print, calibrate and profile your monitor regularly, always verify that print settings are specified correctly, and use quality papers. However, there is no substitute for experience. Experiment with a variety of settings and options—and if at first you do succeed, consider yourself very lucky!

Congratulations! You've completed another Lightroom lesson. In this lesson you learned how to set up your own sophisticated print layouts.

In the process, you've explored the Print module and used the control panels to customize a print template—refining the layout and output settings and adding a background color, text, borders, and an identity plate to your printed page.

In the next chapter you'll look at ways to publish and share your photos, but before you move on, take a few moments to refresh your new skills by reading through the review questions and answers on the following pages.

Review questions

1 How can you quickly preview the preset print templates, and how can you see how your photos will look in each layout?

2 What are the three print template layout styles, and how can you check which type of template you have chosen?

3 When you're working with the Print Setup / Page Setup dialog box, why is it better to leave the Scale setting at 100%?

4 For what purposes is Draft Mode Printing appropriate?

5 What is the difference between a Saved Print collection, a photo collection, and a saved custom print template?

6 What is Soft Proofing?

Review answers

1 Move the pointer over the list of templates in the Template Browser to see a thumbnail preview of each layout displayed in the Preview panel. Select your images in the Filmstrip and choose a template from the list; the Print Editor view shows how your photos look in the new layout.

2 Single Image / Contact Sheet layouts can be used to print multiple photos at the same size on a single sheet. Based on an adjustable grid of image cells that are all the same size. They range from contact sheets with many cells to single-cell layouts such as the Fine Art Mat and Maximize Size templates. Picture Package layouts repeat a single image at a variety of sizes on the same page in cells that can be moved and rezized Custom Package layouts are not based on a grid; they enable you to print multiple images at any size on the same page, even arranged so that they overlap.

The Layout Style panel indicates whether a layout selected in the Template Browser is a Custom Package, Picture Package, or Single Image / Contact Sheet template.

3 Lightroom automatically scales your photos in the print layout template to fit the specified paper size. Changing the scale in the Print Setup / Page Setup dialog will result in the layout being scaled twice so your photos may not print at the desired size.

4 Draft Mode Printing results in high speed output at a relatively low quality, which is an efficient option for printing contact sheets or for assessing your layout before you commit it to high quality photo paper. The contact sheet templates are preset for Draft Mode Printing.

5 A photo collection is merely a virtual grouping of images to which you can apply any template or output settings you wish, whereas a Saved Print output collection links a selection of images to a particular template and specific layout and output settings. A saved print template preserves your customized layout and output settings but includes no images; you can apply the template to any selection of images. A Saved Print collection links the template and all its settings to a particular set of images.

6 Soft Proofing is a way to check on-screen how your photos will look when printed, or perhaps output for use on the Web. Lightroom uses color profiles to simulate the result of printing to specific printers with particular types of ink and paper—or of saving your images to a different color space as you might do with pictures intended for the Internet—enabling you to make the appropriate adjustments to your photos before exporting copies or committing to printing.

10 PUBLISHING YOUR PHOTOS

Lesson overview

Lightroom offers several easy-to-use options for sharing your photos. The Publish Services feature enables you to share images directly from the Library module. You can create Publish Collections to help you manage the files you've handed off to a client, to sync photos to your iPhone, or to upload images directly to a photo sharing website. The Web module provides a range of customizable gallery layout templates and all the tools you need to build a striking website, preview it in a browser, and upload it to your web server.

In this lesson, you'll learn the techniques and skills you need to publish photos from the Library and to create your own web gallery:

- Publishing images to a photo sharing website
- Using Publish Collections and re-publishing updated images
- Distinguishing between HTML and Flash® gallery templates
- Choosing and customizing a gallery layout template
- Rearranging the order of the images in your gallery
- Specifying the output settings and adding a watermark
- Previewing your web gallery
- Saving your customized templates and presets
- Uploading your gallery to a web server

 You'll probably need between one and two hours to complete this lesson.

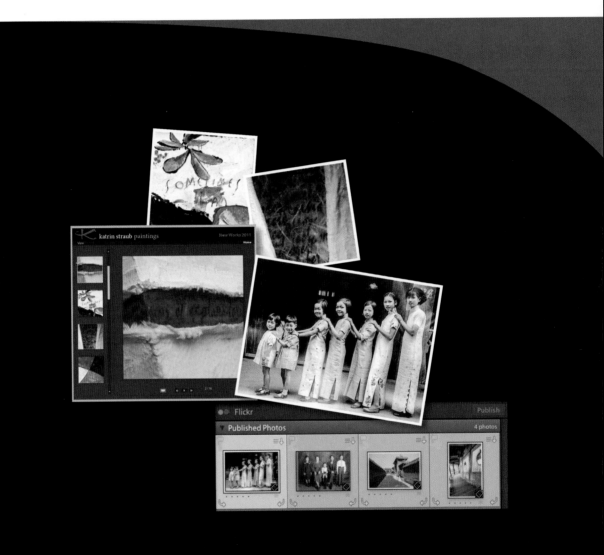

Use the Publish Services feature to share your photos directly from the Lightroom Library module, or choose from HTML and Flash templates in the Web module to quickly generate sophisticated interactive web galleries. Post images to a photo sharing site, sync photos to your iPhone, or upload an interactive gallery directly to a web server—all without leaving the Lightroom workspace.

Getting started

This lesson assumes that you are already familiar with the Lightroom workspace and with moving between the different modules. If you find that you need more background information as you go, refer to Lightroom Help, or review the previous lessons in this book.

Before you start on the exercises in this section, make sure that you have correctly copied the Lessons folder from the CD in the back of this book onto your computer's hard disk as detailed in "Copying the Classroom in a Book files" on page 2, and created the LR4CIB Library Catalog file to manage the lesson files as described in "Creating a catalog file for working with this book" on page 3.

1 Start Lightroom.

2 In the Adobe Photoshop Lightroom - Select Catalog dialog box, make sure that the file LR4CIB Library Catalog.lrcat is selected under Select A Recent Catalog To Open, and then click Open.

3 Lightroom will open in the screen mode and workspace module that were active when you last quit. If necessary, switch to the Library module by clicking Library in the Module Picker at the top of the workspace.

Importing images into the library

The first step is to import the images for this lesson into the Lightroom library.

1 In the Library module, click the Import button below the left panel group.

2 If the Import dialog box appears in compact mode, click the Show More Options button at the lower left of the dialog box to see all the options in the expanded Import dialog box.

3 At the top of the Source panel at the left of the Import dialog box, activate the option Include Subfolders; then, navigate to and select the LR4CIB > Lessons > Lesson 10 folder. Ensure that all the Lesson 10 images are checked for import.

4 In the import options above the thumbnail previews, select Add so that the imported photos will be added to your catalog without being moved or copied. Under File Handling at the right of the expanded Import dialog box, choose Minimal from the Render Previews menu and ensure that the Don't Import Suspected Duplicates option is activated. Under Apply During Import, choose None from both the Develop Settings menu and the Metadata menu and type **Lesson 10** in the Keywords text box. Make sure that your import is set up as shown in the illustration below, and then click Import.

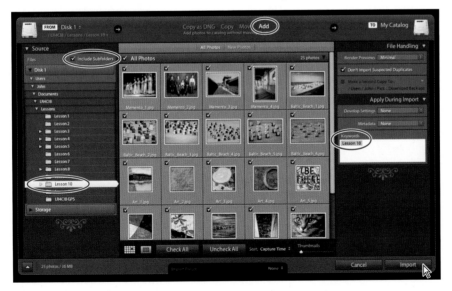

The images are imported from the four subfolders nested inside the Lesson 10 folder, and now appear in the the Library module, in both the Grid view and the Filmstrip across the bottom of the Lightroom workspace.

Publishing photos from the Library

We live in a connected world where, for many of us, sharing our images with family and friends, posting to photo sharing websites, or handing off photos online to a client are almost daily occurrences.

The new Publish Services panel enables you to publish your images directly from the Library module by creating Publish Collections that help you manage your shared images by keeping track of whether or not they've been updated to the most current versions. A Publish Collection can be used to manage the images you've handed off to a particular client, to publish images to your iPhone sync folder, or to upload images directly to a photo sharing website.

In Lightroom 4, the Publish Services panel incorporates direct connections to Facebook and Flickr, so that sharing images to your favorite website is as simple as drag and drop. You'll also find a link to Lightroom Exchange to help you find more services online. Adobe is working to support developers creating Publish Services plug-ins that will enable direct access to other popular photo sharing websites.

Setting up a Flickr account

In this exercise, you'll set up a Flickr account and publish a selection of photos.

1   Expand the Publish Services panel, if necessary, by clicking the triangle to the left of the panel's name; then, click Set Up in the Flickr header.

The Lightroom Publishing Manager dialog box appears.

2 Under Publish Service, type your name in the Description text box.

3 Under Flickr Account, click Log In. A dialog box appears, asking you to give Lightroom permission to upload images to Flickr. Click Authorize.

Your default web browser opens. You will be asked to sign in to Yahoo, and then your browser will open the Flickr sign-in page.

4 Type a screen name for your Flickr account and click Create A New Account.

5 Flicker asks you to confirm the request from Lightroom to link to your Flickr account. As you arrived at this page from Lightroom, click Next as shown in the illustration below.

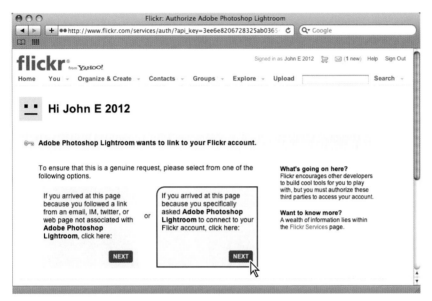

6 On the next screen, click "OK, I'll Authorize It" to authorize Lightroom to access all content in your Flickr account, to upload, edit, replace, and delete photos in your account, and to interact with other Flickr members.

7 Close the browser page, and then click Done to return to the Lightroom Publishing Manager dialog box.

8 Set up the options in the Lightroom Publishing Manager dialog box as follows:

- Under Flickr Title, choose Filename from the Set Flickr Title Using menu.

- Under File Settings, drag the Quality slider to set a value of 75.

- Scroll down, if necessary, to see the Output Sharpening options. Click the check box to enable sharpening, and then choose Screen from the Sharpen For menu, Choose Standard from the Amount menu.

- Ensure that the Watermarking option is disabled.

- Under Privacy and Safety, make sure the Public option is activated.

9   Leave the options for renaming, resizing, video and metadata unchanged and
     click Save to close the Lightroom Publishing Manager dialog box.

In the Publish Services panel, the activated Flickr
service displays the name you assigned in step 2.
The service now contains a single Photostream.
An image count of 0 at the right indicates that the
new Photostream does not yet contain any photos.

Publishing photos to Flickr

In this exercise you'll add a selection of images to your Flickr Photostream.

1   In the left panel group, expand the Folders panel. Collapse other panels, if
     necessary, so that you can see both the expanded Folders and Publish Services
     panels, as shown in the illustration below.

2   In the Folders panel, expand the Lesson 10 folder and click to select the
     subfolder named Batch1.

3   Choose Edit > Select All or Ctrl-click / Command-click to select all four images,
     and then drag the selected photos to your newly created Photostream, listed
     under Flickr in the Publish Services panel.

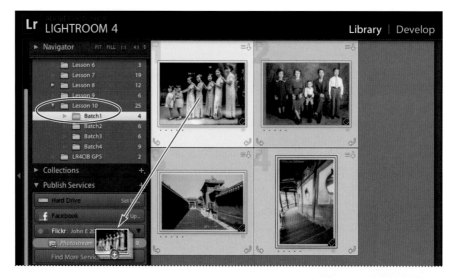

4   Click the new Photostream entry under Flickr in
     the Publish Services panel.

The work area displays the four images in this Publish
Collection under the header New Photos To Publish.

5   Click the Publish button at the bottom of the left
     panel group.

A progress bar appears in the upper left of the workspace as the images are uploaded to Flickr. The work area becomes a split screen, showing which images have been published and which are yet to be published.

6 Wait until the publish process is complete and all four photos are listed as published; then, right-click / Control-click the entry for your new Photostream in the Publish Services panel and choose Show In Flickr from the menu.

Publishing photo comments

Your Publish Services connection allows for two-way interaction between Lightroom and Flickr.

1 On your Flickr web page, click the photo Memento_1.jpg to see the image enlarged. Type a comment in the text box below the enlarged image and click Post Comment.

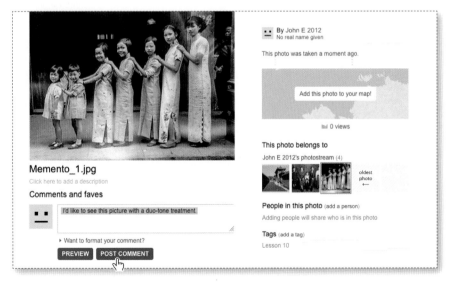

2 Switch back to Lightroom and click the Refresh Comments button (⟳) at the left of the header of the Comments panel in the right panel group. Watch the progress bar at the top left of the workspace as Lightroom connects to Flickr and updates your Publish Collection.

3 When the process is complete, click to select the image Memento_1.jpg under the Published Photos header in the work area.

4 In the right panel group, expand the Comments panel. The comment you posted on your Flickr page has been downloaded to Lightroom.

▶ **Tip:** To post a comment to an image in your Flickr Photostream from within Lightroom, click the Flickr listing in the Publish Services panel, select a published photo, type your comment in the Comments panel, and then press Enter / Return.

Re-publishing a photo

Publish Services helps you keep track of images that have been modified since they were published, so you can easily make sure that you are sharing the latest versions.

1 With your Flickr Photostream selected in the Publish Services panel, and the image Memento_1.jpg selected in the work area, expand the Quick Develop panel in the right panel group.

2 From the Saved Preset menu at the top of the Quick Develop panel, choose Lightroom B&W Toned Presets > Split Tone 3. In the work area, the edited image is now displayed under the header Modified Photos To Re-Publish.

3 Click the Publish button in the bar at the top of the work area to re-publish the modified photo. A dialog box appears asking if you wish to replace the photo on Flickr, and warning that, with a free Flickr account, any comments attached to an image will be deleted when the image is replaced. Click Replace.

4 Right-click / Control-click your Photostream under Flickr in the Publish Services panel and choose Show In Flickr from the menu.

Tip: With a Flickr Pro account, any comments and ratings attached to your photos on Flickr will be preserved when you re-publish images. For more detail on the advantages of a Flickr Pro account, click Help on the Flickr web page.

You may need to wait a few moments while your Flickr page is updated to show the re-published, duo-tone version of the image Memento_1.jpg. If you don't see your re-published photo, try reloading the page in your browser.

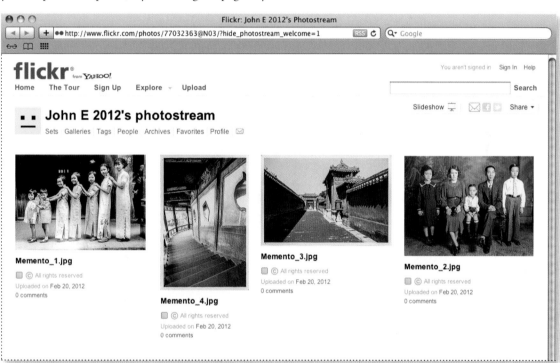

Creating a new Photoset on Flickr

The Publish Services panel offers several options for working with your Flickr account from within Lightroom; let's look at another of them.

1 In the Folders panel in the left panel group, expand the Lesson 10 folder, if necessary, and then click to select the subfolder named Batch2.

2 Choose Edit > Select All or Ctrl-click / Command-click to select all six images in the Batch2 folder.

3 Right-click / Control-click your new Photostream in the Publish Services panel and choose Create Photoset from the context menu.

Tip: The context menu for your Flickr Photostream also offers the option to create a Smart Photoset: a publish collection which will update itself to include any new photos imported to Lightroom that match its search criteria.

4 In the Create Photoset dialog box, type **Baltic Beach** as the name for the new set. Ensure that the Include Selected Photos option is activated and the option Make New Virtual Copies is disabled, and then click Create.

A listing for your new Photoset appears, nested inside the Flickr service in the Publish Services panel, and the central work area displays the six Baltic_Beach images under the header New Photos To Publish.

5 Click the Publish button below the left panel group, or in the bar above the work area, and then wait while the new set of images is uploaded to Flickr.

6 To view the newly published set of images online, right-click / Control-click your new Photoset in the Publish Services panel and choose Show In Flickr from the menu. When you're done, return to Lightroom.

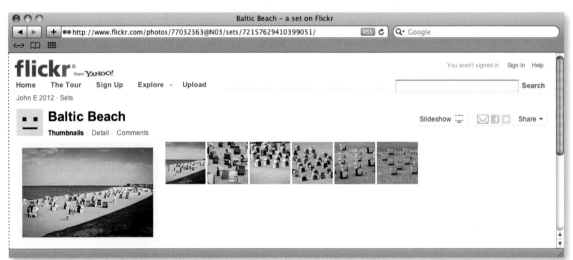

Sharing images to Facebook

The Publish services panel also incorporates a direct connection to Facebook.

1 In the Publish Services panel, click the Facebook connection Set Up button.

2 Under Facebook Account in the Lightroom Publishing Manager dialog box, click Authorize On Facebook. Click OK.

Your default web browser opens. If you are already logged in to Facebook, your Home page opens. If you are not logged in, you'll see the Facebook Login page. If you don't have a Facebook account, you can get started by clicking the Sign Up For Facebook link at the bottom of the login page.

3 Sign up or log in to Facebook, and then follow the prompts to allow Facebook to communicate with Lightroom. When you're done, return to the Lightroom Publishing Manager.

4   Type **Albums** in the Description text box under Publish Service. Under the Facebook Album header, click Create New Album. Type **Cool Cats** as the name of the new album; then, click OK. Choose the new album from the pop-out Album menu. Leave the rest of the default settings as they are and click Save to dismiss the Lightroom Publishing Manager.

5   In the Folders panel, click to select the subfolder Batch3, nested inside the Lesson 10 folder. Choose Edit > Select All, or Ctrl-click / Command-click to select all the images in the Grid view or Filmstrip. Drag the six selected photos to your newly created Cool Cats album, listed under the Facebook connection in the Publish Services panel.

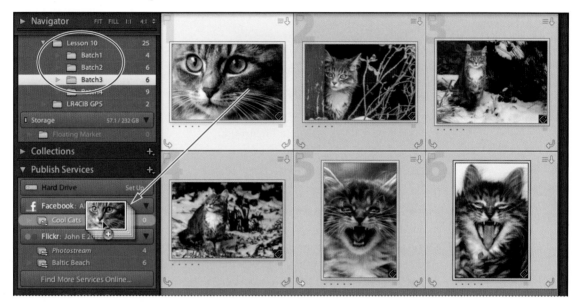

6   Click the Cool Cats album under Facebook in the Publish Services panel; then, click the Publish button below the left panel group, or in the header bar.

A progress bar appears in the upper left of the workspace as the files are uploaded to your Facebook page and the work area becomes a split screen that shows which images have already been published and which have yet to be uploaded.

7 Wait until the publish process is complete and all six photos are listed as published; then, right-click / Control-click your new album in the Publish Services panel and choose Show Album In Facebook from the menu.

▶ **Tip:** Your Facebook Publish Services connection allows for two-way communication between Lightroom and Facebook. Select a published image in your Facebook collection and click the Refresh Comments button (⟳) in the Comments panel header to download the latest comments from Facebook. Type in the Comments panel; then, press Enter / Return to post your comment to your Facebook album.

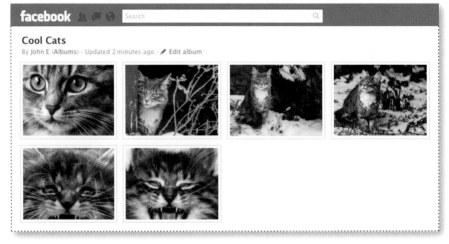

8 When you're done, return to Lightroom.

Exporting photos to Adobe Revel

If you're using Lightroom on Mac OS and you have a subscription to Adobe Revel™, you can export images from Lightroom directly to your Adobe Revel libraries (or carousels), giving you access to your photos from your iPhone or iPad without storage or syncing issues. Simply select the images you want to export in the Library module Grid View, choose File > Export, and then choose Adobe Revel from the Export To menu at the top of the Export dialog box.

For more information about Adobe Revel, see the Adobe Revel product page at http://www.adobe.com/products/revel.html.

Publishing photos to your hard disk

The Publish services panel also enables you to create publish collections on your hard disk; then, Lightroom will keep track of which images have been updated since the collection was published, just as it does for a collection published online.

You can create a new publish collection for each of your clients, making it easy to check whether they have the most current versions of the photos you hand off, or set up a publish collection that will enable you to publish images to your iPhone sync folder with drag and drop convenience.

1 In the Publish Services panel, click Set Up at the right of the Hard Drive header.

2 In the Lightroom Publishing Manager dialog box, type **Sync to iPhone** in the Description text box under Publish Service.

3   Under Export Location, choose My Pictures Folder / Pictures Folder from the Export To menu. Activate the Put In Subfolder option and type **iPhone** as the name for the new subfolder.

4   Under File Settings, set a Quality value of 50. Review the other options in the Lightroom Publishing Manager dialog box, leaving the settings unchanged for the moment, and then click Save.

A listing for your new iPhone publish collection appears under the Hard Drive header; the image count shows that the collection does not yet contain any photos.

5   In the Folders panel in the left panel group, click to select the Lesson 10 folder. If you don't see any photos, choose Library > Show Photos In subfolders.

6   Choose Edit > Select All to select all twenty-five images in the Lesson 10 folder, and then drag the selected photos to your newly created iPhone entry in the Publish Services panel.

7   Click the iPhone entry in the Publish Services panel. The Lesson 10 photos in the new publish collection are displayed in the work area under the header New Photos To Publish. Click the Publish button at the bottom of the left panel group or in the header bar and wait while Lightroom processes the images.

8   Right-click / Control-click iPhone collection in the Publish Services panel and choose Go To Published Folder from the context menu.

An Explorer / Finder window opens showing the twenty five published images in the new iPhone folder.

9   Close the Explorer / Finder window and return to Lightroom.

The Lightroom Web module

Another great way to share and showcase your photos is to use the Lightroom Web module to design, preview, and upload your own web gallery.

In the Web module, you'll start by using the Template Browser in the left panel group to preview the wide range of gallery layout templates. When you've made your choice from the Template Browser, the Gallery Editor view in the central work area shows how your images look in the selected gallery layout.

In the Gallery Editor view, your gallery is fully interactive, performing exactly as it will on the web.

You'll use the panels in the right group to customize the gallery template. You can change the layout, the color scheme, or the background, and add text, borders, or effects. With a single click, you can preview your gallery in a web browser or upload it to your web server without leaving Lightroom.

Assembling photos for an online gallery

In the following exercises you'll create a web portfolio based on one of the Lightroom Flash templates to showcase some photographs of paintings. The first step in creating a web gallery is to isolate the images you want to use from the rest of your catalog.

1 In the Folders panel, select the folder Batch4, nested inside the Lesson 10 folder.

The fact that the selected image source is a folder without subfolders means that you'll be able to rearrange photos in the Grid view or the Filmstrip to create a custom order for your gallery, but you won't be able to exclude an image from the selection without removing it from the catalog.

The solution is to create a collection to group the photos for your project, where you can rearrange the image order—just as you can with a single folder—and also remove an image from the virtual grouping, without deleting it from your catalog.

Tip: You can reorder photos in a collection by simply dragging the thumbnails in the Grid view or in the Filmstrip. Your custom display order will be saved with the collection.

A collection has a permanent listing in the Collections panel, making it easy to retrieve a selection of images at any time, even if they're stored across multiple folders, as could be the case if you had assembled the images for your gallery by means of a complex search of your library.

2 Check that the Lesson 10 > Batch4 folder is still selected in the Folders panel; then, press Ctrl+A / Command+A or choose Edit > Select All.

3 Click the New Collection button (⊕) in the header of the Collections panel and choose Create Collection from the menu. In the Create Collection dialog box, type **Paintings** as the name for the collection, and make sure that Top Level is selected in the Placement options. Under Collection Options, activate Include Selected Photos and disable Make New Virtual Copies; then, click Create.

In the Collections panel, your new collection automatically becomes the active image source; the image count to the right shows that it contains nine photos.

Choosing a template in the Web module

1   Keeping the Paintings collection selected in the Collections panel, choose
     Edit > Select None; then, press Ctrl+Alt+7 / Option+Command+7, or click
     Web in the Module Picker to switch to the Web module.

2   In the Layout Style panel at the right, select the Lightroom HTML Gallery.
     In the Template Browser at the left, the default HTML gallery template is
     activated, the Preview panel shows a thumbnail of the selected design, and the
     Gallery Editor view shows how your images will look in that layout. From the
     Use menu in the Toolbar below the Gallery Editor, choose All Filmstrip Photos.

3   Hide the Filmstrip, if necessary, so that you can
     see the Preview panel and as much as possible of
     the list of templates in the Template Browser.
     Move the pointer down the list to preview the
     different template designs in the Lightroom
     Templates folder. Note the HTML or Flash icon
     in the lower left corner of the layout preview
     indicating the gallery type for each template.

4   When you've finished previewing the gallery
     templates in the Template Browser, click to select
     the template Flash Gallery (Default).

The Gallery Editor view in the work area shows your
images displayed in the new template layout.

Distinguishing between HTML and Flash templates

In the Template Browser you'll find both HTML and Flash templates. As you move the pointer down the list of gallery templates, you'll see a preview of each template layout in the Preview panel.

An icon in the lower left corner of the layout preview indicates the gallery type. Once you click to select a template in the Template Browser, the gallery type is also shown in the Layout Style panel in the right panel group and at the right of the Toolbar below the Gallery Editor view.

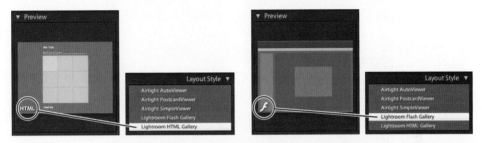

Templates of either type can be customized to show your work in its best light. You can add text and effects to your layout and change the color scheme, the background, and the image size.

The HTML gallery templates enable you to produce simple web sites that are compatible with most browsers. The HTML pages generated can be customized further in an HTML editor.

Flash templates can produce more sophisticated web galleries, including animations, slideshows with smooth transitions, and other special effects. However, Flash galleries require that the viewer has the appropriate Adobe Flash Player plug-in installed. Should security settings be in place to block scripts and ActiveX controls, your audience may have to click through warning messages in the web browser before being able to see the gallery.

5 In the Gallery Editor view you'll notice that the default Lightroom Flash gallery has its own navigation controls below the large image. Click the Play button to view the gallery slideshow.

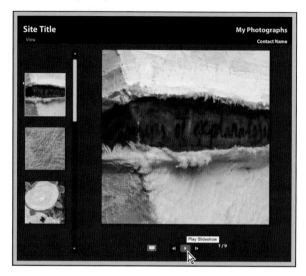

6 To stop the slideshow, click the Pause button.

Rearranging the order of your images

Note: The order of the images in the Grid view and the Filmstrip determines their display order in a Web gallery.

After seeing your slideshow in action, you may wish to change the order in which the images appear in the web gallery. In this exercise, you'll move two of the images so that the slideshow alternates between cool and warm colors.

1 Click the Library Grid button (⊞) at the top left of the Filmstrip, or press G on your keyboard, to return to the Grid view in the Library module.

2 Make sure that the Paintings collection is still selected in the Collections panel; then, choose Edit > Select None.

Note: Dragging an image that is part of a multiple selection will move all the selected images. If all images in a collection are selected you will not be able to rearrange their order.

3 In the Grid view, drag the image Art_8.jpg to position it between the first two thumbnails. Release the mouse button when the vertical black line appears to indicate an insertion point between the images Art_1.jpg and Art_2.jpg.

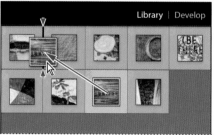

4 In the Filmstrip, drag the image Art_2.jpg, now in the third position, to the right. Release the mouse button when a vertical black line appears to indicate an insertion point between the last two images Art_7.jpg and Art_9.jpg.

5 Click Web in the Module Picker. Click the Play button to review the slideshow in the Gallery Editor view. Click the Pause button to stop the slideshow.

You can rearrange the order of images in the Filmstrip while you're working in any of the Lightroom modules, as long as your image source is a collection or a folder without subfolders. When you re-order photos in the Filmstrip in the Web module, the Gallery Editor view in the work area may be slow to reflect the changes. If necessary, you can refresh the Gallery Editor view by choosing Web > Reload.

Customizing your web gallery

You can save time when creating your web gallery by starting with the layout template closest to the design you have in mind. Once you've made your choice, you can use the Site Info, Color Palette, Appearance, Image Info, and Output Settings panels in the right panel group to customize the template. You can add text, choose backgrounds and color schemes, and tweak the layout to change the look and feel of your gallery. In the following exercises, you'll customize the text in your gallery template, adjust the layout, place a logo, and add a watermark to the images.

Replacing text

In the Site Info panel you can add a website title, a collection description, contact information, and web or e-mail links. The information you enter in the Site Info panel will appear on your website.

1 If the Site Info panel is currently collapsed in the right panel group, expand it by clicking the triangle beside its name.

2 Click the default Site Title text in the Site Info panel and type a title for your site. Press Enter on your keyboard to update the title displayed in your layout in the Gallery Editor view. In a web browser, the site title will also appear in the title bar of the browser window.

3 Click the triangle beside Site Title and note the entries in the Site Title menu. Lightroom keeps track of your entries for each of the text boxes in the Site Info panel. Instead of retyping information each time you create a new web gallery, you can choose previously entered details from this list.

4 As an alternative to working with the Site Info panel, you can edit the text in your gallery directly in the Gallery Editor view in the work area. Click the Collection Title (My Photographs) in the top right corner of the Gallery Editor view and type a new title. Press Enter and both the gallery preview and the corresponding entry in the Site Info panel will be updated.

5 In the Site Info panel, delete the default text under Collection Description. Additional information about the images in your web gallery can be entered here. In this particular template, the viewer can access those details by clicking View below the site title and choosing About These Photos from the menu.

The last two items in the Site Info panel are Contact Info and Web Or Mail Link. Your web or email address will become an active link on your website, so the viewer's browser will either jump to the specified web page or launch their default e-mail application.

Enter an e-mail address like this: mailto:user@domain.com, or a web address in the following format: http://www.domain.com.

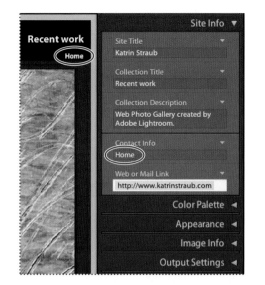

Tip: As illustrated here, you could create a link to a Home page where you can offer the viewer links to the other galleries that you've created in Lightroom.

Changing colors

The controls in the Color Palette panel enable you to change the color scheme for your website. You can set the color for every element in your layout: background, borders, header, menu bar, and text.

Choosing colors that work well together and look good on any system may seem a major challenge, but a few simple rules might help you to stay within a safe color palette:

- Use dark text on light backgrounds.
- Use light text on dark backgrounds.
- Don't rely on differences in color to convey essential information.

In this exercise you'll change the color of the text for the site and collection titles, but the same technique applies to any of the color settings.

Tip: When choosing colors, particularly for base elements such as the background, borders, and headers, remember that neutral colors will compete less with your images. If you want to get serious about designing color schemes, Kuler® from the Adobe labs can be an invaluable tool (http://labs.adobe.com/technologies/kuler/).

1   Expand the Color Palette panel by clicking the triangle next to its name. If necessary, you can collapse other panels to make more space.

2   In the Color Palette, click the Header Text color swatch to open the Lightroom Color Picker.

Tip: You can simplify the way you work with the side panel groups by setting the panels to Solo Mode, which automatically collapses all the panels in the group other than the one you're working with. Right-click / Control-click any panel header, and toggle Solo Mode in the context menu.

► **Tip:** If you see a hexadecimal value displayed in the lower right corner of the Color Picker rather than the RGB values shown in the illustration at the right, click RGB below the vertical color slider.

3   In the Color Picker, drag the slider at the right almost to the top, and then click a bright red in the large color field on the left. We chose a color with RGB values of R: 90%, G: 10%, B: 15%. You can enter these RGB values directly by clicking the number and typing a new value. The new color appears in the Header Text color swatch in the Color Palette panel and is applied to both the site and collection titles in the Gallery Editor view.

4   Close the Color Picker and collapse the Color Palette panel.

Tweaking the layout of a web gallery

You can adjust your gallery layout using the Appearance panel. The options available in the Appearance panel differ for Flash and HTML galleries.

For an HTML gallery, the Appearance panel offers the options shown in the illustration to the right. You can add borders or drop shadows to your images and display an index number in the background of each image cell. Change the number of rows and columns used on the index page with the Grid Pages controls, which will indirectly determine the size of the thumbnail images in the grid. The minimum grid is three by three—if your gallery contains more than nine images additional index pages will be generated. You can also set the size of the page and the width of a photo border for the enlarged view of an image.

These options give you great flexibility in customizing the look and feel of your HTML gallery. For a Flash gallery the options in the Appearance panel are more restricted.

1 In the right panel group, expand the Appearance panel; then click the double triangle beside Layout, and choose the Scrolling layout option from the menu.

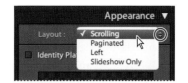

The Scrolling layout displays a scrollable row of index thumbnails beneath an enlarged image view.

2 In the Appearance panel, click the double triangle beside Layout, and choose the Paginated layout option from the menu.

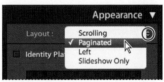

The Paginated layout displays thumbnails organized as an index beside an enlarged image view. Navigation controls below the thumbnails provide easy access to additional index pages.

3 Under Thumbnail Images in the Appearance panel, click the double triangle beside Size and choose Medium from the menu.

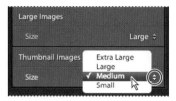

The gallery preview is updated in the Gallery Editor view. Depending on the number of images in your collection and the size of your Lightroom workspace window, the new thumbnail size may affect the number of index pages for your gallery.

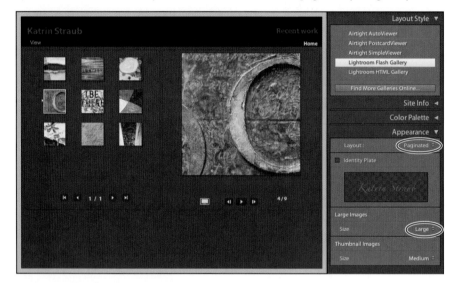

4 In the Appearance panel, click the double triangle beside Layout, and choose the Slideshow Only layout option from the menu.

The Slideshow Only layout displays only the enlarged image with controls for navigating through the collection and playing a gallery slideshow.

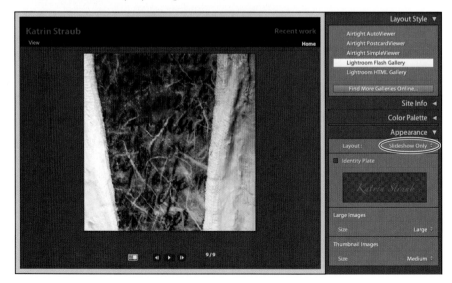

5 In the Appearance panel, click the double triangle beside Layout, and choose the Left layout option from the menu to return to the default layout for this gallery template, with a scrolling column of thumbnails to the left of the enlarged image view.

6 Click the View Slideshow button () below the enlarged image view to hide the index thumbnails and view a slideshow that will display only the enlarged images.

The View Slideshow button switches the gallery temporarily to Slideshow Only mode—it is available in all of the Flash gallery layout options except the Slideshow Only layout. When the View Slideshow button is clicked, it changes to the View Gallery button (▦).

7 Click the View Gallery button (▦) to return to the selected gallery layout, complete with index thumbnails.

Personalizing your web gallery

Next, you'll personalize your web gallery by placing a logo in the header area.

1 In the Appearance panel, activate the Identity Plate option; then click the white triangle at the lower right of the Identity Plate preview pane and choose Edit from the menu.

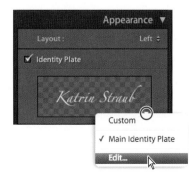

2 In the Identity Plate Editor dialog box, activate the option Use A Graphical Identity Plate, and then click the Locate File button.

3 In the Locate File dialog box, navigate to the Lesson 10 folder and select the file Web_Identityplate.png. Click Choose, and then click OK.

Tip: For best results use an image that is no more than 60 pixels high so that it will not need to be scaled to fit your layout template. In this case we used an image with a height of 46 pixels.

The new identity plate appears in the gallery preview and in the Identity Plate preview in the Appearance panel. The identity plate will replace the site title on your web page, but when the gallery is viewed in a web browser, the text you entered as the Site Title will still be displayed in the title bar of the browser window.

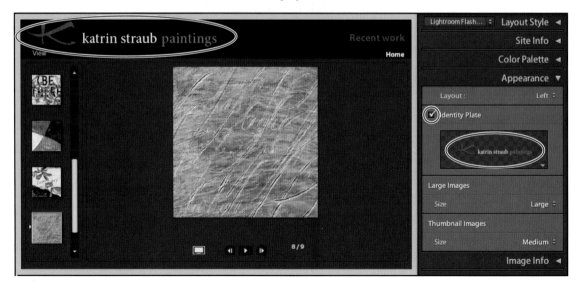

Working with identity plates

You can personalize your slideshows, Web presentations, and print layouts—and the Lightroom workspace itself—by adding your own identity plate.

A **Styled Text Identity Plate** will display the text you enter in the Identity Plate Editor dialog box. You can choose from the menus below the text box to specify the font characteristics.

A **Graphical Identity Plate** uses a graphic that is no more than 60 pixels high, in any of the following file formats: PDF, JPG, GIF, PNG, TIFF, or PSD (Windows) and JPG, GIF, PNG, TIFF, or PSD (Macintosh). The resolution of graphical identity plates may be too low for printed output. Choose Save As from the Enable Identity Plate menu, and give your identity plate a name.

To display your identity plate in the Lightroom workspace, choose Edit > Identity Plate Setup / Lightroom > Identity Plate Setup. In the Identity Plate Editor dialog box, activate the Enable Identity Plate option and choose one of your saved identity plates from the menu to the right.

Choose from the pop-up menus on the right side of the dialog box to change the font style, size and color for the Module Picker. The first color swatch sets the text color for the active module; the second swatch sets the text color for the others.

—From Lightroom Help

Providing more information

You can display information about the images in your web gallery by choosing from a range of options in the Title and Caption menus in the Image Info panel. Show specific details retrieved from the metadata of each image, apply the same text to all the images at once, or display your images without any text information at all.

> **Note:** The title text will be displayed immediately below the enlarged image view. The caption appears below the title in a smaller font size.

You can also set up a text template that will combine information drawn from different sources to compose titles and captions for your images automatically. In this exercise, you'll add a title and caption to the first image in the collection.

1 Expand the Image Info panel in the right panel group. Make sure that both the Title and Caption options are activated.

2 Click on the double triangle beside Title to see the list of options. The same choices are available in the Caption menu. Most of the options display information retrieved from an image's metadata.

> **Tip:** Choose the Custom Text option to add "boilerplate" text that will be displayed with every image.

3 From the Title menu, choose Title. From the Caption menu, choose Caption.

Next, you'll need to edit the image metadata from which the Title and Caption information will be drawn. You can do this in the Library module.

4 Press G to switch to the Grid view in the Library module.

5 Choose Edit > Select All or press Ctrl+A / Command+A. Expand the Metadata panel in the right panel group. In the Title text box, type **Soliloquy**, and then press Enter / Return. Click to confirm that you want to apply the change in metadata to all the selected images. In the Caption box, type **mixed media on canvas**; then, press Enter / Return and click to confirm the changes.

6 Choose Edit > Select None or press Ctrl+D / Command+D; then, select the first image in the series. In the Metadata panel, change the Title to **Soliloquy 1**. Select each of the other eight images in turn and add sequential numbers to their Title metadata.

7 To switch to the Web module, press Ctrl+Alt+7 / Command+Option+7.

The title and caption details drawn from the images' metadata are now displayed under the enlarged view of each painting.

Specifying output settings

In the Output Settings panel you can control the image quality and the sharpness of the JPEG images generated for your web gallery. You can also choose to add a watermark to your images—a minimal protection when publishing your work.

▶ **Tip:** It's always worth experimenting with the image quality settings; for some images a lower setting might be sufficient, resulting in a website that loads faster.

1 In the right panel group, collapse the Image Info panel and expand the Output Settings panel. Drag the Quality slider to set the image quality to 70%, or alternatively, click the value to the right, type **70** and press Enter. In most cases, an image quality setting of 70% to 80% strikes a good balance between file size and image quality.

2 Activate the Sharpening option at the bottom of the Output Settings panel. Click the double arrow to open the Sharpening menu and choose Standard.

You won't see the changes to these settings reflected in the images in the gallery preview; both the image quality and sharpening settings will not be applied until Lightroom exports the image files for your website.

Watermarking images

With the Watermark Editor interface, Lightroom makes it easy to watermark your images for export, printing, publishing, or for a web gallery.

You have the choice of applying a simple text watermark—ideal for a copyright message or your business name—or importing an image file such as your company logo to be applied as a graphic watermark.

For a text watermark you can specify a font and the text color, and for both watermark styles you can adjust the opacity and either use precise scaling and positioning controls or work directly with your watermark in the watermarking preview.

1 In the Filmstrip, select all the images in your web gallery. In the Output Settings panel, activate the Watermarking option. Click the double arrow to open the Watermarking menu and choose Edit Watermarks to open the Watermark Editor dialog box.

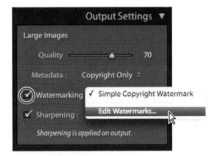

The default watermark style is a simple text copyright watermark. In the Watermark Editor dialog box you have the opportunity to enter your own message and specify the font, style, alignment, and color of your text. On Mac OS, you also have the option to set up a drop-shadow effect for your watermark text.

▶ **Tip:** For both watermark styles you can use the Watermark Effects controls at the right of the Watermark Editor dialog box, where you can adjust the opacity of your watermark as well as its size and placement. Alternatively, you can move or resize your watermark directly in the watermarking preview; a bounding box and handles will appear around the watermark when you move the pointer over the preview. Use the left and right arrows at the top of the dialog box to change the image in the preview pane.

2 Under Image Options at the top right of the Watermark Editor dialog box, click Choose to select an image file to be used as a graphic watermark.

3 In the Open / Choose A File dialog box, navigate to and open the Lesson 10 folder. Select the file watermark_K.png, and then click Choose.

4 At the right of the Watermark Editor dialog box, scroll down if necessary and expand the Watermark Effects controls. Use the sliders or type new values to set up the Watermark Effects controls as shown in the illustration below. Set the opacity value to **50**, proportional sizing value to **25**, and both the horizontal and vertical inset values to **3**. Leave the Anchor setting at the default so that the wateremark appears in the lower left corner of the image. For our purposes, you won't need to use the Rotate buttons to reorientate the watermark image.

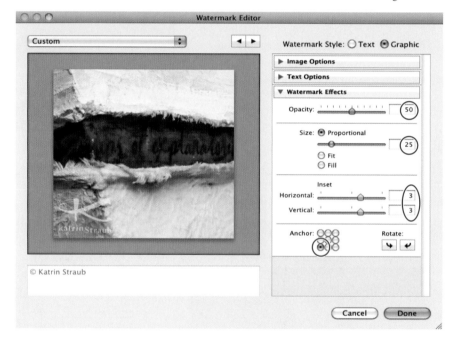

5 Use the left and right arrow buttons at the top of the Watermark Editor dialog box to cycle the image in the watermarking preview and decide whether the settings are effective for all the images in the collection. Make any adjustments you wish to make.

6 Choose Save Current Settings As New Preset from the Custom menu above the watermarking preview. In the New Preset dialog box, type **web portfolio** as the name for your new preset, and then click Create. You could now apply the same watermark settings to another collection of images quickly and easily.

7 Click Done to close the Watermark Editor dialog box. The watermark appears on the images in the gallery preview and the web portfolio preset is indicated beside Watermarking in the Output Settings panel.

This concludes the section on customizing the look and feel of your web gallery. You've changed the site title text, added a Home page link, learned how to adjust the color scheme and the layout, personalized your web page by placing a graphic identity plate, and finally added titles, captions and a watermark to the images.

It's time to save all these modifications as a custom template that you can use as a starting point the next time you create a web gallery, but first let's preview your gallery in your web browser.

Previewing the gallery

To enable you to preview your gallery as it will appear on the Web, Lightroom generates the web pages and all the necessary image files in a temporary folder on your hard disk, and then opens the main page of the gallery in your default web browser.

1   To preview the gallery in your default web browser, click the Preview In Browser button below the left panel group, or choose Web > Preview In Browser.

While Lightroom generates the necessary files, a progress bar appears in the upper left corner of the Lightroom workspace. You can cancel the Preview In Browser command at any time by clicking the small cross icon (x) at the right end of the progress indicator—but for this exercise, let the process run its course.

2   Once Lightroom has finished generating the necessary files, your web gallery opens in your default browser.

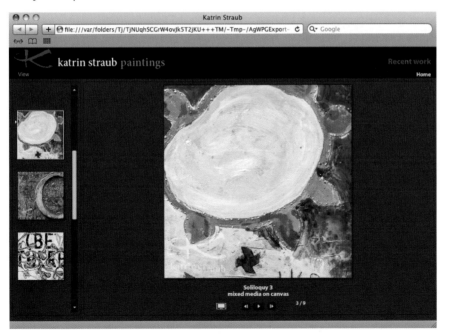

> **Tip:** You should always preview your gallery in this way before uploading it to your website. Check that the navigation controls work as expected, examine the image quality, and confirm that your photos appear in the correct order. Finally, you should resize the browser window to see how well the gallery layout adapts to different display sizes.

3 To check how your web gallery performs in the browser, run these simple tests:

- Click the Play button in the group of navigation controls below the large image to start the gallery slideshow.

- Click the Pause button to stop playback.

- Use the scroll bar to scroll down the list of small thumbnail images on the left. Click a thumbnail to view the enlarged image on the right.

- Click the word View just below the identity plate at the upper left of the gallery layout, and then choose Slideshow from the menu.

- Click the Next Image and Previous Image buttons on either side of the Play button to move from one image to the next.

- Click the View Gallery button at the left of the navigation controls below the large image to leave the slideshow mode and return to the gallery layout with the column of thumbnail images on the left.

- Resize your browser window to see how the gallery works at different sizes.

- Examine the image quality.

- Make sure the titles, captions, and watermarks are displayed correctly.

- Click the Home button to see if it links correctly to your home page. (You'll need an active Internet connection to test this.)

4 When you're done, close the browser window and return to Lightroom.

Saving your custom template

Having spent time and effort modifying the gallery layout, changing the color scheme and text style, adding titles, captions, an identity plate, and watermarks, you should save your design as a custom web gallery template. The new template will be listed under User Templates in the Template Browser panel, where you can access it easily in case you need to rework or extend your gallery, or should you wish to use your customized template as a starting point for creating a new layout. You can create additional folders in the Template Browser to help you manage your custom templates.

1 With your customized web gallery still open in the Web module, click the Create New Preset button (+) in the header of the Template Browser panel in the left panel group. Alternatively, choose Web > New Template.

2 In the New Template dialog box, type **My Flash Web Portfolio**. Leave the default User Templates folder selected in the Folder menu and click Create.

Your customized web gallery template is now listed under User Templates in the Template Browser panel.

3 In the Template Browser panel right-click / Control-click the User Templates folder and choose New Folder from the context menu. In the New Folder dialog box, type **My CIB Templates** as the name for the new folder; then click Create.

4 In the Template Browser panel, drag the My Flash Web Portfolio template from the User Templates folder into your new My CIB Templates folder.

Tip: To delete a selected template, click the Delete Selected Preset button (-) in the header of the Template Browser. You cannot delete the Lightroom templates. To delete a folder from the Template Browser, first delete all the templates inside it—or drag them into another folder; then right-click / Control-click the empty folder and choose Delete Folder from the context menu. You cannot delete the default templates folders.

Creating a Saved Web Gallery

Since you entered the Web module, you've been working with an *unsaved web gallery*, as is indicated in the bar across the top of the Slideshow Editor view.

::: Unsaved Web Gallery	Create Saved Web Gallery

Until you save your gallery design, the Web module works like a scratch pad. You can move to another module, or even close Lightroom, and find your settings unchanged when you return, but if you click a new gallery template—or even the one you started with—in the Template Browser, the "scratch pad" will be cleared and all your work will be lost.

Converting your project to a Saved Slideshow not only preserves your layout and output settings, but also links your layout to the particular set of images for which it was designed.

Your web gallery is saved as a special kind of collection—an *output collection*—with its own listing in the Collections panel. Clicking this listing will instantly retrieve the images you were working with, and reinstate all of your settings, no matter how many times the web gallery scratch pad has been cleared.

1 Click the Create Saved Web Gallery button in the bar at the top of the Gallery Editor view, or click the New Collection button (➕) in the header of the Collections panel and choose Create Web Gallery.

Tip: Once you've saved your gallery, any changes you make to the layout or output settings are auto-saved as you work.

2 In the Create Web Gallery dialog box, type **Web Portfolio** as the name for your saved presentation. In the Placement options, activate Inside and choose the collection Paintings from the menu; then, click Create.

Your saved web gallery appears in the Collections panel, marked with a Saved Web Gallery icon (⊞), and nested inside the original source collection, Paintings. The image count shows that the new output collection, like the source, contains nine photos. The title bar above the Slide Editor displays the name of your saved gallery.

Depending on the way you like to work, you can save your web gallery at any point in the process; you could create a Saved Web Gallery as soon as you enter the Web module with a selection of images or wait until your presentation is polished.

Exporting your gallery

Now that you're happy with your gallery and you've saved the template, you can export the website to your hard disk. You can run the exported website from your laptop if you need to present your work where there is no Internet connection, or burn the exported files to a CD-ROM as a working backup or to send to a client.

1 Select My Flash Web Portfolio from the My CIB Templates folder in the Template Browser panel and click the Export button below the right panel group, or choose Web > Export Web Photo Gallery.

2 In the Save Web Gallery dialog box, navigate to your Lesson 10 folder. Type **My Web Gallery** in the File Name / Save As text box, and then click Save.

Lightroom will create a folder named My Web Gallery inside the Lesson 10 folder and generate all the necessary image files, web pages, subfolders and support files within that folder. If you have many images in your gallery, this operation might take a while—a progress bar at the upper left of the Lightroom workspace provides feedback as Lightroom completes the process.

3 When the export is complete, double-click the file index.html in the folder My Web Gallery inside your Lesson 10 folder. Your gallery opens in your default web browser. When you're finished reviewing the exported gallery, close the browser window and return to Lightroom.

Uploading your gallery to a web server

In the last exercise of this lesson you'll learn how to upload your web gallery to a server from within Lightroom. To do this, you'll need to know your FTP server access information. You can get these details from your Internet service provider.

1 In the Web module, expand the Upload Settings panel in the right panel group.

2 From the FTP Server menu in the Upload Settings panel, choose Edit.

3 In the Configure FTP File Transfer dialog box, enter the server address, your username and password, and the server path.

> **Tip:** For security reasons, don't activate the Store Password In Preset option unless you are the only person with access to the computer you're using.

4 From the Preset menu, choose Save Current Settings As New Preset.

5 In the New Preset dialog box, enter a name for your FTP server preset, and then click Create.

6 Click OK to close the Configure FTP File Transfer dialog box. You'll notice that the name of your new FTP server preset now appears in the Upload Settings panel, where you can access it at any time from the FTP Server Presets menu.

7   To place the gallery inside a subfolder on your FTP server, activate the option Put In Subfolder and type a name for the subfolder that's relevant to the content of the gallery. This subfolder name will become part of the URL of your web gallery. For example, we used **soliloquies** as subfolder name, so the complete URL might look like this: http://www.katrinstraub.com/soliloquies.

8   Click the Upload button below the right panel group. If you didn't save your FTP server password in the Configure FTP File Transfer dialog box, you'll need to enter it now in the Enter Password dialog box, and then click Upload.

Uploading your web gallery to an FTP server generally takes much longer than exporting it to your local hard disk. You can watch the upload status in the progress bar at the upper left of the Lightroom workspace.

Once the upload is complete, you can enter the URL of your gallery in your web browser and admire your site live on the Internet. Don't send the URL to a client or friends before you've confirmed that everything works as expected!

Congratulations—you've completed this lesson on publishing images. You've learned how to use the new Publish Services feature to publish images to a photo sharing website or to your hard disk. You've built your own web gallery, saved a custom gallery template and created new watermarking and FTP upload presets. Finally, you learned how to export your web gallery or upload it to a web server.

Before you move on to the next lesson, take a moment or two to review some of your new skills by reading through the questions and answers on the facing page.

Review questions

1 Why would you use Publish Services to publish images to your hard disk?

2 Why is it useful to create a collection to group the images that you intend to use for a web gallery?

3 What is the difference between HTML and Flash galleries?

4 Which panels would you use to customize the Lightroom web templates?

5 How do you add a graphic watermark to the images in your web gallery?

Review answers

1 You can create a new publish collection on your hard disk for each client to whom you hand off photos, making it easy to check whether they have the most current versions, as Lightroom will keep track of which images have been updated since the collection was published. You can also set up a publish collection that will enable you to publish images to your iPhone sync folder with drag and drop convenience.

2 Grouping your images as a collection not only keeps them all in one place for easy reference—it will also make the process of updating and adjusting your web gallery much more efficient. Once a selection of photos has been saved as a collection it is possible not only to re-order images, as you can with a single-folder image source, but also to exclude an image without deleting it from the catalog.

3 HTML gallery templates produce simple web sites that are compatible with most browsers. Flash templates can produce more sophisticated web galleries, including animations, slideshows with smooth transitions, and other special effects. However, Flash galleries require that the viewer has the appropriate Adobe Flash Player plug-in. Viewers may need to click through security messages in the web browser before being able to see the gallery.

4 The panels in the right panel group—the Site Info, Color Palette, Appearance, Image Info, Output Settings, and Upload Settings panels—contain controls for modifying the gallery layout templates available in the Template Browser.

5 In the Web module, activate the Watermarking option in the Output Settings panel. Click the double arrow to open the Watermarking menu and choose Edit Watermarks to open the Watermark Editor dialog box. Under Image Options in the Watermark Editor dialog box, click Choose to select an image file to be used as a watermark.

11 MAKING BACKUPS AND EXPORTING PHOTOS

Lesson overview

Lightroom makes it easy to back up and export all the data connected with your image library. You can create backup copies to external storage during import, have Lightroom schedule automatic backups of your catalog file, and perform full or incremental backups of both your photos and develop settings. Export files in a range of formats—from images optimized for on-screen viewing to archival copies.

In this lesson you'll learn a variety of techniques to help you to manage your image library, minimize the impact of accidental data loss, and streamline your workflow:

- Backing up your catalog file
- Backing up the entire image library
- Making incremental backups
- Exporting metadata
- Exporting photos for on-screen viewing
- Exporting photos to be edited in another application
- Exporting photos for archival purposes
- Using export presets
- Setting up automated post-export actions

 You'll probably need between one and two hours to complete this lesson.

Safeguard your photographs and develop settings against loss using Lightroom's build-in backup tools. Back up just your catalog file, or your entire photo library, complete with develop settings and copies of your master files. Export photos in different file formats for multimedia presentations, for further editing in an external image editor, as e-mail attachments, or to be burned to CD or DVD for archival purposes.

Getting started

This lesson assumes that you are already familiar with the Lightroom workspace and with moving between the different modules. If you find that you need more background information, refer to Lightroom Help, or review the previous lessons.

Before you begin, make sure that you have correctly copied the Lessons folder from the CD in the back of this book onto your computer's hard disk as detailed in "Copying the Classroom in a Book files" on page 2, and created the LR4CIB Library Catalog file to manage the lesson files as described in "Creating a catalog file for working with this book" on page 3.

1 Start Lightroom.

2 In the Adobe Photoshop Lightroom - Select Catalog dialog box, make sure the file LR4CIB Library Catalog.lrcat is selected under Select A Recent Catalog To Open, and then click Open.

> **Tip:** The first time you enter any of the Lightroom modules, you'll see module tips that will help you get started by identifying the components of the Lightroom workspace and stepping you through the workflow. Dismiss the tips by clicking the Close button. To reactivate the tips for any module, choose [*Module name*] Tips from the Help menu.

3 Lightroom will open in the screen mode and workspace module that were active when you last quit. If necessary, switch to the Library module by clicking Library in the Module Picker at the top of the workspace.

The first step is to import the images for this lesson into the Lightroom library.

4 In the Library module, click the Import button below the left panel group.

5 If the Import dialog box appears in compact mode, click the Show More Options button at the lower left of the dialog box to see all the options in the expanded Import dialog box.

6 Under Source at the left of the expanded Import dialog box, navigate to and select the LR4CIB > Lessons > Lesson 11 folder. Ensure that all six images in the Lesson 11 folder are checked for import.

7 In the import options above the thumbnail previews, select Add so that the imported photos will be added to your catalog without being moved or copied. Under File Handling at the right of the Import dialog box, choose Minimal from the Render Previews menu and ensure that the Don't Import Suspected Duplicates option is activated. Under Apply During Import, choose None from both the Develop Settings menu and the Metadata menu, and type **Lesson 11** in the Keywords text box. Make sure that your import is set up as shown in the illustration below, and then click Import.

The six images are imported from the Lesson 11 folder and now appear in both the Grid view of the Library module and in the Filmstrip across the bottom of the Lightroom workspace.

Preventing data loss

The importance of a good backup strategy is often only understood too late. How much damage would be done if your computer was stolen right now? How many files would be irrecoverably lost if your hard disk failed today? How much work and money would that cost you? You can't prevent a disaster from happening but it *is* in your power to reduce the risks and the cost of recovery. Backing up regularly will reduce the impact of a catastrophe and save you time, effort, and money.

Lightroom delivers a range of options that make it easy to safeguard your photo library; as for the rest of the files on your computer, you really should have your own backup strategy in place.

Backing up the catalog file

The Lightroom catalog file stores a great deal of information for the photos in your library—not only the locations of the image files, but the metadata attached to them, including titles, captions, keyword tags, flags, labels, and ratings, together with all your developing and output settings. Every time you modify a photo in any way, from renaming the file during import to color correction, retouching, and cropping—all your work is saved to the catalog file. It records the way your images are grouped and ordered in collections, and records the publishing history, slide-show settings, web gallery designs, and print layouts associated with them as well as your customized templates and presets.

Unless you back up your catalog, you could lose hundreds of hours of work in the event of a hard disk failure, accidental deletion, or a corrupted library file—even if you do have copies of your original images stored safely on removable media. You can set Lightroom to initiate a regular backup of your catalog file automatically.

1   Choose Catalog Settings from the Edit / Lightroom menu. On the General tab, choose When Lightroom Next Exits from the Back Up Catalog menu.

2 Click OK / the Close button (⊖) to close the Catalog Settings dialog box; then quit Lightroom.

3 In the Back Up Catalog dialog box, click the Choose button to change the folder where the backed up catalog will be stored. Ideally the backup should be located on a different disk than your original catalog file; for the purpose of this exercise you can select the LR4CIB folder on your hard disk. In the Browse For Folder / Choose Folder dialog box, select the LR4CIB folder as the backup directory and click OK / Choose.

4 Make sure the options Test Integrity Before Backing Up and Optimize Catalog After Backing Up are activated. It's a good idea to keep these options activated whenever you back up your catalog; it would defy the purpose of a backup if your original catalog file was not in good working order. Click Back Up.

Each time you back up your catalog, Lightroom will create a complete copy of the catalog file in the directory you specified, inside a new folder with a name composed from the date and time of the backup. To save space on your backup drive, you can either delete your older backup files or compress them. Catalog files compress very effectively; you can expect a compressed catalog to be as small as 10% of the size of the original. Make sure to decompress the file before attempting to restore your catalog from the backup.

Should your catalog be accidently deleted or become corrupted, you can now restore it either by copying the backup file to your catalog folder or by creating a new catalog and importing the contents of your backup file. To avoid inadvertently modifying your backup file, it's preferable not to open it directly from the Lightroom File menu.

Note: Backing up the catalog file in this way does not make backup copies of the original image files or the preview images that Lightroom displays in the workspace. The previews will be regenerated as your catalog file is restored from the backup, but you'll need to back up your original image files separately.

5 Start Lightroom. In the Adobe Photoshop Lightroom - Select Catalog dialog box, make sure that the file LR4CIB Library Catalog.lrcat is selected under Select A Recent Catalog To Open, and then click Open.

6 Choose Edit > Catalog Settings / Lightroom > Catalog Settings.

7 In the Catalog Settings dialog box, click the General tab and set your preferred backup frequency by choosing from the Back Up Catalog menu.

8 Click OK / the Close button (⊖) to close the Catalog Settings dialog box.

Exporting metadata

The catalog is a central storage location for all the information associated with every image in your library; exporting and distributing the catalog file's content is another strategy that will lessen the impact if your catalog file is lost or damaged. By saving the information from the catalog file that is specific to each photo to the respective image file on your hard disk—and keeping this exported information in sync with your catalog file, which can be done automatically—you have, in effect, a distributed backup of the metadata and develop settings for each of your photos.

When a photo has changes to its metadata that have not yet been saved to the original image file—such as the keyword tag you applied to the images for this lesson during the import process—its image cell in the Grid view and the Filmstrip is marked with the Metadata File Needs To Be Updated icon (≡⬇).

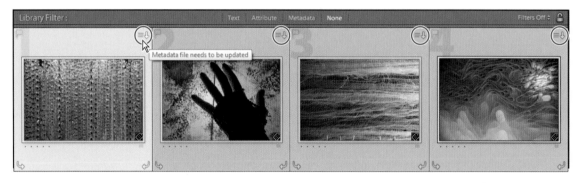

1   If you don't see the Metadata File Needs To Be Updated icon (≡⬇) in the Grid view image cells, choose View > View Options. On the Grid View tab in the Library View Options dialog box, activate the Unsaved Metadata option under Cell Icons. Click the Close button to close the Library View Options dialog box.

2   Select the first image in the Grid view. Right-click / Control-click the thumbnail and choose Metadata > Save Metadata To File from the context menu. After a brief processing time, the Metadata File Needs To Be Updated icon disappears.

3   Ctrl-click / Command-click to select the other five photos, and then click the Metadata File Needs To Be Updated icon (≡⬇) in the image cell of any of the selected images. Click Save in the confirmation dialog box to update the image files on your hard disk.

After a brief processing time, the Metadata File Needs To Be Updated badge disappears from each of the image cells.

If you edit or add to an image's metadata in another application, such as Adobe Bridge or the Photoshop Camera Raw plug-in, Lightroom will show the Metadata Was Changed Externally icon (≡⇧) above the thumbnail in the Grid view. To accept the changes and update your catalog file accordingly, choose Metadata > Read Metadata From Files. To reject the changed metadata and overwrite it with the information in your catalog file, choose Metadata > Save Metadata To Files.

You can update the metadata for a batch of modified images—or even for the entire catalog with all its folders and collections—by selecting the images or folders to be updated and choosing Metadata > Save Metadata To Files as you did in step 3.

You can use the Metadata Status filter in the Filter bar to quickly find those photos in your library with changes made externally to the master files on disk, any image with a metadata conflict—with unsaved changes made by both Lightroom and another application since the file's metadata was last updated, those with unsaved changes made in Lightroom, or images with metadata that is up to date.

For DNG, JPEG, TIFF, and PSD file formats—which have defined spaces within the file structure where XMP information can be stored separately from the image data—Lightroom writes metadata into the image file itself. In contrast, changes made to camera raw images are written into a separate *XMP sidecar file* that records the metadata and develop settings exported to the image from Lightroom.

Many camera manufacturers use proprietary and undocumented formats for their Raw files, some of which become outdated as new ones appear. Because of this, storing the metadata in a separate file is the safest approach, avoiding the possibility of corruption in the Raw file or loss of the metadata exported from Lightroom.

You can configure the Catalog Settings (in the Edit / Lightroom menu) so that metadata is exported automatically whenever a Raw image is modified. Although you might notice some slowing in performance as Lightroom writes information to the hard disk, you'll always have an up-to-date copy of the metadata from your catalog stored in the sidecar file.

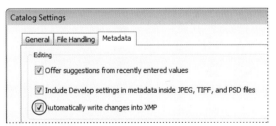

However, XMP information exported in this way contains only the metadata specific to the individual images: keywords, flags, labels, ratings, and develop settings. It does not include higher-level data relevant to the catalog as a whole such as information relating to stacks, virtual copies, and settings used in presentations.

Backing up the library

In the first exercise you backed up your catalog without the image files. In the second, you updated your images files with metadata and develop information from the library catalog catalog. In this exercise you'll export your entire Lightroom library: images, catalog, stacks, collections—the works!

Exporting images as a catalog

When you export your photos as a catalog, Lightroom creates a copy of the catalog file and gives you the option to make copies of the master files and the image previews at the same time. You can choose to export the entire library, or just a selection of your images, as a catalog. Exporting images in this way is ideal for moving your photos together with all the associated Lightroom catalog information from one computer to another. You can use the same technique to restore your entire library from a backup after a data loss.

1   In the Catalog panel, click All Photographs, and then choose File > Export As Catalog.

Ideally, you should save your backup files to a hard disk other than the one that stores your catalog and the master image files—but for this exercise, you can save the backup files to the LR4CIB folder on your hard disk.

2   In the Export As Catalog dialog box, navigate to the LR4CIB folder you created on your hard disk. Type **Backup** in the File Name / Save As text box, disable Export Selected Photos Only and activate Export Negative Files and Include Available Previews. Click Save / Export Catalog.

An initial progress bar is displayed while the new catalog is being created, which should only take a few seconds. Lightroom then begins copying all the image files associated with this catalog to the new location as a background task.

3 While you wait for the export to be completed, watch the progress bar in the upper left the Lightroom workspace.

4 When the export process is complete, switch to Windows Explorer / the Finder and navigate to the LR4CIB folder. Open the new Backup folder.

● **Note:** You may see a different set of folders than is shown in the illustration, depending on which lessons you've already completed.

You can see that the folder structure nested inside the Backup folder replicates the arrangement of folders you see in the Folders panel. All the master images in your Lightroom library have been copied into these new folders and the file Backup.lrcat is a fully functional copy of your original catalog.

5 In Lightroom, choose File > Open Catalog. In the Open Catalog / Open dialog box, navigate to the new Backup folder inside the LR4CIB folder. Select the file Backup.lrcat, and then click Open. If the Open Catalog dialog box appears, click Relaunch. Lightroom will open the backup catalog.

6 Other than the filename in the title bar of the workspace window, this catalog will be almost indistinguishable from your original. Only some minor status information has been lost. For example, you can see that the Previous Import folder in the Catalog panel is now empty.

7 Some of your preferences have been reset to defaults which may differ from the choices you've made for your LR4CIB catalog. Choose Catalog Settings from the Edit / Lightroom menu. Click the General tab in the Catalog Settings dialog box. You can see that the backup frequency has been reset to the default. Click Cancel / the Close button (●) to close the Catalog Settings dialog box.

8 Choose File > Open Recent > LR4CIB Library Catalog.lrcat to return to your original catalog. If the Open Catalog dialog box appears, click Relaunch.

9 If the Back Up Catalog dialog box appears, click Skip Now.

Doing incremental backups

In the usual course of events, the majority of the images in your library will remain unchanged between backups. An incremental backup will save you time by replacing only the backup copies and catalog entries of images that have been modified since the last backup.

Although Lightroom does not have an incremental backup command, you can achieve the same effect by regularly updating your existing backup with just those files in your main catalog that have been modified since the last backup.

1 In the Folders panel, select the Lesson 11 folder. Apply star ratings to two or three of the images in the Grid view. This will be the incremental change to your library for the purposes of this exercise.

2 Choose File > Open Recent > Backup.lrcat to switch to the Backup catalog. If the Open Catalog dialog box appears, click Relaunch.

3 Choose File > Import From Another Catalog. In the Import From Lightroom Catalog dialog box, navigate to the LR4CIB folder. Drill down to the LR4CIB Library/LR4CIB Library Catalog folder. Inside that folder, select LR4CIB Library Catalog.lrcat, and then click Open / Choose.

4 In the Import From Catalog dialog box, make sure the Show Preview option is activated. Choose Metadata And Develop Settings Only from the Replace menu under Changed Existing Photos. Disable the option Preserve Old Settings As A Virtual Copy. Scroll down in the Preview panel to confirm that only the images you modified in step 1 are selected for import.

● **Note:** When you're adding new images to your backup library, choose Copy New Photos To A New Location And Import from the File Handling menu. Click the Choose button to specify your current Backup folder as the destination for the copied files.

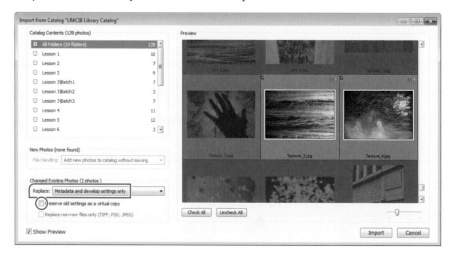

5 Click Import. You can see that the modified images have been updated with the ratings you applied in the master catalog. You have just performed an incremental backup.

6 Click All Photographs in the Catalog panel, and then choose Edit > Select All or press Ctrl+A / Command+A. Choose Metadata > Save Metadata To Files or press Ctrl+S / Command+S. This will export the metadata and develop settings for each photo in the backup library to the backup image file or its XMP sidecar, as an extra precaution against data loss.

7 To return to your original catalog, choose File > Open Recent > LR4CIB Library Catalog.lrcat. If the Open Catalog dialog box appears, click Relaunch.

8 If the Back Up Catalog dialog box appears, click Skip This Time.

Exporting photos

The backup techniques we have discussed so far all produce backup files that can be read only by Lightroom or another application that is capable of reading and interpreting the exported XMP metadata. If you wish to send your work to somebody who doesn't have Lightroom installed on his or her computer, you'll first need to convert the images to an appropriate file format. This is comparable to saving a Word document as plain text or as a PDF document for distribution; some of the functionality is lost but at least the recipient can see what you're working on. Your choice of file format will depend on the purpose for which the images are intended.

- To export a photo for use as an e-mail attachment intended to be viewed on screen, use the JPEG file format and minimize the file size by reducing the resolution and dimensions of the image.

- To export an image to be edited in another application, convert the photo to either the PSD or TIFF file format at full size.

- For archival purposes, export the images in their original file format or convert them to DNG.

Exporting JPEG files for on-screen viewing

For this exercise, you'll use a saved preset to edit the lesson images before you export them so that you'll be able to see at a glance that your develop settings have been applied to the exported copies.

1 In the Folders panel, select the Lesson 11 folder; then, choose Edit > Select All. From the Saved Preset menu at the top of the Quick Develop panel, choose Lightroom B&W Toned Presets > Split Tone 4.

2 With all six images still selected in the Grid view, choose File > Export.

3 Under Export Location in the Export dialog box, choose Specific Folder from the Export To menu, and then click the Choose button below it to specify a destination folder *(see illustration after step 4).* Navigate to your Lessons folder, select the Lesson 11 folder, and click OK / Choose.

4 Activate the Put In Subfolder option and type **Export** as the name for the new subfolder. Disable the option Add To This Catalog.

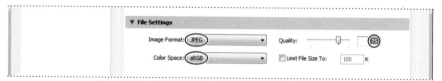

5 Under File Naming in the Export dialog box, click the checkbox to activate the Rename To option; then, choose Date - Filename from the menu.

6 Under File Settings, choose JPEG from the Image Format menu and set a Quality value of between 70% and 80%—a range that generally makes an acceptable compromise between image quality and file size. From the Color Space menu choose sRGB. The sRGB color space is a good choice for images intended to be viewed on the web—or in other circumstances where you are unsure what form of color management is used, if any at all.

7 Scroll down in the Export dialog box, if necessary, so that you can see the Image Sizing controls. Activate the Resize To Fit option and choose Width & Height from the menu. Enter **750** for both width (W) and height (H) and choose Pixels from the units menu. This will proportionally scale each image so that its longest side is 750 pixels. Activate Don't Enlarge to avoid smaller images being upsampled. Set the Resolution to **72** Pixels Per Inch—although resolution settings are in general ignored for on-screen display. The reduction in file size is the result of reducing the total number of pixels that make up the image.

8 In the Output Sharpening settings, activate the Sharpen For Screen option and set the Amount to Standard. In the Metadata options, activate the Copyright Only option. Note the other options available under Metadata; even with the All metadata option selected, you can still protect your privacy by removing GPS location information. Disable Watermarking. Choose Show In Explorer / Show In Finder from the After Export menu under Post-Processing.

9 Click Export; then, watch the progress bar on the left side of the top panel in the Lightroom workspace. When the export process is complete, your Export folder inside the Lesson 11 folder will open in Windows Explorer / the Finder.

Using export plug-ins

You can use third-party Lightroom plug-ins to extend almost any aspect of Lightroom's functionality, including the export options.

There are export plug-ins available that enable you to upload photos directly from within Lightroom to your SmugMug, MobileMe, Zenfolio, Shutterfly or Picasa Web accounts, amongst others. Worth mentioning also are the plug-ins for SlideShowPro, and iStockPhoto.

Other plug-ins add search criteria to the Filter bar, enable you to automate and compress backups, help you to create photo-collages or design and upload web galleries, give you access to professional effects and filters, or let you work with Photoshop-style layers in the Develop module.

Click the Plug-in Manager button in the lower left corner of the Export dialog box, and then click Plug-in Exchange to browse Lightroom Exchange online, where you'll find plug-ins from third-party developers offering additional functionality or helping you to automate tasks, customize workflows, and create stylish effects.

You can search the available Lightroom plug-ins by category, browsing for camera raw profiles, develop presets, export plug-ins, and even web gallery templates.

Note: To have Lightroom notify you by playing a sound when the export process is complete, choose a sound from the menu under Completion Sounds on the General tab in the Preferences dialog box.

10 In Windows Explorer, show the Preview Pane or click Slideshow view to see a preview of the images in the folder. In the Mac OS Finder, select an image in Column view or in Cover Flow to see its preview. You can see that the duo-tone preset has been applied to these copies of the lesson photos during the export process. The copies are 750 pixels wide and have much reduced file sizes.

11 Delete the images from the Export folder, and then return to Lightroom. With the six images still selected, choose Photo > Develop Settings > Reset to revert all six images to their original colors.

Exporting as PSD or TIFF for further editing

1 In the Grid view, choose Edit > Select None, and then click to select the image Texture_1.jpg. In the right panel group, expand the Quick Develop panel and choose Lightroom Color Presets > Cross Process 2 from the Saved Preset menu.

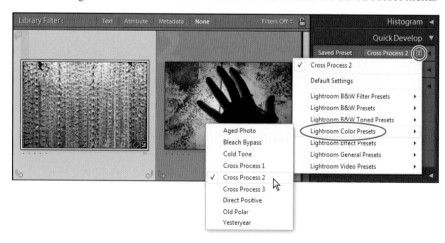

2   Choose File > Export. In the Export dialog box, you'll notice that all your settings from the previous exercise are still in place.

3   In File Settings, choose TIFF from the Image Format menu. When saving in TIFF format, you have the option to apply ZIP data compression—a lossless form of compression—to reduce the resulting file size. From the Color Space menu, choose AdobeRGB (1998).

▶ **Tip:** To export more images using the same settings that you used for the previous export (and without calling up the Export dialog box) choose File > Export With Previous.

When you intend to edit an image in an external application after exporting it, you should use the AdobeRGB (1998) color profile rather than the sRGB color profile. The AdobeRGB (1998) color profile has a larger color gamut, which results in fewer colors being clipped and the original appearance of your images being better preserved. The ProPhoto RGB color gamut is even larger, capable of representing any color from the original raw image. However, to correctly display images using the AdobeRGB (1998) or ProPhoto RGB color profiles on screen you need an image editing application capable of reading these color profiles.

You'll also need to turn color management on and calibrate your computer display. Without taking these measures, your images will look bad on screen with the AdobeRGB (1998) color profile—and even worse with ProPhoto RGB.

▶ **Tip:** Choose your preferred external editor, file format, color space, bit depth, compression settings, and file naming options on the External Editing tab of the Preferences dialog box. In the Lightroom workspace, choose Photo > Edit In, and then choose your preferred external image editing application from the menu. Lightroom will automatically export an image in the appropriate file format, open it in the external editor, and add the converted file to the Lightroom library.

4   Change the image format to PSD. Choose 8 Bits/Component from the Bit Depth menu. Unless you have a particular need to output 16 bit files as part of your workflow, 8-bit files are smaller and compatible with more programs and plug-ins, but do not preserve fine tonal detail as well as 16-bit files. Lightroom actually operates in a 16 bit color space but by the time you're ready to export images you've usually already made any important corrections or adjustments that were necessary, so you won't lose much in terms of editing capability by converting the files to 8 bits for export.

5   In Image Sizing, disable Resize To Fit; to preserve all the image information for further editing, we wish to export every pixel of the original image.

6 Leave the Output Sharpening and Metadata settings unchanged. If you have Adobe Photoshop CS2/CS3/CS4/CS5 installed on your computer, choose Open in Adobe Photoshop CS2/CS3/CS4/CS5 from the After Export menu in the Post-Processing options. Alternatively, choose Open In Other Application, and then click Choose to select your preferred image editor. Click Export.

7 Wait until the export is complete and the photo has opened in the external editor. The image has been exported with the BW Creative - Cyanotype preset that you applied in the Quick Develop panel. Its dimensions are the same as those of the original Raw image—4288 by 2848 pixels.

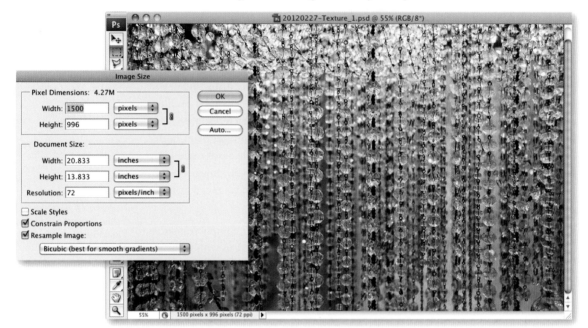

8 Quit the external editor, delete the file from the Export folder in Windows Explorer / the Finder, and then return to Lightroom.

Exporting as Original or DNG for archiving

● **Note:** When you choose to export images in DNG file format you have additional options that affect the way the DNG files are created, but the original image data remains essentially unchanged.

1 In the Folders panel, click the Lesson 6 folder. In the Grid view, select the Raw image DSC_0299.NEF, a photograph of a stone church.

2 Choose File > Export. In the Export dialog box, leave the Export Location unchanged, but disable the renaming option under File Naming.

3 In File Settings, choose Original from the Image Format menu. Note that there are now no other File Settings, Image Settings, or Output Sharpening options available; Lightroom will export the original image data unaltered.

4 In the Post-Processing options, choose Show In Explorer / Show In Finder from the After Export menu; then, click Export.

5 Wait until the export process completes and the Export folder inside the Lesson 11 folder opens in Windows Explorer / the Finder. In the Windows Explorer / Finder window, note that an XMP sidecar file has been saved together with the copy of the original RAW image. This XMP file records changes to the image's metadata as well as its detailed editing history.

6 In Windows Explorer / the Finder, delete both files from the Export folder, and then return to Lightroom.

Using export presets

Lightroom provides presets for commonly performed export tasks. You can use a preset as is or as a starting point for creating your own.

If you find yourself performing the same operations over and over again you should create your own presets to automate your workflow.

1 Click the Lesson 11 folder in the Folders panel. In the Grid view, select any of the images in the Lesson 11 folder and then choose File > Export.

2 In the list of presets on the left side of the Export dialog box, choose For Email from the Lightroom Presets.

3 Examine the settings associated with this preset. With the current File Settings, an exported file will be an sRGB JPEG file with a Quality setting of 60 (%). Under Image Sizing, the exported image is set to be scaled down so that its longest side will be 500 pixels. Output Sharpening and Watermarking are disabled and the Metadata options are set to export copyright details only. Note that there are no export location or post-processing settings.

▶ **Tip:** For more detail on exporting photos as e-mail attachments, see "Sharing your work by e-mail" on page 47.

Lightroom will export the image directly to an e-mail, so there are no export location settings associated with this preset. Post-processing options are also unnecessary; Lightroom automatically generates an e-mail and attaches the photo, and your e-mail will be sent from within Lightroom, with no need to launch an e-mail client.

4 In the list of presets on the left side of the Export dialog box, click to select the Burn Full-Sized JPEGs export preset.

5 Note the changes in the export settings. CD / DVD is now selected in the Export To menu at the top of the Export dialog box, instead of Email (so, once again, export location settings are redundant). Under File Settings, the JPEG Quality setting has been set to 100 (%).

6 Scroll down in the Export dialog box to examine the rest of the preset options. Under Image Sizing, the Resize To Fit option is disabled, and the file will be exported with all of its metadata intact, including GPS location information.

You can adjust any of the preset settings if you wish, and then save your custom configuration as a new preset by clicking the Add button below the Presets list.

Once again, there are no post-processing options; if you go ahead and click the Export button, Lightroom will automatically open the Choose Burner / Burn Disc dialog box, where you can nominate your disk burner and specify the burn speed before clicking Burn.

Setting up post-processing actions

You can streamline your export workflow by setting up automated post-processing actions. For example, if you prefer to set up an e-mail in your default e-mail client, you could have Lightroom automatically launch your mail application and prepare a new message with the exported image attached.

1 Choose For Email (Hard Drive) from the Lightroom Presets. For this preset, Lightroom exports the file to disk at an appropriate file size for e-mailing.

2 Under Export Location in the Export dialog box, choose Specific Folder from the Export To menu, and then click the Choose button below it to select your Lesson 11 folder as the export destination. Activate the Put In Subfolder option and type **For Email** as the name for the new subfolder. Disable the option Add To This Catalog.

3 In the Post-Processing options, choose Go To Export Actions Folder Now from the After Export menu.

Lightroom opens a Windows Explorer / Finder window with the Export Actions folder already selected. The next step in setting up your automated export is to place a shortcut or alias for your e-mail application into this folder.

4 Open a second Windows Explorer / Finder window and navigate to the folder containing your e-mail application. Right-click / Control-click the e-mail application, choose Create Shortcut / Make Alias from the context menu, and then drag the new shortcut or alias into the Export Actions folder. When you're done, return to the Export dialog box in Lightroom.

5 In the Post-Processing settings, choose the new shortcut or alias to your e-mail application from the After Export menu.

With the current settings you could export an image as a small JPEG file and Lightroom would automatically launch your e-mail application and open a new message with the image already attached. But first, there's one more step that can help automate the process even further.

Creating user presets

You can save your customized export settings as a new user preset. Export presets are always available from the File menu (File > Export With Preset) where you can start your export without having to open the Export dialog first.

1   Click the Add button in the lower left corner of the Export dialog box. In the New Preset dialog box, type **To My Email and Attach** as the name for your new preset, choose User Presets from the Folder menu, and then click Create.

In the Export dialog box, your new preset is now listed under User Presets.

2   Click Cancel to close the Export dialog box without exporting any images.

3   Select one or more images in the Grid view and choose File > Export With Preset > To My Email And Attach.

The export process will begin immediately. When exporting is complete, your e-mail application will be launched automatically and will open a new message with your exported photo or photos already attached; all you need a to do is to enter the recipient's e-mail address and you're ready to send.

Review questions

1 What are the two basic components of your photo library that need to be backed up?

2 How can you move a selection of images or your entire image library with all the associated catalog information from one computer to another?

3 How can you do an incremental backup of your photo library?

4 How would you choose between file formats for exporting your photos?

5 What is a post-processing action?

Review answers

1 The two basic components of the image library are the original image files (or master files) and the library catalog file, which records all the metadata and the complete editing history for every image in the library as well as information about collections, user templates and presets, and output settings.

2 On one computer, use the Export As Catalog command to create a catalog file together with copies of the original images and the available previews. On the other computer, use the Import From Catalog command.

3 Once you have created a full backup of the library using Export As Catalog, you can switch to the backup catalog regularly and use the Import From Catalog command to update it. You can configure the import settings so only those images that have been modified since the last backup are imported from the main catalog. In this way, you can keep your existing backup catalog updated incrementally—avoiding the more time consuming process of making a full new backup.

4 The appropriate choice of a file format depends on the intended use of the exported images. To export images for on-screen viewing as e-mail attachments, you'd use the JPEG file format and minimize the file size. To export an image to an external image editing application you'd use PSD or TIFF and export the image at full size. For archival purposes, export the images in their original format or convert them to DNG.

5 A post-processing action is a preset that can help to automate your workflow. You can choose a preset that will automatically burn your images to a CD or DVD after export, or one that will launch your e-mail application and attach your exported images to a new message. You can save your own action presets, which will be listed beside the Lightroom presets in the Export dialog box.

INDEX

showing and hiding, 58, 71
Top Label option, 121
top panel, 15
tracking, 235
Treat JPEG Files Next To Raw
    Files As Separate Photos
    option, 86
Trim Video button, 103, 181
type
    fine-tuning baseline, 235
    fine-tuning kerning, 235
    fine-tuning leading, 235
    fine-tuning tracking, 235
Type panel, 234

U

undoing changes, 195
Unrated option, 169
Unsaved Metadata option,
    121, 340
Upload button, 332
Upload Settings panel, 331
upsampling images, 346
Use Defaults button, 75
Use Defaults option, 121
Use Second Monitor button,
    60

V

vibrance, 42
video
    capturing frames from, 181
    editing, 180
    importing and viewing, 103
    playback control bar, 103
    setting poster frame, 181
    trimming, 103, 181
video files, 91
View Gallery button, 321, 328
view modes, 70, 119
view options, 73
View Slideshow button, 321

virtual copies, 32, 200–202,
    341

W

warm colors, 186
watched folder, 108
watermarking, 325
    Watermark Editor dialog
        box, 325, 333
web galleries
    customizing, 315
Web module, 23
white balance, 179
    about, 185–186
White Balance Selector, 186
white point, 185
Widescreen slideshow
    template, 248
work area, 15, 70
workflow, 24
workspace
    customizing, 16
    overview, 14

X

XMP metadata, 149, 159
XMP sidecar file, 341

Z

zoom levels, 123
Zoom To Fill option, 271

Production Notes

The *Adobe Photoshop Lightroom 4 Classroom in a Book* was created electronically using Adobe InDesign CS3. Art was produced using Adobe InDesign, Adobe Illustrator, and Adobe Photoshop.

References to company names in the lessons are for demonstration purposes only and are not intended to refer to any actual organization or person.

Team credits

The following individuals contributed to the development of this edition of the *Adobe Photoshop Lightroom 4 Classroom in a Book*:

Project coordinators, technical writers: John Evans & Katrin Straub

Production: Manneken Pis Productions (www.manneken.be)

Copyediting & Proofreading: John Evans, Katrin Straub and Torsten Buck

Keystroker: Megan Tytler

Designer: Katrin Straub

Special thanks to Victor Gavenda, Eric Geoffroy, Connie Jeung-Mills, Tracey Croom, and Christine Yarrow.

Typefaces used

Adobe Clean, Adobe Myriad Pro, and Adobe Warnock Pro are used throughout the lessons. For more information about OpenType and Adobe fonts, visit www.adobe.com/type/opentype/.

Photo Credits

Photographic images and illustrations supplied by Torsten Buck, John Evans, Roger Mills, Katrin Straub, and Adobe Systems Incorporated. Photos are for use only with the lessons in the book.

Contributors

John Evans has worked in computer graphics and design for more than 25 years, initially as a graphic designer, and then since 1993 as a multimedia author, software interface designer, and technical writer. His multimedia and digital illustration work associated with Japanese type attracted an award from Apple Computer Australia. His other projects range from music education software for children to interface design for innovative Japanese font design software. As a technical writer his work includes software design specifications, user manuals, and more recently copy editing for *Adobe Photoshop Elements 8 Classroom in a Book*, *Adobe Photoshop Lightroom 3 Classroom in a Book*, and *Adobe Creative Suite 4 Classroom in a Book* and authoring for *Adobe Photoshop Elements 10 Classroom in a Book*.

Katrin Straub is an artist, a graphic designer, and author. Her award-winning print, painting, and multimedia work has been exhibited worldwide. With more than 15 years experience in design, Katrin has worked as Design Director for companies such as Landor Associates and Fontworks in the United States, Hong Kong, and Japan. Her work includes packaging, promotional campaigns, multimedia, website design, and internationally recognized corporate and retail identities. She holds degrees from the FH Augsburg, ISIA Urbino, and The New School University in New York. Katrin has authored many books, from the *Adobe Creative Suite Idea Kit* to Classroom in a Book titles for Adobe Photoshop Lightroom 3, Adobe Creative Suite 4, Adobe Soundbooth, and several versions of *Adobe Photoshop Elements Classroom in a Book* and *Adobe Premiere Elements Classroom in a Book*.

Torsten Buck has been involved in the development of software for the design and desktop publishing industries in Japan, China and the United States for almost 20 years. A Masters in Computer Science combined with a passion for typography have shaped a career that took Torsten from the development of ground-breaking Asian font technology in Hong Kong to a position as Head of Type Development at Adobe Systems in the USA. As director of Manneken Pis Productions he has authored a wide range of design software training books.

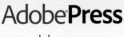